The Fabric of
American Literary Realism

The Fabric of American Literary Realism

*Readymade Clothing,
Social Mobility and Assimilation*

BABAK ELAHI

McFarland & Company, Inc., Publishers
Jefferson, North Carolina, and London

LIBRARY OF CONGRESS CATALOGUING-IN-PUBLICATION DATA

Elahi, Babak, 1965–
　　The fabric of American literary realism : readymade clothing, social mobility and assimilation / Babak Elahi.
　　　　p.　　cm.
　　Includes bibliographical references and index.

　　ISBN 978-0-7864-4119-8
　　softcover : 50# alkaline paper ∞

　　1. American fiction — 19th century — History and criticism.
　　2. American fiction — 20th century — History and criticism.
　　3. Clothing and dress in literature.　4. Realism in literature.　I. Title.
　　PS374.C565E43　2009
　　813'.009355 — dc22　　　　　　　　　　　　　　　　　　　2009000611

British Library cataloguing data are available

©2009 Babak Elahi. All rights reserved

No part of this book may be reproduced or transmitted in any form or by any means, electronic or mechanical, including photocopying or recording, or by any information storage and retrieval system, without permission in writing from the publisher.

On the cover: Man carrying bundle of garments, Bleecker Street, New York City, 1912 (Photograph by Lewis Wickes Hine, Library of Congress)

Manufactured in the United States of America

McFarland & Company, Inc., Publishers
　Box 611, Jefferson, North Carolina 28640
　　www.mcfarlandpub.com

Acknowledgments

My first debt of graditude goes to my mother, Farrah Amini, for her love and wisdom. I am grateful to RIT's College of Liberal Arts for awarding me the Paul and Francena L. Miller Fellowship in order to complete work on this project. This project was also helped along by John Michael, whose careful reading of my work, mentorship, support, and friendship have been indispensable throughout the writing process. I owe a great debt of gratitude to Frank Shuffelton for his wisdom and guidance, and his extensive reading and response to my work. Thanks to Melinda Knight for encouraging me to work on Willa Cather, and for the many ways she helped me through the early part of the process. Thanks to Joan Rubin for encouraging me to write about Anzia Yezierska. Thanks to those who have read and responded to parts of this work at different times, Tom DiPiero, Tyra Seldon, Deborah Uman, Stephen Brauer, Penelope Kelsey, Evelyn Brister, Edward K. Chan, Tim Engstrom, Melissa Bloom, Richard Santana and John Capps, and especially Doris Borrelli for a very careful read of several chapters, and Larry Winnie for his reading and suggestions. Janet Zandy's mentorship and encouragement have helped at key moments in this process, and I thank her sincerely. Thanks especially to John Capps for helping me think through the work of Henry and William James, for discussing John Dewey and Jane Addams with me, and for his intellectual generosity. Special thanks to Afred Vitale for editorial assistance, proofreading, and indexing. Most of all, thank my daughters, Kalila and Roxanne, and my wife, Jennifer Spencer Elahi, for their love, their patience while I worked and wrote, and their sense of humor. They've helped me through this and much else.

Table of Contents

Acknowledgments v
Preface 1

CHAPTER 1
Dress in the North American Political Imagination   9

CHAPTER 2
The Discourse of Dress and Literary Realism in the United States   39

CHAPTER 3
Henry James's Old Clothes   61

CHAPTER 4
From Clothing to Nothing: Annihilating the Self in *Sister Carrie*   82

CHAPTER 5
Dress and Mobility in *The Rise of David Levinsky*   108

CHAPTER 6
The Financial and Sartorial Fictions of Anzia Yezierska   139

CHAPTER 7
The Clothing of the American Frontier: or
How the West Was Worn in Willa Cather   165

POSTSCRIPT
A Scarf, a Shawl, *un Rebozo*   187

Chapter Notes   191
Bibliography   209
Index   217

Preface

IN THE SECOND HALF OF the nineteenth century, clothing production in the United States shifted from the hand craft of making homespun garments to the corporate enterprise of producing ready-made clothes, and eventually to mass-production of factory-made clothing. This technological and economic change from individually tailored dress to an industrialized fashion and clothing system has cultural and social implications. It can be read as a standardization of American national identity, and a radical transformation of how the individual was measured and reproduced. This broad change led to the Fordist model of production/consumption, at the center of which was the new American citizen — middle-class or working-class aspiring to middle-class, second-generation immigrant, dressed in factory-made clothing that she or he helped produce. At the same time, this same historical period — between the development of ready-made clothing in the 1860s to its mass production by the 1880s and early 1900s — also saw the rise of American literary realism, and the establishment of American fiction not only as part of American popular culture, but increasingly as a critically mature aesthetic pursuit. Surprisingly, while political scientists, cultural studies scholars, and historians have examined the development of ready-made mass produced dress and its ideological implications, few literary scholars have examined this history in any broad systematic way. While literary scholars, most notably Anne Hollander and Clair Hughes, have produced book-length studies of clothing in fiction, and while shorter pieces have discussed the gendered or ethnic implication of dress during this period, no scholarship of the American literary realist period explores systematically the coincidental rise of the off-the-rack clothing industry and the establishment of realist literary representation as both high and popular culture. This book attempts to accomplish the latter by bringing existing political histories and cultural studies of dress to an examination of the development of literary realism in the United States, paying close attention to key figures and debates.

Histories of the North American ready-made clothing industry tend to focus on the political stakes of such a shift, debating whether the development of a technology and a culture of consumption democratized America or whether it produced a hierarchy of labor and capital that had often negative political ramifications.[1] One key study, Claudia Kidwell's *Suiting Everyone,* tends to perpetuate notions of American exceptionalism and the myth of social mobility. Kidwell characterizes the "rising classes in early nineteenth-century America" as an "aspiring people who automatically thought of themselves as being as good as everyone else, and who wanted the clothing — but not at the cost of custom-made — to prove it." Kidwell goes on to say that "the common quality of American dress served to obliterate ethnic origins and blur social distinction" (15). However, this view, while important in understanding the significance of ready-made innovations in American ideology, tends to downplay the complications of race, and to ignore the ways in which corporate hierarchies and industrial relationships would, despite the appearance of equality, perpetuate some old stratifications and establish new ones. However, other, more recent studies reveal that while ready-made mass produced clothing standardized identity and produced hierarchies of class, gender, and race, these tendencies were, nevertheless, resisted in different ways by different groups.[2] Some of the most important work on the American garment industry and on the implications of clothing for identity formation come out of Jewish American historical studies. Elizabeth Ewen, Susan Glenn, Barbara Schreier, John Higham, Hadassa Kosak, and Andrew Heinze, among others, have closely examined the important role played by Russian Jewish immigration in the transformation of labor and capital in the United States at the turn of the twentieth century. These studies explore a range of questions from the transformation of the clothing industry itself to the importance of immigrant workers in resisting structures of class and ethnic dominance to the significance of clothing in processes of assimilation (and resistance to it) for both men and women.[3] Thus, historians, political scientists, and sociologists have paid close attention to how material culture had both symbolic and real significance for the United States between the 1860s and the 1920s.

Scholars of American literary realism have paid close attention to questions of material culture and consumption in the Gilded Age. For the past two decades, these critics have argued that far from being either a successful or a failed attempt at mimesis, realism was, itself, involved in processes of "production" or "incorporation" of American culture. Walter Benn Michaels has argued that realism involved "a commitment to production so complete" that it requires the production of the self.[4] Building upon and responding to Michaels and others, Amy Kaplan argues that realism did not simply attempt to represent faithfully a "*ready-made* setting," nor did it attempt to "compensate for the absence of a complex social *fabric*," but, rather, "realists contribute to the construction of a cohesive public sphere."[5] The language of "production," construction, and of the social fabric suggests an awareness of material culture and economic relations that continues to inform more recent studies of key American realist texts, such as Robert Seguin's reading of *Sister Carrie* in the context of labor and leisure. Seguin responds to the historicization of realism by arguing that "if periodizing concepts such as consumer society are to be historically meaningful, they must refer to mass consumption."[6] Modes of production-consumption that took root in the United States between the 1860s and the 1920s produced "an ineluctable dismantling of any notion of collective agency." When a Fordist system such as this takes hold, "collective modes of social organization and interaction" become "atomize[d] and disperse[d]" and subsumed to the point that "both the subject, at the level of the individual, and the domain of the collectivity suffer together." Because realist narrative relies on "those limited and anthropomorphizing units known as 'characters,'" it is always caught in the problem of depicting collective agency through individual desires, and, thus, tends to fall into the tendency of muddling the two and losing touch with both (Seguin 50). Literary analysis of realism, then, tends to focus on the space between the discursive production and reproduction of individual identity and the broad social and cultural construction of social reality.

Thus, it is clear that in the scholarship on American realism, the lessons of cultural historians about mass culture and consumption have been guiding principles. The foundational work of Alan Trachtenberg, J.T. Jackson Lears and Richard Wightman Fox has established certain assumptions for literary historians and American studies scholars, assumptions about the "incorporation of America," as Trachtenberg puts it, and about American consumer culture and the shaping of individual identity. In discussing how material developments of urbanization, mass transport, communication, governmental "efficiency," professionalization, and financial organization turned earlier forms of economic and social association into the dominant corporate form in the United States, Trachtenberg argues that any account of this process must pay close attention to "subtle [cultural] shifts in the meaning of prevalent ideas, ideas regarding *the identity of the individual*, the relation between public and private realms, and the character of the nation."[7] What all of these studies of American realism have in common is the notion that the massive scale changes in processes of production influenced the construction of reality through fiction and the construction of *individual identity*, whether in the characters portrayed in realist fiction or for readers who responded to the work.

If understanding American realism requires an account of how material production and mass consumption affected the formation of individual identity, then it is surprising that no scholars of American realism have written a thorough analysis of dress in the era of American realism. Far from being a particular topic within a wide range of issues at the turn of the twentieth century, clothing is the most significant social, cultural, psychological, and ideological fabric of American society. Clothing marks the space where individual self-production meets broad social construction. As fashion historian Elizabeth Wilson puts it, clothing is the "connective tissue" of the "cultural organism."[8] Other fashion historians, such as Diana Crane, have argued that clothing, "as one of the most visible forms of consumption, performs a major role in the social construction of identity."[9] In addition to Wilson and Crane, Peter Stallybrass has offered some of the most insightful observations about dress and culture in his work, arguing that clothes are particularly important in embodying individual and collective identity in the face of commodification and alienation.[10] Given this significance, and given that the study of realism involves an exploration of social and individual construction of identity, scholarship on the importance of dress in American realism has been limited and scattered.[11] Jewish American writers have been studied in the context of dress, the clothing industry, and assimilation.[12] Furthermore, there are a few important book-length studies of dress and literary representation, but these either focus on a broader context than American realism, or focus on formalist or historicist questions around a single author. In this context, the work of Anne Hollander, Clair Hughes, and Mark Anderson has been very important in developing a critical perspective on clothing and literature.[13] Thus, while literary scholars have occasionally examined the significance of dress in fiction, and while there are a few isolated studies of dress and identity in specific realist texts, no study has explored the implications of the fact that the production of mass-produced ready-to-wear clothing and the emergence of a mature form of mimetic literary representation developed simultaneously in the United States. This book attempts to do so by placing broader discourses of dress (from commercial, philosophical, social Darwinist, and sociological frames) alongside the development of realism all within the historical context of the development of ready-made garment production, particularly as it accelerated in the 1880s. As American realists attempted to "produce" identity and to construct social reality, clothing took on important symbolic and material significance in debating and defining American national identity for writers of fiction and within public discourse.

Realism is important precisely because it was during this era that both text and textile became commodified, and as authors represented conspicuous consumption of clothes they registered anxieties about the conspicuous consumption of communication media, including stories in magazines and novels published by commercial presses. Realists like Dreiser, Yezierska, and Cahan employed a literary rhetoric and style attuned to *both* the symbolic and material significance of clothes as the tissue of social organisms — both collective organisms (such as ethnicity, gender, and class) as well as more technical constructions of the nation that contributed to or challenged the myth of social mobility. The realities of clothing production — immigrant labor, expanding markets, standardization and uniformity of styles, transformations in images of gender, national origin, ethnicity, and class — pushed these writers to represent the vested body in often new and sometimes troubling ways. Examined in terms of the question of national identity, these writers seem to be exploring the tension between unity and uniformity. Ready-made identity threatened to produce a uniform national self. On the one hand, this provoked anxiety for those like Henry James, who prized distinction in dress as he did in art. James's modernist valorization of "distinction," could not abide the sameness of mass consumption. For James, *both* immigrants and native-born Americans lost out in a ready-made culture because the former lost their authenticity while the latter lost the interest (in both its epistemological or aesthetic sense and its financial sense) gained by difference and distinction. Uniformity of identity was troubling for others because it erased racial difference: the right clothes could make Jews white. For Cather, this indecipherability between immigrant and native could unravel the nation and its culture. As social mobility posed both promises and threats about the shape of national identity and culture, American literary realists looked to and depicted clothing as the screen on which hopes and anxieties could effectively be projected. Looking back, it is clear that today's tensions between a global fashion market and fragmented style cultures based on youth, ethnicity, and sexuality pose very different problems for the representation of dress. However, an examination of fictions of the American fabric during the rise of the ready-made industry can help us begin to understand this contemporary scene as well.

In what follows, the first three chapters explore the literary, ideological, and social implications of an emerging ready-made clothing industry. As America was transformed from a "homespun" society into a ready-made consumer culture, various popular and professional discourses, including that of literary realism, responded to and participated in the shaping of a ready-made society and culture. Chapter 1 examines the emergence of an ideology of simple dress in the nineteenth century in the United States. Clothing can be understood as a recurring symbol of how American identity is fashioned, going back to some of the earliest accounts of exploration and continuing to contemporary times. Contrasts between nakedness and adornment, simple clothes and fancy dress, have been at the heart of how Americans imagine their own democratic national identity. Chapter 1 also argues that a public and literary discourse of dress emerged in the United States in tandem with the shift from homespun clothing to ready-mades. An awareness of these connections between discourse and practice allow for a counterintuitive comparison of Horatio Alger, Jr.'s rags-to-riches narratives and Henry David Thoreau's notions of simple dress. Alger and Thoreau seem to be and are in some ways diametrically opposed to one another on the question of dress. However, both re-imagine a basically Franklinian conception of the individual in society, and the individual's property and person within the wider political economy.

The second chapter explores the expansion of the discourse of dress in the second half of the nineteenth century. In this period, economists and sociologists like Thorstein Veblen, social Darwinists, historians and art historians, psychologists, philosophers like William James, and women's advice columnists linked clothes to both personal and national identity. From this survey of clothing discourse, Jane Addams emerges as one of the few thinkers of her time to imagine a more materialist and at the same time more democratic theory of dress and society at the turn of the twentieth century. She attempted to use clothing production and consumption as a way of telling the history of the immigrant laborers she worked with in the Chicago slums. This chapter examines American realism and its relation to clothing and social mobility within this broader discursive context. In order to historicize the literary representation of clothing in this period, Chapter 3 compares Henry James's late work with his early story from 1868, "A Romance of Certain Old Clothes." In his youth, James was haunted by the weight of a barren cultural past in North America, just as his female characters are haunted by the ghostly handmade dresses of their personal history. But by the turn of the twentieth century, in his belated return to the U.S. he was terrorized by an industrial American culture peopled by immigrants, just as his characters are hounded by new clothes and new Americans.

By contrast, Theodore Dreiser's realism offers, as explained in Chapter 4, a more stark portrayal of an increasingly consumerized American society. Thus, this chapter focuses on a key text in American realism and naturalism, *Sister Carrie*. As the central text in debates over defining the success or failure of literary realism in the United States, *Sister Carrie* offers a way of understanding important questions of class, gender, commodity, and identity central to these debates. In his *Sister Carrie*, Dreiser traces both upward and downward mobility partly as a function of his characters' wardrobes. At the same time, he explores what Thorstein Veblen calls the "spiritual" function of clothing, or what William James (so unlike his brother) saw as the potentially positive psychological function of the materiality of clothing. It is this deeper debate over the relative psychological, social, and, even, democratic function of American material culture (and clothing in particular) that this analysis of literary representations of clothing hopes to uncover. Dreiser, on the surface, seems to offer a hard hitting critique of an increasingly materialistic culture. However, his understanding of the relationship between material culture and the inner lives of his characters is much more complex than it may seem. Hurstwood's and Carrie's relationships to their clothes represent a particular kind of alienation at work in American culture at the beginning of the twentieth century: one that turned the individual's *material* connections to a community, a past, and a locality into that individual's *abstract* relation to exchange value. Just as the industrial economy turned objects and materials into commodities, it also turned people into value.

The two chapters that follow this reading of *Sister Carrie* address the importance of ethnicity, specifically the response of Russian Jewish immigrant writers to both literary realist and broader social discourses of race, assimilation, clothing, commodity, and currency in the United States. Anzia Yezierska and Abraham Cahan's literary portrayals of assimilation conveyed both the material and metaphorical importance of clothing in the lives of immigrants.[14] Cahan wrote his fictional "Autobiography of an American Jew" partly in response to the 1913 textile workers' strike in New York where he worked as a journalist and newspaper publisher. In its full-length development into a novel, *The Rise of David Levinsky* (1917) examined the tradeoffs the title character faces after leaving his Jewish *shtetl* and becoming a clothing industry tycoon in the United States. The material rise of Levinsky is in many ways his spiritual decline. However, Levinsky seems divided between a Jamesian attack on consumerism and a Dreiserian cultural analysis of material culture. Ultimately, Cahan re-tailors the literary representation of the American subject as much as his title character is re-tailored, and assimilated into an American. Similarly, Yezierska attempts to imagine a process of assimilation that weaves the sacred culture of the past into the material culture of the American present and future. Yezierska's novels — especially *Arrogant Beggar*— attempt to tailor a new sense of self created out of the threads of past and present, sacred and profane, tradition and modernity. Yezierska reshapes the fabric of American realism by exploring the questions of credit and debt control to the immigrant's assimilation into the North American Middle Class. In her novels we see clearly how fashion is related to finance and how ethnic vestments are exchanged for American investments.

Finally, Willa Cather's novels of the American West and Southwest can be read as a compendium of American pioneer "fashions" as well as a critique of conspicuous consumption. In this final case study, it becomes clear that Cather performs in fiction what Theodore Roosevelt and Frederick Jackson Turner did with history: she tries to imagine a post–Reconstruction and post-immigrant America guided by what she describes in *The Song of the Lark* as a feeling of empire. However, while Roosevelt imagines a racially narrow notion of the new America united by imperialism *and* assimilation, Cather broadens the ethnic category of whiteness, and she accomplishes this, to a great extent, through a deft representation of clothes — preferring the handmade over the mass-produced and linking these crafts and artifacts to a mythic conception of the nation. What she does share with Roosevelt is an imperialist vision of the United States, a vision that attempts to weave different European ethnicities ("Bohemian," French, Spanish, and Scandinavian) into the fabric of a new American society. Once again, clothes become key symbols of this transformation.

1. Dress in the North American Political Imagination

IN A.D. 1528, A SPANIARD WASHED ashore on the North American mainland, probably on the Gulf coast of present-day Texas. Somehow, in the course of the shipwreck, Álvar Núñez de Cabeza de Vaca had been stripped of his clothes. He came to America naked, divested of his European garb along with its social, cultural, and political values. Cabeza de Vaca might be considered the first European-American. In a very real sense, his might be the first case of assimilation. Unlike Columbus or Cortés who remained more distinctly loyal to Europe in their projects of conquest, Cabeza de Vaca seems to have developed a deep affinity for this brave new world. An early instance of "going" native, Cabeza de Vaca's reinvention of self constitutes a literal and metaphorical divestiture, the shedding of European clothes:

> No clothing against the weather might appear the worst. But for us poor skeletons who survived it, it was not. The worst lay in parting little by little with the thoughts that clothe the soul of the European, and most of all of the idea that a man attains his strength through dirk and dagger, and serving in your Majesty's guard. We had to surrender such fantasies till our inward nakedness was the nakedness of an unborn babe, starting life anew in the womb of sensations which in themselves can mysteriously nourish. Several years went by before I could relax in that living plexus for which even now I have no name; but only when at last I relaxed, could I see the possibilities of a life in which to be deprived of Europe was not to be deprived of too much.[1]

This observation — that a European identity was dispensable — is conceptually radical and rhetorically simple, and its guiding metaphor is still alive almost five hundred years later: clothing and nakedness as symbols of vested and divested cultural interest, as emblems of cultural identity. In the film adaptation of Luis Valdez's play *Zoot Suit*, the trickster character, El Pachuco, played by Edward James Olmos, represents a similar dialectical symbolism of dress. Marked as morally ambiguous by his zoot suit (which changes color from black to white to red at key moments in the film), El Pachuco is stripped of his clothing at the film's climax. Humiliated, and cringing into a fetal position, El Pachuco slowly rises to his full stature wearing a loincloth, emerging as a mythic rebirth of an Aztec archetype, a high priest. Basing his play and the film on actual historical events, including the ritualized stripping of a young Chicano by Anglo attackers, Valdez taps into the dialectic between clothing and nakedness, or in this case, between modern sub-cultural style and premodern religious vestment. Valdez restores to dress its symbolic power. Like Cabeza de Vaca, El Pachuco sheds his clothes and is reborn. Each sheds one identity like (and along with) a garment. Shedding the clothing of tradition and of the European past has been a powerful symbol of American national identity.

The Naked and the Dressed: Imagining the American as a New Man

In the context of Western European civilization, disrobing or dropping the veil revealed, for many philosophers and playwrights, an authentic autonomous individual liberated from the frauds, limitations, and bonds of tradition. Shakespeare, Montesquieu, Edmund Burke, Goethe, and Karl Marx all used this metaphor to imagine the new cultural manners, social structures, and political ideas of a society breaking away from the past. Marshall Berman argues that in the sixteenth century a new discourse of modernity emerges according to which

> the false world is seen as a historical past, a world we have lost (or are in the process of losing), while the true world is in the physical and social world that exists for us here and now (or is in the process of coming into being). At this point a new symbolism emerges. Clothes become an emblem of the old, illusory mode of life; nakedness comes to signify the newly discovered and experienced truth; and the act of taking off one's clothes becomes an act of spiritual liberation, of becoming real [Berman 106].

The emergence of this metaphor in early modern Europe coincides with the conquest and exploration of the Americas. Thus, while Berman's comments about modernity are focused on Europe, the "New World" allowed for an even more powerful context to describe the nakedness of the modern subject. Divestiture — both taking off clothes and selling off financial as well as cultural worth — becomes particularly important when it is a symbol not only of transformation within a single society, but of movement from one culture to another. Europeans divest themselves of the European past and are reborn in their New-World nakedness.

The publication of Thomas Carlyle's *Sartor Resartus* in the United Sates, with the aid of Ralph Waldo Emerson, in 1836 marks a moment of crisis in this conception of American identity in terms of simple dress. According to Kerry McSweeny and Peter Sabor, Carlyle proposed that "the clothing fashioned by society and by religious institutions must be removed and replaced entirely" (Carlyle, xv). With Carlyle, then, we begin to see the difficulties of using nakedness or even sartorial simplicity as a metaphor for modernity. Carlyle adds to the discourse of shedding the clothes of social conformity, the additional stage of donning the clothes that suit the inner self more precisely, and of a whole philosophy of clothes as a way of understanding the fabrication of society. Indeed, his combination of transcendentalism with materialism (or "Descendentalism") has a profound influence on Emerson and Henry David Thoreau. Emerson begins his essay "Nature," for example, by asking "why should we grope among the dry bones of the past, or put the living generation into masquerade out of its faded wardrobe?" Published the same year as Carlyle's *Sartor Resartus*, Emerson's "Nature" uses the metaphor of a new wardrobe for a new people to express his desire for "our own works and laws and worship" (Emerson 32).

Despite its mediation through two narrative devices — a narrating English editor re-tailoring the manuscripts of the fictitious German transcendentalist philosopher, Diogenes Teufelsdröckh (God-born Devil's-shit) — Carlyle's philosophical statement on clothes suggests a transcendentalism tempered, often ironically, by a materialism. "Man's earthly interests" he ventriloquizes through the voice of the German philosopher, "are all hooked and buttoned together, and held up, by Clothes" (Carlyle 41). At first glance, Carlyle's philosophy, mediated though it may be, seems to espouse a transcendentalism in which the true self is veiled by the body-as-garment and by clothes, themselves. In considering the question, "Who am *I*," Carlyle's alter-ego, Tuefelsdröckh, sounds very much like Emerson calling for "self-trust" in "The American Scholar" and "Self-Reliance," where the self being trusted is one with the universe:

> With men of a speculative turn ... there come seasons, meditative, sweet, yet awful hours, when in wonder and fear you ask yourself that unanswerable question: Who am *I*; the think that can say "I" (*das Weden das sich Ich nennt*)? The world, with its loud trafficking, retires into the distance; and, through the paper-hangings, and stone-walls, and thick-plied tissues of Commerce and Polity, and all the living lifeless Integuments (of Society and a Body), wherewith your Existence sits surrounded,— the sight reaches forth into the void Deep, and you are alone with the Universe, and silently commune with it, as one mysterious Presence with another [42].

The tissue of society — including clothes — falls away, and what seems to be revealed is the authentic self: "Perhaps not once in a lifetime does it occur to your ordinary biped, of any country or generation, be he goldmantled Prince or russet jerkined Peasant, that his Vestments and his Self are not one and indivisible; that *he* is naked, without vestments, till he buy or steal such, and by forethought sew and button them." Carlyle's Teufelsdröckh explains that "there is something great in the moment when a man first strips himself of adventitious wrappages; and sees indeed that he is naked, and, as Swift has it, 'a forked straddling animal with bandy legs;' yet also a Spirit, and unutterable Mystery of Mysteries" (45). In this philosophy, all material is a form of clothing, the physical garment covering the metaphysical world: "All visible things are Emblems" and "all Emblematic things are properly Clothes, thought-woven or hand-woven." In the end, "Whatsoever sensibly exists, whatsoever represents Spirit to Spirit, is properly a Clothing, a suit of Raiment, put on for a season, and to be laid off" (56–7). Thus, viewed through these instances, the transcendentalism of Carlyle is one that echoes the metaphor of the clothed conformity of society and the naked authenticity of the individual soul.

However, the materiality of clothes impinges upon this mystifying association of the individual with the cosmos. Carlyle, through his "editor," laments the fact that no philosopher or scientist has produced an epistemology or a philosophy of clothes: "How, then, comes it, may the reflective mind repeat, that the grand Tissue of all Tissues, the only *Tissue*, should have been quite overlooked by Science — the vestural Tissue, namely, of woolen or other Cloth; which Man's Soul wears as its outmost wrappage and overall; wherein his whole other Tissues are included and screened, his whole Faculties work, his whole Self lives, moves, and has its being?" (4). Teufelsdröckh's manuscripts answer this call by producing a *Spirit of Clothes* after Montesquieu's *Spirit of Laws*, and in this text the German philosopher comes to the conclusion that "In all his Modes and habilatory endeavors an Architectural Idea will be found lurking; his Body and the Cloth are the site and materials whereon and whereby his beautiful edifice, of a Person, is to be built" (28). Indeed, Carlyle moves toward an analysis of clothes that anticipates not only Henry David Thoreau, whose description of clothes as "outmost cuticle and mortal coil" echoes both in rhythm and idea Carlyle's phrase "outmost wrappage and overall," but also Thorstein Veblen whose discussion of the human need for clothes as a higher spiritual need echoes another Carlyle phrase: "The first spiritual want of a barbarous man is Decoration; as indeed we still see among the barbarous classes in civilized countries" (31).

Carlyle's most famous phrase from this book is, perhaps, the following: "Clothes gave us individuality, distinctions, social polity; Clothes have made Men of us; they are threatening to make Clothes-screens of us" (32). And this phrase does suggest the privileging of a naked authenticity above a clothed alienation. However, ultimately Carlyle begins to move modernity toward a discourse in which the new self is not a naked self, but one that is better — meaning more rationally — clothed. In *Sartor Resartus* Carlyle distinguishes between Sansculottism and Adamitism. Sansculottism, literally "without breeches," was a term "used to describe radical republicans among the Paris poor who gave up the knee-breeches associated with the *ancien régime* and adopted trousers as a symbol of the new era" (Carlyle 251). Carlyle writes, "Teufelsdröckh, though a Sansculottist, is no Adamite: and much perhaps as he might wish to go forth before this degenerate age "as a Sign," would nowise wish to do it, as those old Adamites did, in the state of Nakedness" (47). Thus, in addition to the symbolic dichotomy between nakedness and dress, the history of the discourse of modernity in the U.S. involves material and legal distinctions between written and unwritten sumptuary laws and a sartorial republicanism or liberalism that called for moderation, equality, even uniformity of clothes.

Homespun Ideology

It is no longer nakedness, but simple, unadorned, homemade dress that symbolizes the new American citizen for whom republican virtue and democratic ideals are more important than the pomp and adornment of old-world institutions of church and state. The Puritans left Europe behind, but they retained their own particular European sumptuary laws. Strictures and limitations on dress constituted the material expression of abstract differences and hierarchies.[2] By the revolutionary period, the material importance of clothing gave much more weight to the political as opposed to religions significance of costume. According to Michael Zakim, "Homespun clothing became a means of revolutionary agitation in colonial America. A patriot donned these unrefined products of household labor to renounce imperial hubris and promote its antithesis, domestic manufactures" (11). Homespun ideology advanced the notion that by manufacturing its own clothing from domestically produced textiles, every household in the American colonies could contribute to the nation's economic and political independence from England and its cultural independence from France. In contrast to seventeenth-century Anglo-American sumptuary laws that legally and materially buttressed Puritan ideals of providence and of the elect, the ideals of the early republic promoted the homespun ideology that called for simple dress as a common uniform (the simple dark suit made from homespun wool) that sartorially marked national identity, and promoted an economics of independence.[3] The idea was that each man could make himself as he made his own clothes, and that a nation of such men could make their own country an independent and free one. The shift from Puritan sumptuary regulation to sartorial republican simplicity was a shift from an ideology of status and subordination to one of anonymity and relative autonomy. The former aimed at hierarchy while the latter toward self-fashioning.

However, this contrast between Puritan and republican values can be misleading. For instance, John Winthrop, whose grandfather was a well-to-do clothier, uses the key metaphor of "knitting" to describe how a hierarchy of economic order can become a democratic congregation and polity. As early as the Puritan context, then, the English-speaking conception of the nation was a paradoxical mixture of hierarchy and democracy. Thomas Jefferson advocated the wearing of homespun as a political act, and James Buchanan, according to Patricia Cunningham, once stated that his proudest moment as an ambassador was "when [he] stood amidst the brilliant circle of foreign ministers and other court dignitaries, in the simple dress of an American citizen" (Cunningham 195). By the middle of the nineteenth century, what had begun as a direct political act of defiance against colonial rule — the adoption of homespun as a way of declaring economic as well as sartorial independence from England and Europe more generally — had become a style of self-fashioning. American modernity was not so much about the naked essence of the modern self, but, rather, the unadorned and simply garbed universal self.

Later, these complex paradoxes were expressed as contrasts between sentimental endorsement of sartorial democracy and critical dissent against newer modes of production. In the nineteenth century, new technologies of clothing production, standardization of size and fit, and transformations in the "efficient" employment of labor combined to complicate the ideology of simple dress. This is not to say that technological change determined ideological or cultural attitudes. In fact, one of the aims of this chapter is to show how homespun ideology developed, as Zakim has argued, alongside and in dialectic with technological change. However, it is important to take note of these changes and how a new discourse of dress framed and guided those changes. By the 1830s, clothing for both men and women, but especially for men, was no longer made for someone in particular (made to order), but, rather, made for anyone (ready-made). And after the Civil War clothing could be made for everyone (mass-produced ready-made).[4] These changes involved technological change but also ideological discourse, particularly the Franklinian image of the simply-dressed citizen, and, later, as we shall see, the ideological debate between Alger's myth of social mobility through sartorial transformation, and Thoreau's challenge to the emerging factory system. Thoreau's speculation on dress led him, eventually, to consider, at least briefly, the unfairness of capitalist production. Alger's mythology of democratic dress would cover what Thoreau attempted to lay bare.

By 1789, the introduction of mechanized yarn spinning, brought to the States from England by Samual Slater, established the first material bases for the transformation of homespun ideology into the rhetoric of a ready-made society. In 1993, the same year that Eli Whitney invented the cotton gin, Slater and two associates established the first yarn mill in the United States.[5] Other innovations, such as the invention of the inch tape measure in 1820 and techniques of standardization (which would culminate during the Civil War), allowed garment makers to speak of a uniformity and standardization of size. According to Kidwell, "Men preoccupied with business no longer felt the need to dress with individuality. Clad now in sober black, which seemed appropriate to the new industrial world, they had come to look alike. Everyone was in a hurry, agreeable to a uniform sameness of dress..." (37). Thus, one can speak of the investment of America as part of what Alan Trachtenberg has described as the "incorporation of America," the restructuring of national culture (along with the national economy, polity, and ethnicity) after the model of corporate organization of labor and capital into large systems. Such incorporation also results in the structuring of subjective experience into these systems. American investment (in both the financial and sartorial sense) can expand and complicate our understanding of American incorporation because clothes exist at that space where material culture, money, and the body itself— the individual corpus of the corporate nation — co-exist. To be clothed in a consumer item produced through a thoroughly incorporated system is to wear the nation literally on one's sleeve.

By the end of the eighteenth century, simplicity in dress had become a symbol for republican virtue, democratic ideals, and economic independence in the United States. Benjamin Franklin, for example, contrasted the pretentious imitation of European fashion with the honest coarse cloth and modestly designed garments of the model American citizen. This contrast became an important ideological statement that often linked sartorial simplicity with direct unadorned language, hard work, and moral rectitude. The economic underpinnings of simple dress were, however, complex and even contradictory. Simplicity, for example, didn't always mean affordability. In fact, one of the causes for Revolutionary American resistance to fine European fashions can be found in the United States' protest against cheaply imported French and British cloth. While it is tempting to see this resistance to European fashions as a resistance to European class hierarchies, this was not always the case. American resistance to European fashions was sometimes defended on the basis of the more Puritan privileging of social order. As Michael Zakim has observed, "Fourteen Penny Stuffs ... spawned a miasma of social pretension, and with it, a betrayal of the civic order. The natural hierarchy was obfuscated by people dressing beyond their rank." As early as 1722, Franklin linked "economic goods with the public good" in intoning against cheap imitations of upper class finery. In condemning cheap imitation of fancy dress, Franklin was endorsing existing class hierarchies (Zakim 17). Simple dress may have been a symbol of republican virtue, but it was not an emblem of economic democratization or of social mobility. Americans should dress within their means.

The ideal of simple dress in North America did not espouse or encourage real democratization, but rather served as an ideology that produced the myth of social mobility, at least in the Franklinian mold of virtuous self-help and melioration. Unadorned fashion opened the way towards what Michael Zakim has called a "postsumptuary world." Franklin's ideological position was that social hierarchies were natural, but that individuals could transcend them; this transcendence, however, was to be accomplished not through imitation of fine dress, but through virtue, austerity, and hard work. Franklin "eventually became the colonies' leading publicist for the distinctly nonpuritan idea that virtue could be acquired through regular habits." This transformation of the Puritan ethic into a post–Puritan civic faith in the accumulation of personal wealth could also be expressed through representations of clothing. In commenting on this postsumptuary ideal in his pseudonymously published newspaper columns, Franklin described his image of the honest citizen dressed in simple clothing: "He appear'd in the plainest Country Garb; his Great Coat was coarse and looked old and thread-bare; his Linnen was homespun; his Beard perhaps of Seven Days Growth, his Shoes thick and heavy, and every Part of his Dress corresponding." The homespun linen, the heavy shoes, and the beard point to the social values of independence, austerity, and thrift. By the beginning of the nineteenth century, through a proliferation of images like this one, homespun ideology would become what Zakim calls "a foundation myth of simpler and more frugal times designed to help establish the basis for social order in a secularizing, postsumptuary world" (Zakim 18). Homespun ideology solved a basic dilemma at the heart of American national identity — the conflict between the value of capitalist acquisition on the one hand, and the ideals of democracy and equality on the other. Commerce might corrupt, but it also had the potential to civilize by encouraging both industry and frugality (Zakim 19). It is in its ability to combine industry with frugality that the ideology of homespun materials solves the American paradox between acquisitiveness and democratic ideals.

Two figures can be seen as emblematic of the nineteenth-century continuation of and response to Franklin's postsumptuary America: Henry David Thoreau's authorial persona in *Walden*, and Horatio Alger, Jr.'s Richard

Hunter — the hero of the Ragged Dick stories. Thoreau's *Walden* takes Franklin's notion of virtuous self-improvement to its logical and radical conclusion. In Thoreau's dissenting revision of the independent citizen, improving the self does not, at bottom, mean becoming prosperous or accumulating wealth. Rather, by becoming self-reliant and evolving out of his natural context, the individual demands and enacts the improvement of his society as a whole. Living within one's means is not, for Thoreau, the way to wealth, but the path to a "more perfect" polity. The individual is invested in the nation not as a share within a financial stock, but, rather, as a radical part that can change the whole. Alger, on the other hand, produces a sentimentalized fictional version of Poor Richard in Ragged Dick.[6]

Before the Civil War, the ideal of American citizenship was often embodied in the image of the self-sufficient individual dressed in handmade garments of homespun wool. However, by the late 1860s, because of changes in technology and labor, including the standardization of measurements resulting from war mobilization, and because of the growth of an American market for consumer goods, the ideal image of the American citizen changed. Now, the relatively uniform identity of a citizen in ready-made garments became the emblem of democratization. These were iconic figures, presented in printed word and image.[7] Citizenship was no longer a matter of sumptuary laws, material wants, and social distinctions as it had been in the Puritan era of congregational citizenship, nor was it the ideal of economic and political independence espoused by Ben Franklin. However, the ideals of social mobility, opportunity, and self-transformation were deeply influenced by both of these earlier conceptions of the national self. America's industrialization, urbanization, and expansion were accompanied by a change in notions of American identity, and yet these notions of identity were in tension with earlier conceptions of the self invested in society: the ready-made self continued to be informed by ideals of the homespun self. However, ultimately, in the postwar years, an ideal American citizen was no longer a changeless and abiding individual confined to certain boundaries of culture and society; rather, the American was a protean and socially mobile subject.

In the new discourses of advertising and popular narrative in the United States, new notions of the self became widely available, including images of clothing and the increasingly popular narrative of rags to riches. During these years marked by war and the acceleration of industry, American literature — both high and low, both dissenting and sentimental — was coming into its own, and American homespun ideology was giving way to an American ready-made culture. Homespun clothing and ready-made dress have *both* been read as symbols for the democratization of American culture. Thus, the transition from one to the other marks an important shift in self-conceptions of national identity in the United States. This awareness can be seen in these two different works, both coming out of New England Unitarian ideas, but separated by war, and by different ideological motives. Homespun conceptions of citizenship were still grounded in Jeffersonian ideals about the nation's measured agrarian expansion. Like Jefferson's blueprint for a nation of independent farmers, the basically Franklinian notion of the homespun citizen was based on the image of independent vested individuals. By contrast, the ready-made citizen was part of an emerging expression of urban citizenship beginning to be embodied in popular narratives like the Ragged Dick stories. While Thoreau and Alger dealt with the question of capitalism differently, both confronted the emergent hegemony of markets by at least acknowledging their pragmatic reality. Moreover, both Thoreau and Alger anticipated some aspects of American realism, including Thoreau's dissenting view of what Theodore Dreiser would later call the "conventional expression of morals" (*Carrie* 73) and what Carol Nackenoff has read as Alger's ambivalent response to the Gilded Age, for if there is something sentimental in the realism of the late nineteenth century, there is some social criticism in the Alger tales as well.

It would seem, then, that Thoreau is the radical and dissenting extension of Franklinian ideals, and Alger the conservative and sentimental expression of the same. However, such a reading would dismiss certain basic affinities between these two very different figures. Both, whether through Alger's more conservative vision or Thoreau's more radical one, imagined a new kind of subject — one that could undergo transformation. No easy dichotomy can be made between Alger and Thoreau on this head. Alger's Ragged Dick becomes the respectable Richard Hunter through honesty, hard work, acquisition of literacy, and embracing his more noble characteristics, ones he already possesses but that are buried under bad economic habits. But even these habits are driven by noble qualities: generosity with friends, for example. Dick, like Cinderella, gains clothes that better express who he already is: his inner worth, including his loyalty as a friend and his honesty. But in some ways, Dick's story reverses the Cinderella myth in that Dick gains some of his best qualities — at least those best suited for prosperity in a modern capitalist world — by wearing new clothes: frugality, the habit of saving money, but spending it wisely when necessary, investing in his education. These qualities and habits come about only *after*, and, it can be argued, as a result of dressing properly. His first respectable suit of clothes comes as a gift, and the look of respectability helps him gain other tangible benefits. Thoreau, too, charts the transformation of the individual as a molting, a natural change wrought by work and conduct but expressed in a change of clothes. But this change comes at a necessary moment in the individual's life. Thus, while Thoreau and Alger present very different literary expressions of and changes to the Franklinian ideal, both do so through the creation of what we might call the protean subject. For Alger, the self is transformed to fit into normative models; for Thoreau, the self *transforms* those models.

Fashioning the Self Out of Nature

Thoreau argued for self-fashioning in ways that espouse and at the same time critique and revise American homespun ideology. He privileges what he calls the "possibility of change," arguing that "there are as many ways as there can be radii from one center" (266). This discussion of "change" rises out of Thoreau's famous critique of lives led in "quiet desperation" (263). Regret comes not from transgressing social mores, but, rather, from sheepishly following commonly accepted standards: "if I repent of anything, it is very likely to be my good behavior," that is, behavior dictated by "what my neighbors call good" (266). Thus, from the outset, *Walden* is a description of iconoclastic self-fashioning—the act of embracing change, or what Thoreau calls the "miracle" of change (266).

The possibilities of iconoclastic self-fashioning are endless, the self is protean, but there is only one center. Thoreau's geometrical metaphor presents the idea of oneness in multiplicity or multiplicity out of unity, *e pluribus unum*. For Thoreau, the center of the infinite radii of iconoclastic self-fashioning is not society, but nature. The self must be created from the ground up, from the bare necessities of life toward its fruits. Thoreau bases his discussion of the protean subject on natural history, discussing how "*Nature* is as well *adapted* to our weakness as to our strength" (266 emphases added). The radius that is Thoreau's own narrated life at Walden moves outward from the basic material economy of the first section toward the reading and aesthetic delights of its later sections.

Like Cabeza de Vaca, whose nakedness (or absence of clothing) is the emblem of American identity, Thoreau begins by stripping everything away. The first human necessity Thoreau identifies beyond the basic needs of "brute creation," "Food and Shelter," (267) is clothing (followed by fuel). It is a way of keeping in "vital heat" (276), and constitutes the first tool for the social construction of self. But the movement from a state of nature to a state of society is inevitable. What is important about clothing is that it is common to both; garments occupy the precise evolutionary moment when the individual moves from a state of nature to a state of society because clothes are both necessary and supplementary.[8]

Thoreau attempts to balance an evolutionary fatalism with the infinite possibilities of individual "free-will," and clothes allow for a useful prop upon which to balance this argument. He bases his sartorial speculations upon natural philosophy:

> Darwin, the naturalist, says of the inhabitants of Tierra del Fuego, that while his own party, who were well clothed and sitting close to the fire, were far from too warm, these naked savages, who were farther off, were observed, to his great surprise, to be streaming with perspiration at undergoing such a roasting [268].

Balancing the demands of life in a state of nature with the potentiality of a life of free-will requires rhetorical acumen. As part of this rhetorical dexterity, Thoreau questions how things have evolved in humanity's social, as opposed to natural, state: our current society was far from inevitable. In fact, Thoreau suggests that with the ever-increasing social significance of clothes, "men degenerate" (rather than evolve), needing more and more clothing, more and more fuel, to stay warm and to feel protected. He condemns the "accumulated dross" of industrialized life, and contrasts this life from "a life of simplicity, independence, magnanimity, and trust" (270).

Thoreau's account of self-fashioning is addressed to those who know they are discontented, but this discontent is a discontent not with the natural order of things, but with human perversion of that order. He addresses those who see social evolution as having diverged from natural evolution. However, the remedy to this discontent is not wealth, as Franklin would have claimed, but contentment within one's means. But rather than passively accepting ones place in the social order, contentment turns out to be a form of radical resistance to production and consumption. Specifically, for Thoreau, the problem is the process of selling and buying. His main purpose in retreating into the woods is "to avoid the necessity of selling" (274). The hypothetical anecdote Thoreau uses to make this point is that of an Indian who weaves baskets and hopes to sell them. He sees that "the lawyer had only to weave arguments, and by some magic wealth and standing followed." So the Indian decides to weave baskets, but he "had not discovered that it was necessary for him to make it worth the other's while to buy them, or at least make him think that it was so" (274). However, while wanting to avoid the base requirements of useless commerce — the socially normative exercise of exchange value — Thoreau does not avoid what he calls "strict business habits" which he says are "essential for every man." Thoreau's emphasis seems to be on *habits* rather than *business*. Thoreau is interested more in the *discipline* of business than in its profits, but this discipline does not fit the individual to the social order, but, rather, makes the individual an agent of social transformation. And, furthermore, that social transformation, for Thoreau, is one that brings society back into line with natural requirements.

Thus, even Thoreau's dissent against commonly accepted opinion draws on an important strain within American thought — the ideal of self-improvement through self-reliance. As such, he, in fact, reiterates fairly conventional notions of simple dress espoused by Franklin earlier. The discipline of business, its set of habits imposed on the self by the self, not by the boss on his workers, leads to a kind of virtue or self-improvement. Thoreau is himself at the center of his experiment of creating a self through certain imposed habits. And these habits are imposed from a lack of capital, not from its abundance. Clothing plays no small part in this development of a set of business habit that function to fashion a self rather than to accumulate wealth:

> As this business was to be entered into without the usual capital, it may be easy to conjecture where those means, that will still be indispensable to every such undertaking, were to be obtained. As for Clothing, to come at once to the practical part of the question, perhaps we are led oftener by the love of novelty and a regard for the opinions of men, in procuring it, than by true utility. Let him who has work to do recollect that the object of clothing is, first, to retain the vital heat, and secondly, in this state of society, to cover nakedness, and he may judge how much of any necessary or important work may be accomplished without adding to his wardrobe [276].

Thoreau privileges the utility of clothes over their novelty, and their practicality above "the opinions of men." He calls on "him who has work to do," focusing on action rather than image. He follows up this statement by contrasting mannequin-like kings and queens who are vested with a nation's image of itself but have no real substance in and of themselves to serious men whose clothes have practical use because the men themselves are useful men: Kings and queens who wear a suit of clothes just once "are no better than wooden horses to hang clean clothes on" (276–7). Here, Thoreau not only echoes Franklin's privileging of simple dress, he also anticipates the comments of Henry Adams some seventy years later, when Adams would argue that the American self had become a dummy upon which garments were to be hung.[9] Thoreau wanted the clothes to become part of the self, or to grow out of the practices of the individual the way skin or feathers grow on animals and birds.

In Thoreau's conception of the dressed individual, the longer we wear a suit of clothes, the less like a wooden horse or mannequin we become: "Every day our garments become more assimilated to ourselves, receiving the impress of the wearer's character, until we hesitate to lay them aside, without such delay and medical appliances and some such solemnity even as our bodies." Keeping ones clothes for as long as possible transforms those clothes into an essential part of identity, no longer a supplement to that identity. Thoreau contrasts this assimilation of dress to the character and body of the wearer to the more common attitude of his time — that the clothes make the man.

> No man ever stood lower in my estimation for having a patch in his clothes; yet I am sure that there is greater anxiety, commonly, to have fashionable or at least clean and unpatched clothes, than to have a sound conscience. I sometimes try my acquaintances by such tests as this: Who would wear a patch, or two extra seams only, over the knee? It would be easier for them to hobble to town with a broken leg than with a broken pantaloon [277].

In the perverted social state that Thoreau challenged clothes dictate vital activity — the torn suit is like a broken body. Again, Thoreau brings these comments back to the notion of acting as one knows to be good and respectable, not what is considered good and respectful: "Dress a scarecrow in your last shift, you standing shiftless by, who would not sooner salute the scarecrow?" He declares, "It is an interesting question how far men would retain their relative rank if they were divested of their clothes" (277). Clearly, Thoreau is making a post- or anti-sumptuary argument.

But Thoreau is careful to distinguish between outward changes in dress and real transformations in the individual and protean self resulting in the need for different, not necessarily new, clothes. Those who turn a keen eye to their habiliments before they turn their hand to work are changeable wafflers, not men of constant character: "Only they who go to soirees and legislative halls must have new coats, coats to change as often as the man changes in them." Social climbing and conventional notions of respectability drive men to don new clothes. But for those concerned more with hard work and self-reliance, old clothes are best:

> A man who has at length found something to do will not need to get a new suit to do it in; for him the old will do, that has lain dusty in the garret for an indeterminate period. Old Shoes will serve a hero longer than they have served his valet — if a hero ever has a valet — bare feet are older than shoes, and he can make them do [278].

Thoreau complains that no man "ever saw his old clothes — his old coat, actually worn out, resolved into its primitive elements, so that it was not a deed of charity to bestow it on some poor boy, by him perchance to be bestowed on some poorer still, or shall we say richer, who could do with less?" (278). Clothes, like the skin of a snake, must fall away almost of their own accord, or because of the work the wearer does. Again, this is grounded in notions of natural philosophy and natural history. However, he does not see the individual as locked into an unchanging identity, but, rather, advocates evolutionary transformation, and organic change. In this conception of person and clothing, cloth is a living substance, almost a social organ of the human body.

But Thoreau's comments against men who change their clothes as often as they change their minds can be misleading. He recognizes some need for change and transformation. By contrast to inconstant men led by fickle fashion, the man who has found a true vocation chooses and wears clothes as an extension of his labor, and this leads to change. The discussion of such change is grounded in a discussion of the self, the individual, the "I." In the opening pages of *Walden,* Thoreau describes his own rhetorical position as one that embraces the first person — he will write as an *I*. It is almost as if he is donning simple unadorned rhetorical attire. This image of the unadorned self becomes personified and material later when he explains the nature of the self and its relation to dress. While this self should not be changeable — not inconstant — it can be protean, or at least evolutionary. Indeed, Thoreau's most famous comments about being wary of "enterprises that require new clothes" address directly the question of the self transformed:

> I say, beware of enterprises that require new clothes, and not rather a new wearer of clothes. If there is not a new man, how can the new clothes be made to fit? If you have any enterprise before you, try it in your old clothes. All men want, not something to *do with*, but something to *do*, or rather something to *be*. Perhaps we should never procure a new suit, however ragged or dirty the old, until we have so conducted, so enterprised or sailed in some way, that we feel like new men in the old, and that to retain it would be like keeping new wine in old bottles. Our moulting, like that of the fowls, must be a crisis in our lives. The loon retires to solitary ponds to spend it. Thus also the snake casts its slough, and the caterpillar its wormy coat, by an internal industry and expansion; for clothes are but our outmost cuticle and mortal coil. Otherwise we shall be found sailing under false colors, and be inevitably cashiered at last by our own opinion, as well as that of mankind [278–9].

While on the one hand Thoreau attacks those who would change clothes with their changing loyalties or changeable convictions, he, nevertheless, conceives of a self that is subject to change or that is changed by his or her actions. Notice the contrast between Thoreau's use of the word "enterprise" as a noun and as a verb. It is not the job, the social position, or the division of labor in a political economy that is important, but, rather, the individual's work and life. When a change of clothes does occur, it should be a metamorphosis: like the "caterpillar" emerging from "its wormy coat." Thoreau carefully distinguishes, then, between the fop or even the politician who "needs" a new coat for every soiree and legislative hall, and the self-reliant and enterprising man who *works* his way out of old clothes and into new ones.

Thoreau contrasts what he calls "our outside and often thin and fanciful clothes" from the "thicker garments" of the body itself. The first constitute "our epidermis, or false skin," the latter comprise "our cellular integument, or cortex." The thin outside clothes "partake not of our life, and may be stripped off here and there," while the figuratively thicker garment (the body) is "constantly worn" (279). And yet, according to this earlier commentary on transformation from the inside out, even the body of the self can change. Central to Thoreau's construction of the self is independence, but this independence is dependent on work, and is measured in both currency and costume:

> While one thick garment is, for most purposes, as good as three thin ones, and cheap clothing can be obtained at prices really to suit customers; while a thick coat can be bought for five dollars, which will last as many years, thick pantaloons for two dollars, cowhide boots for a dollar and a half a pair, a summer hat for quarter of a dollar, and a winter cap for sixty-two and a half cents, or a better be made at home at nominal cost, where is he so poor that, clad in such a suit, *of his own earning*, there will not be found wise men to do him reverence?" [279–80].

Through a combination of homespun and ready-mades, a man of modest means may be dressed respectably. What is important here is that Thoreau mixes and matches the costume of the independent individual. Thoreau lists some of the clothes as purchased — probably from slop shops common at the time, or from newly emerging ready-made shops, not yet producing on a mass scale but for local markets — but also suggests that some can be made at home at a "nominal cost." Here we have the individual somewhere between the homespun figure of Ben Franklin's imagination and the ready-made and standardized individual of the next century that we will find in the work of Theodore Dreiser and Abraham Cahan.

If clothing is such an essential aspect of self-fashioning, then homespun is the truest way to fashion a self. What then of the individual in factory-made clothes? Thoreau's discussion of clothing and work leads to his dissent against the spirit of capitalism as it was developing around mid-century. His discussion of his own modest life at Walden Pond, with his lack of capital investment and his attempt "to be at once pilot and captain, and owner and underwriter" of his business affairs, leads him eventually to a critique of the emerging factory system that would, within quarter of a century, overtake the United States ideologically and materially. Thoreau concludes his discussion of dress on the subject of the factory system, anticipating in other ways these later writers who were concerned with the sartorial self in an industrialized America. The factory system was well established in England by the 1830s but was in its early stages in the United States, fostered through speculative clothing production and the development of clothing emporiums which were beginning to appear as early as 1815 but that did not take on economic significance until mid century. "If the clothing industry had an actual birth, it was in the emporiums and warehouses that appeared in New York and in other American seaboard entrepots after the end of the War of 1812 and the reopening of European trade in 1815." As an important innovator in this rising business of dress, James Burk approached his actions with a new "ethos of accumulation ... guided by the anticipation of what would sell tomorrow rather than by what was available today.... The goods were now a means of generating capital rather than vice versa, and clothing was simply a current, and currently convenient, means for Burk to do so" (Zakim 41). Clothing manufacturers, not all of whom were skilled tailors, began to sell greater quantities of more cheaply produced clothing. Men like Stewart, Burk, Brooks, Williams, and Witmarsh "now saw their chance to succeed in business by buying cheap and selling at small margins. It clearly mattered far less to them precisely what they were selling" (45). This new system required cheaper production methods, including cheap labor, and Thoreau was aware of this.

> I cannot believe that our factory system is the best mode by which men may get clothing. The condition of the operatives is becoming every day more like that of the English; and it cannot be wondered at, since, as far as I have heard or observed, the principal object is not that mankind may be well and honestly clad but, unquestionably, that the corporations may be enriched [281–2].

For Thoreau, the industrialization of clothing production was responsible for the mis-measure of man in two ways: by measuring body instead of character, and by undervaluing labor in pursuit of profit. National identity, for Thoreau, suffered as a result of both of these errors. A ready-made individual took the place of a homespun self.

Alger's Ready-Made Individual

An industrially produced, popular, sentimental, and often didactic literature would drown out Thoreau's dissenting voice by the 1860s when popular novels provided a venue for what Nackenoff calls Alger's pedagogical representations of enterprising young men. At the same time, the mechanization of clothing manufacture initiated by mechanized yarn and cotton production at the end of the eighteenth century would accelerate, partly as a result of the Civil War. During that conflict "chest and height measurements of over one million conscripts were taken.... Following the war, the army's study was made available to the manufacturers of civilian clothing" (Kidwell, 105). This produced a mass of statistics that could and was used by commercial manufacturers to establish standard measurements for the male body. There is an interesting historical irony here that must be noted: a conflict that had almost divided the nation, resulted in the standardization of measuring the individual American citizen, in effect unifying the men of America under a set of reproducible sizes and proportions. By 1879, Albert Bolles, writing in his *Industrial History of the United States*, would note that "everyone can secure an excellent fit at any ready-made clothing store.... A good fit can be obtained, even for dress suits" (quoted in Kidwell, 105).

Through the middle and latter part of that century, then, the expansion of the ready-to-wear market became a sign for American democracy. For example, in documenting the history of their own company, Brooks Brothers especially noted that their clientele included Abraham Lincoln, "for whom we made, among other things, an overcoat on the occasion of his second inaugural. The quilted lining of this was embellished ... with an embroidered design of an eagle holding in its beak a pennant inscribed, 'One Country, One Destiny.'"[10] The label sums up nicely the ideological use of clothing in American popular culture: Lincoln's *custom-made* suit represents the democratic ideal to be found in the movement toward a *ready-to-wear* market in Brooks Brothers' description of their industry. And yet, the inscription itself could be read as much in terms of manifest destiny as it could in terms of union and equality and democratic ideals. This use of clothing to represent social identity and to stand for American democracy was an important part of nineteenth and early twentieth century fiction as well in the United States. In both its material and literary history, the rise of ready-to-wear clothing was as ambiguous as the label on Lincoln's coat. Did it suggest union in equality or the colonization and the assimilation of difference? As we shall see in the case of Cather, for example, clothes — from handmade to store-bought — suggest both Whitmanesque democratic vistas (or vestments) *as well as* manifest destinies.

Thus, it is not surprising that a key component of Alger's pedagogical narratives, written in the 1860s, was the significance of well-fitting, clean attire as a means to social mobility. By mid century, ready-made clothing production was an important part of America's growing economy, and it transformed the symbolic meaning of simple dress. Simplicity was no longer crafted at home from domestically produced wool, nor even purchased from custom-made tailors' shops, but, rather, manufactured in workshops in New York and textile factories in Massachusetts, and sold to anyone who could afford the ever-decreasing cost of acquiring a new suit. The myth of identity that Alger produced for Americans beginning in the 1860s presented the availability of affordable clothing as a means to social mobility and economic independence. In this process, distinction and uniformity, identity and anonymity, independence and standardization went hand in hand. Alger advocated some of the same basic ideas that Thoreau presented — self-reliance and hard work. But for Alger, the good opinion of others and normative expectations mattered. What is interesting is that both seem to advocate a basic utility and modesty in dress. But in Alger's rags-to-riches myth, a change in clothing usually precedes or serves as a catalyst for, rather than following and expressing the transformation of self. Dick Hunter acquires a new suit of clothes before he acquires the good business habits that lead him to success. In the Alger myth there is a relationship between materials and money: rags are transformed into riches; clothing becomes currency; vestment becomes investment.

Within the first few pages of *Ragged Dick*, Alger points our attention to Dick's clothes — his ragged attire. When a gentleman asks Dick what tailor he patronizes, criticizing the "fit" of his worn clothes, Dick responds by telling him that he acquired his coat from George Washington, himself:

> He wore it all through the Revolution, and it got torn some, 'cause he fit so hard. When he died he told his wider to give it to some smart young feller that hadn't got none of his own; so she gave it to me. But if you'd like it, sire, to remember General Washington by, I'll let you have it reasonable.

Then, when the gentleman asks about Dick's pants — whether they, too, are from Washington, Dick replies: "No, they was a gift from Lewis Napoleon. Lewis had outgrown 'em and sent 'em to me,— he's bigger than me, and that's why they don't fit" (41). Dick's ironic reference to the president's coat does more than provide comic relief. From the outset of the novel, the joke links dress to national identity, even if seemingly ironically. Even the Napoleon pants, though not part of American national identity, ascribe symbolic significance to clothing. Most important perhaps are the fit and condition of the clothes — too big and baggy, worn to rags. The actual condition of the clothes underscores Dick's economic condition, whereas his joke points to his high aspirations. Clearly, what Dick needs is something to bridge the gap between his material conditions and his latent moral aspirations, expressible only through the subconscious vehicle of a joke about his clothes.

The following passages present moral economic instruction to help Dick bridge that gap. Dick earns enough to dress well, but he spends it all on extravagant entertainment and food, often treating his friends to dinners: "There were not a few young clerks who employed Dick from time to time in his professional capacity, who scarcely earned as much as he, greatly as their style and dress exceeded his. Dick was careless in his earnings" (43). Thus, being careful with one's earnings means, presumably, spending at least a portion of them on "style and dress." Instead, Dick spends his profits on the theatre, restaurants, and gambling: "He was fond of going to the Old Bowery Theatre, and to Tony Pastor's" (43). And later, he repeats this to Frank: "I needn't have been Ragged Dick so long if I hadn't spent my money in goin' to the theatre, and treatin' boys to oyster-stews, and bettin' money on cards, and such like.... One time I saved up five dollars to buy me a new rig-out, cos my best suit was all in rags, when Limpy Jim wanted me to play a game with him" (75). As the narrative proceeds, we learn that dressing well is not just another extravagance, but, rather, has the potential of curbing bad economic habits. Throughout the novel, the narrative imparts moral lessons, and many of these center on clothes as the most important material expression of character, wealth, and identity.

The question raised in this novel is whether Dick's character is merely revealed when he acquires the proper attire, or whether that character emerges in part because of the attire. Do the clothes make this man, or was he always a diamond in the rough? Answering this question can help us understand the wider context in which Thoreau's philosophy of self circulated. Thoreau's fairly dynamic notion of the transformation of self—and the changing of clothes—was just one possible answer to the question of the self in a democratic society. Alger's myth of rags to riches was a more conservative conception of the self, one that suggested a fairly stable, rather than dynamic notion of the individual in society. The self, in Alger, is produced through the individual's honesty and hard work, assisted by the kind help of strangers, and through the democratizing influence of the ready-made clothing industry. Dick's transformation is impossible without the availability of clothes for himself and for his tutor and friend, Henry Fosdick. Some of these clothes are provided as gifts—from wealthy strangers—and some, like the clothes Dick provides for Henry, are bought from the ready-made clothing shops that were, by the 1860s, an important part of the New York economy. Philanthropic strangers and cheaply available clothes help Dick on his way to wealth.

Dick's wardrobe does not admit him to the finest restaurants, but by Chapter 4, Dick acquires one of his most important assets—a new set of clothes given to him as a gift from Frank Whitney and his father (a modern fairy godfather for an industrial age), whom Dick has helped by offering to guide Frank through New York while his father attends to business. In fact, the giving of clothes as gifts is a figure that recurs twice more in this novel. Dick, himself, once he begins to save money, provides a new suit of clothes to his friend and tutor, Henry Fosdick. And later, James Rockwell gives Dick a new suit of clothes as a reward for saving his son from drowning. What is important here is that for Dick, vestments are investments. The clothes he acquires from the Whitneys open the door to a respectable residence. The clothes Dick gives to Henry allow Henry to gain employment and, thus, ease Dick's own burden of supporting this young friend who has book learning, but has less street smarts and business savvy than Dick. In all three cases, clothes suggest a transformation. This is similar to, but also very different from, Thoreau's sense that a change of clothes should result from "enterprising" or working in such a way that the wearer of clothes is, himself, transformed.

The first transformation for Dick is less this kind of molting than a Cinderella-like transformation with the help of a fairy godfather. Dick, himself, notes this when he can barely recognize himself in the mirror: "By gracious

... that isn't me.... It reminds me of Cinderella ... when she was changed into a fairy princess" (58). Alger turns the Cinderella myth upside down: In the Cinderella narrative, the protagonist is eventually arrayed in a costume befitting her essentially good nature. Anne Hollander suggests a reverse reading of Cinderella in her analysis of clothes as social signifiers. She argues that dress can "succeed so well in pretending that it truly transforms the aspiring pretender into his ideal." This is the reverse of Cinderella because "her rags are supposed to hide but not diminish her loveliness and virtue." Her "magic finery" and the "fitting slipper" simply reveal the moral fineness already there. Cinderella "keeps the same self" through the wardrobe change. But in more realist representations, "rags obviously cannot be 'seen through' to something lovely underneath because they themselves express and also create a tattered condition of soul." In these more realistic narratives, the "habit of fine clothes produces personal grace from the outside in" (*Seeing through Clothes*, 443). Hollander distinguishes between the realist novel of the nineteenth century, and the fairy-tale of the eighteenth and seventeenth centuries.

> The Cinderella myth ... expresses the dear idea that ugliness and bad behavior cannot be transformed by exquisite finery, whereas Balzac relentlessly demonstrates that they can indeed when the motivation is strong and the method is efficiently studied. A truer-to-life fairy tale — perhaps because it comes from the acute nineteenth-century Hans Christian Andersen — is the story of the ugly duckling transformed into a swan, achieving beauty through self-knowledge and patience. Had the stepsisters been beautiful and Cinderella ugly, the seventeenth-century Perrault fairy tale would have had all the basic elements of a novel such as *Jane Eyre* [444].

In Alger's version of the reverse Cinderella myth, decent clothes can make a person better from the outside in. This is not to say that Dick begins the story as a bad person. Rather, it is to say that good habits and good motives can be acquired, and that they are more readily acquired *after* one dons good clothes. This is a distinct move away from Thoreau's notion that we change our clothes only through work, work that can change us internally. Both Thoreau and Alger imagine the individual as having the potential for change, but Alger moves the source of that change closer to the surface and shifts the motive for that change from nature to society. In the case of Fosdick, the transformation *is* closer to what Thoreau describes — Henry Fosdick has worked as a scholar, a teacher, and thus, in a sense, earned his stripes, while Dick seems to have magically changed his spots. The final example — of Dick acquiring new clothes, again — occurs as a result of a kind of baptism, as if Dick is born again. What Alger presents in this narrative of mobility is a cross between the fairy-tale like transformation — in which a character becomes, in some essential way, what he always has been — and the Thoreauvian idea that the individual's sartorial change is the result of radically changed actions.

Alger revises the Cinderella myth by placing it squarely within an industrial age of labor, capital, entrepreneurship, and social mobility. Mr. Whitney gives Dick what is basically Franklinian advice:

> You know in this free country poverty in early life is no bar to a man's advancement.... So you see, my lad, that my studious habits paid me in money, as well as in another way.... If you try to learn, you can, and if you ever expect to do anything in the world, you must know something of books.... All labor is respectable, my lad, and you have no cause to be ashamed of any honest business ... earn your living in the way you are accustomed to, avoid extravagance, and save up a little money if you can [108–9].

Dick does, eventually, acquire the literacy and virtue that allow him to rise in what Alger describes as a dangerous, though ultimately fair, world of commerce. In the meantime, however, even before Dick has had a chance to develop an internal change through diligent study, he acquires an outward change that is similar to what Hollander calls the reversal of the Cinderella myth. Simply donning the new clothes gives Dick a new sense of self: "Perhaps it was the new clothes he wore, which made him feel a little more aristocratic. At all events, instead of patronizing the cheap restaurant where he usually procured his meals, he went into the refectory attached to Lovejoy's Hotel, where the prices were higher and the company more select. In his ordinary dress, Dick would have been excluded, but now he had the appearance of a very respectable, gentlemanly boy, whose presence would not discredit any establishment" (113). On the one hand, Alger describes the reverse of the Cinderella story—the clothes he wore made him "feel a little more aristocratic." On the other hand, he reinforces the basically conservative side of the Cinderella myth—the clothes simply reveal what is already fine about Dick.

This notion that Dick already has within him those qualities that make a young man like Frank respectable is reinforced when Dick has to decide which set of clothes to wear as his work clothes as a bootblack: "A question now came up for consideration. For the first time in his life Dick possessed two suits of clothes. Should he put on the clothes Frank had given him, or resume his old rags?" Alger's narrator tells us that Dick "had rather a contempt for good clothes, or *at least he thought so*" (120, emphasis added). Dick is not so much becoming a different person as much as he his understanding his own inner identity better, because "now, as he surveyed the ragged and dirty coat and the patched pants, Dick felt ashamed of them. He was unwilling to appear in the streets with them" (120). Shame becomes an important quality that Dick acquires—or that emerges—with his consciousness of personal style and sartorial identity.

But in addition to acquiring a healthy sense of shame (or, simply, in addition to becoming virtuous), Dick also acquires, along with the new clothes, economic smarts: "Yet, if he went to work in his new suit, he was in danger of spoiling it, and he might not have it in his power to purchase a new one. *Economy* dictated a return to the old garments" (120). What Dick realizes, however, is that looking respectable has its own economic value: "Dick tried them [the old clothes] on, and surveyed himself in the cracked glass; but the reflection did not please him" (120). Dick decides that these clothes "don't look 'spectable" and decides to wear his new clothes. This is an investment in more ways than one, because not only do the new clothes give him access to the world of commerce and wealth (restaurants where wealthier people eat), they force him to pursue profits more vigorously.

New clothes not only make Dick look different and feel different, they also make him act differently. For example, because he wants to keep his clothes clean, he is no longer willing to sleep on the streets or in doorways: "with his new clothes, he was unwilling to pass the night out of doors. 'I should spile 'em,' he thought, 'and that wouldn't pay'" (114). Not only do the new clothes change his habits — of spending money on entertainment rather than lodging — but they also make him think in terms of investment: "that wouldn't pay." His clothes, as much as his ability to pay, buy his way into a lodging house, and because he is able to offer his room to Henry Fosdick, his new clothes lead indirectly to his acquisition of literacy.

Like Theodore Dreiser's heroine Caroline Meeber after him, Alger's hero gives himself an allowance for clothing: "I must try to earn a little more ... to pay for my room, and to buy some new clo'es when these is wore out" (120). Alger gives us a detailed account of Dick's expenditures and his savings: "In fact he had formed the ambitious design of starting an account at a savings' bank, in order to have something to fall back upon in case of sickness or any other emergency, or at any rate as a reserve fund to expend in clothing or other necessary articles when he required them" (121). Dick's emerging consciousness — his sense that decent attire is something to be desired — can be contrasted to the foil to Dick's character: Micky MaGuire. "Now Micky was proud of his strength, and of the position of leader which it had secured him. Moreover he was democratic in his tastes, and had a jealous hatred of those who wore good clothes and kept their faces clean. He called it putting on airs, and resented the implied superiority" (122). When Dick appears in the neighborhood wearing fine new clothes, Micky takes notice and offence. "My eyes! ... Jim, just look at Ragged Dick. He's come into a fortun', and turned gentleman. See his new clothes?" (123). Dick's desire to keep a savings account is linked to expenditure on clothes, at least in part. Thus, it is not simply that good habits come *after* the acquisition of good clothes in this narrative. Good clothes motivate good habits.

Mistaken Identity and Transformations of Self

Dick's first sartorial transformation involves a change that is skin deep, but, perhaps, no more than that: "Clean clothes and a dirty skin don't go very well together," says Mr. Whitney to Dick after giving him his son Frank's clean and relatively new clothes as a gift (57).

> Instantly Dick was seized with a fancy for witnessing Johnny's amazement at his change in appearance. He stole up behind him, and struck him on the back.
>
> "Hallo, Johnny, how many shines have you had?"
>
> Johnny turned round expecting to see Dick, whose voice he recognized, but his astonished eyes rested on a nicely dressed boy (the hat alone excepted) who looked indeed like Dick, but so transformed in dress that it was difficult to be sure of his identity [60].

The fact that Dick is unrecognizable suggests that clothes were an essential part of the self—so assimilated to identity that a change of clothes was a change of person. This passage also distinguishes between aural identity and visual identity. The latter trumps the former. What Dick looks like overwhelms the clearly recognizable voice that Johnny hears.

This case of mistaken identity is repeated later when one of his customers does a double take upon seeing Dick "as if his face seemed familiar." Dick notes, "He would have knowed me at once if it hadn't been for my new clothes ... I don't look much like Ragged Dick now" (78). An even more important instance of a similar misrecognition occurs later when Dick goes to the offices of Mr. Greyson to return the change he had promised this costumer from the day before. When Greyson finds Dick in his office, he doesn't recognize the bootblack who had served him the day before: "'Did you wish to speak to me, my lad?' said he to Dick, whom in his new clothes he did not recognize" (132). He comments on the clothes directly: "But you don't look like the boy I employed. If I remember rightly he wasn't as well dressed as you" (132). Dick replies, in characteristic jocularity, "No ... I was dressed for a party, then, but the clo'es was too well ventilated to be comfortable in cold weather" (132). Greyson invites Dick to church, and, again, Dick's entry into respectable society is aided by his new clothes. It is really Dick's honesty—that he did, indeed, return Mr. Greyson's change—that is most important here, but his new clothes facilitate his acquainting himself with a dignified and prosperous businessman. Dick's wearing of new clothes changes how he feels about himself in this situation: "Dick felt in very good spirits. He seemed to be emerging from the world in which he had hitherto lived, into a new atmosphere of respectability, and the change seemed very pleasant to him" (133).

Toward the end of the novel, the question of mistaken identity takes on a different cast. Dick must re-assume his old identity by putting on his ragged clothes when he receives a letter from Frank, who never learned Dick's full name (Richard Hunter), addressed to Ragged Dick. The figure of "Ragged Dick" takes on a semi-official stamp because of this letter waiting for Dick at the post office and advertised in the newspaper, where Dick's friend and tutor, Henry Fosdick, sees it. In order to be recognized as the addressee, Dick changes out of his new suit and back into his Washington coat and Napoleon pants so that when he collects his letter, the postal official will recognize him as Ragged Dick. Henry suggests, "Suppose you wear the old clothes you used to a year ago, when Frank first saw you? They won't have any doubt of your being Ragged Dick then" (196). Dick's feelings are mixed. He wants to retrieve the letter, but he has now acquired "considerable more pride in a neat personal appearance than when we were first introduced to him." And yet, he has "carefully preserved, for what reason he could hardly explain," the "long disused Washington coat and Napoleon pants" (196).

The dilemma Dick faces in donning his old, ragged identity is emblematic of the difficulty of self-transformation as Thoreau and others imagined it in the nineteenth century, and as such transformation is related to clothes. While Dick's transformation is a "rise" in social status and in commonly conventional notions of acceptability and respectability, his old self is difficult to discard completely. Clothes, as one of the most intimate forms of property — indeed a form of property that is indistinguishable from identity (having and being coincide in our clothes) — are difficult to discard even when the fall into disuse. Moreover, Dick must revive this identity in order to reclaim his relationship with Frank — the letter is addressed to Ragged Dick not to Richard Hunter, Esquire.

This transformation from street Arab to respectable boy is accomplished, in large part, through a change of clothes, but also through "enterprise," as Thoreau might describe it. Dick has "enterprised" in so many ways — through hard work, study, heroic action (in saving a boy from drowning), in generosity — that he is thoroughly transformed, from the inside out but also from the outside in. The final instance of this transformation is most vividly presented in Dick's act of writing his first letter. The narrative has followed Dick not only from rags to respectability, but also from textile to text, from labor to literacy. This is a central part of the Horatio Alger myth; it is, in part, what we imply when we call a story "Algeresque." And it is an essential part of immigrant narratives, like those of Anzia Yezierska and Abraham Cahan to be discussed later.

Dick as Business Guide: Navigating the Ready-Made Clothing Industry

As a guide to living and thriving in urban industrial America, *Ragged Dick* includes scenes that educate the young reader about the language and potential pitfalls of a commercial marketplace. The setting of New York allows Alger to portray the development of a whole system of retail commerce with its own language, a language that any enterprising young man should learn. In his depiction of the city, Alger includes descriptions of the ready-made retail trade that was emerging in the city after the Civil War. In Chapter Five, as Dick leads Frank on a tour of the city, the two boys proceed through "Chatham Street, walking between rows of ready-made clothing shops, many of which had half of their stock in trade exposed on the sidewalk" (63). As Michael Zakim has shown, the ready-made clothing retail trade was in full swing by the 1860s. Entrepreneurs like A.T. Stewart, to whom Dick later refers, had capitalized on the market for cheap off-the-rack clothes. Dick shows that one of the things he has learned in his life on the streets is a familiarity with the language of trade in an industrialized nation.

Advertising was a big part of the ready-made clothing market, and Alger takes note: "The proprietors of these establishments stood at the doors watching attentively the passers-by, extending urgent invitations to any who even glanced at the goods, to enter" (63). Part of the advertising strategy of these stores also involved hiring "walking advertisers" like the narrator of Edgar Allan Poe's story, "The Business Man," a man by the name of Peter Proffit whose first entrepreneurial venture is to hire himself out as one of these human advertisements. He wears clothes produced by the shop, and invites potential customers to frequent the establishment, earning his salary on commission. Poe's ironic tale descends into increasingly absurd business ventures including the "Eye-Sore trade" (manipulation of property values), the "Assault-and-Battery business" (provoking assault in order to litigate), "Organ-Grinding" and, finally, cat-tail sales. The suggestion in Poe's story is that business in America was becoming bizarre. Alger, on the other hand, merely places his characters in the context of consumption and the bustling business life of the city. Poe's was a satire on entrepreneurship, while Alger's description of the clothing market and advertising was a moral guide, as Nackenoff observes. Part of this moral guidance was to encourage young boys *not* to emulate "goody-goody boys" who "never win life's prizes," but rather boys who have had difficult times and are "plucky" and "manly," with, in this case, some street smarts (Alger quoted in Nackenoff 24).

When one of the salesmen for a ready-made shop announces, "We're selling off at less than cost," Dick responds: "Of course you be. That's where you makes your money.... There aint nobody of any enterprise that pretends to make any profit on his goods" (63). Alger encourages his young readers to learn the grammar of commerce and advertising, not to be ignorant of it. Frank notes that "Clothes seem to be pretty cheap here." But Dick is quick to explain the concomitant cheapness in design and manufacture: "Yes, but Baxter Street is the cheapest place.... Johnny Nolan got a whole rig-out there last week, for a dollar,— coat, cap, vest, pants, and shoes. They was very good measure, too, like my best clothes that I took off to oblige you" (64). Dick refers, of course, to his George Washington coat and his Napoleon pants that were ragged and fit badly. Thus, the discourse of advertising and retail sales in a big city requires a basic understanding of business, including the rhetoric of advertising, the cost of raw materials, overhead costs, and quality control. While Dick receives the proper social training from wealthy benefactors, he teaches, in return, a basic knowledge of the market which he understands through hard work and hard knocks.

In his role as a savvy guide to big business in the big city, Dick draws attention to the names of great industrialists of the day. In fact, here, it would seem, Alger enters into the same debate that Thoreau entered when he commented on the New England factory system. Indeed, there's an edge of satire to Alger's references to figures like Horace Greeley that makes his critique, as conservative as it may be, of production and divisions of labor quite similar to Thoreau's. For example, Dick comments that Horace Greeley "always go[es] there [to Baxter Street] for clothes" (64). Michael Zakim describes Horace Greeley as "one of nineteenth-century America's great champions of industrial progress." In his 1872 *Great Industries of the United States*, Greeley saw the development of ready-made clothing as a key event in American industrial history—a catalyst of change. Greeley was, perhaps, the first historian to explain the origin of ready-to-wear clothes in the "slops"— shops that sold used or what we call today "irregular" garments. Such shops catered to "those who could not afford to employ a tailor or buy better articles." Greeley argued that from such beginnings, the ready-made industry became more and more respectable. By the 1850s "there [were] thousands of men, even among those who are most fastidious in matters of dress, who never think of being measured for a suit of clothes, but who go to a clothier and supply themselves from his stock" (Greeley in Zakim 7). According to Zakim, this history of the social rise of a new industry reflected Greeley's own political program of democratic progress (Zakim 7). Alger takes Greeley to task through Dick's jocular reference to the great industrialist's clothes and to his support of potentially unscrupulous business practices: "When Horace gets a new suit, I always have one made just like it; but I can't go the white hat. It aint becomin' to my style of beauty" (64). The joke includes a reversal of the democratizing influence of ready-mades because Dick has his "tailor" custom design his clothes to resemble Greeley's ready-mades.

Conclusion

Dick's comments on the great industrialists of his day include references to those who sold text and textiles: the founder of *The New York Herald*, James Gordon Bennett, as well as one of the first clothing retailers in New York, A.T. Stewart. What is most important about these references is that they outline a business ethics. And this business ethics is very clearly Franklinian. In one important passage, Mr. Whitney reveals his own past to Dick in a pastiche of Franklin's didactic autobiographical voice. Whitney even reveals that he, like Franklin, worked as a printer and advanced in the world by reading as much as he could:

> I entered a printing-office as an apprentice, and worked for some years. Then my eyes gave out and I was obliged to give that up.... But there was one thing I got while I was in the printing-office which I value more than money.... A taste for reading and study.... So you see, my lad, that my studious habits paid me in money, as well as in another way [108–9].

When Dick secures a tutor for himself, he finds someone whose father was a printer (134). Dick emulates those who have risen in society. However, he also warns against those who have abused the Protestant ethic — those like James Gordon Bennett or A.T. Stewart.

Dick's own model of prosperity is more modest. By dressing well, Dick puts himself in situations and develops habits that make him prosper. In this sense, Alger's notion of how the individual changes is not so different from Thoreau's conception of the protean self. Moreover, both Alger and Thoreau include critiques of industrial capital in their work — Thoreau in a direct comment on the emerging factory system and Alger through his remarks on industrialists such as Astor, Stewart, Bennett, and Greeley. However, Alger's critique of society is motivated simply by what he sees as a better version of society. Thoreau, on the other hand, challenges the social through what he presents as the natural order of things. As literary and disciplinary discourses on dress emerged later in the century, both Thoreau's natural history of dress and Alger's economic morality of dress would be developed further. However, literary realists attempted to critique and revise any simple notion that clothes made the man. They saw their own work as being implicated in the same market forces that beset their characters with an insatiable desire for mass produced materials of consumption.

As clothing production was transformed, so were ways of talking and writing about clothing. It is interesting that the mass production and circulation of print developed at around the same time as the rise of mass production and consumption of ready-made clothing. The proliferation of magazines and periodicals of all sorts after mid-century occurs alongside, and, in fact, helps to spur the development of ready-to-wear suits, cloaks, dresses, and shirtwaists.[11] A popular as well as specialized discourse of dress developed, as women's advice columnists, historians, professionals in the emerging human sciences of psychology and anthropology, and philosophers began to write about clothing in a variety of ways for a variety of audiences. This new discourse of dress in the United States, the subject of chapter 2 of the present study, produced a language concerned with the self in society. As American realism established new forms of authorship and new ways of reading, American fiction also became engaged in this discourse of dress. As clothing production became industrialized, and as both popular images and professional theories of dress became more concerned with understanding the self, American literary discourse shifted, generally speaking, from a discourse of romance and sentiment, to one of realism and naturalism. And yet, as will be clear in the discussion of Henry James in chapter 3, like nonfiction journalism and like clothing, American literary discourse also became commodified. Text and textile were turned into commodities. By the time Fordist mechanisms of mass production/consumption fabricated the illusion of democratized dress, various new disciplines also began to codify clothing and fashion within their new discursive frameworks, and writers of fiction attempted to represent the brutal realities of class difference and industrial social forces in texts that, themselves, were part of the new culture industry. After the middle of the nineteenth century, there seemed to be a proliferation of discourse on dress in response to its political and economic transformation into a mass-produced ready-made commodity. Part of the rhetorical response to these transformations was a literary inquiry and, to some extent, protest in both progressive and reactionary directions.

Literary critical debates over realism in the United States have tended to claim that the realist project fell short of challenging the anti-egalitarian and anti-democratic forces underlying the incorporation of America.[12] As literary realists developed apparently more mimetic ways of depicting dress, the clothed self posed a particularly vexing problem for the limits of realistic representation, especially in the context of the shift from homespun ideology to ready-made democracy. Thus, while in the 1860s, Horatio Alger, Jr., crafted a sentimental myth of social mobility through the material and metaphor of clothing, by the 1890s Abraham Cahan presented an image of clothing that oscillates between the sentimental and satirical. Even in the career of a single author — such as Henry James — one can trace a romantic vision of the ghostly symbolism of dress in a story written just after the Civil War to the materiality of dress in a story written a few years before World War I. Clothing, or, in a strictly literary sense, costuming of characters, is both part of setting and part of character, both mise-en-scene and motivation; it is the very border of individual agency and collective agency. Clothes bear the imprint of our bodies and our habits, and because they do, they are faithful indices of the lives we live — both as individuals and as members of collectives.

Thus, if the period of literary realism in the United States (the 1860s to the 1920s) is marked by the incorporation of America, then by paying attention to clothing we look at a material and cultural space where ruptures of that incorporation could occur. If clothes are, according to fashion historian Elizabeth Wilson, "the connective tissue of our cultural organism," then they are absolutely essential to processes of incorporation (12). Indeed, incorporation is impossible without investment, both in the economic and in the material sense of both of those words. Actually, Wilson is speaking here not of clothes per se but of fashion as the socio-cultural system of taste and innovation that structures and drives the desire for clothes: all the more reason to attend to the realist novel's attempts to grapple with the significance of clothing in the lives of individuals, of ethnic groups, of classes, of genders, and, ultimately, of the nation. Ambiguities of dress and fashion become instructive when they appear within literary and broader rhetorical struggles over representing individual/collective agency. As the rise of literary realism in the United States coincided with the rise of the mass-produced ready-made clothing industry, specific novelists attempted to negotiate between collective and individual agency, and to represent both the material and metaphoric significance of America's new consumer-driven culture.[13]

2. The Discourse of Dress and Literary Realism in the United States

HALF WAY THROUGH WILLIAM DEAN Howells's *The Rise of Silas Lapham*, the title character, a Civil War veteran and a self-made businessman, faces his greatest challenge when he is invited to a dinner party by his would-be Boston Brahmin in-laws, the Coreys. Almost immediately, the family fixes its attention on the troublesome question of clothes: what shall Silas's wife, Persis, and their daughters, Irene and Penelope, wear? And what, for that matter, will Silas himself wear? Penelope, the more modest of the girls (but the one most appealing to young Corey), gives her own clothes the least thought and decides not to attend, responding to her father's concern by simply stating that if she were to change her mind and attend the dinner she would "go to White's with him and get him to choose her an imported dress." As the night of the dinner draws near, Silas becomes more and more nervous about his own clothes:

> Finally, all that dress-making in the house began to scare him with vague apprehensions in regard to his own dress. As soon as he had determined to go, an ideal of the figure in which he should go presented itself to his mind. He should not wear any dress-coat, because, for one thing, he considered that a man looked like a fool in a dress-coat, and, for another thing, he had none — had none on principle. He would go in a frock-coat and black pantaloons, and perhaps a white waist-coat, but a black cravat, anyway. But as soon as he developed this ideal to his family, which he did in pompous disdain of their anxieties about their own dress, they said he should not go so. Irene reminded him that he was the only person without a dress-coat at a corps-reunion dinner which he had taken her to some years before, and she remembered feeling awfully about it at the time. Mrs. Lapham, who would perhaps have agreed of herself, shook her head with misgiving. "I don't see but what you'll have to get you one, Si," she said. "I don't believe they *ever* go without 'em to a private house."

He held out openly, but on his way home the next day, in a sudden panic, he cast anchor before his tailor's door and got measured for a dress coat [171].

This passage is important for three reasons: the level of detail Howells devotes to a discussion of dress, the fact that this detail appears in a text traditionally identified as central to the development of American realism, and because the passage pays close attention to material culture while serving important formal functions in plot, character development, and theme. The passage marks a pivotal moment in the plot when the newly rich Laphams are finally drawn more completely into the social circle of Boston's upper crust. The commentary on clothes also develops Silas's character as a simple man who eschews questions of adornment and appearance, but is defeated by fashion as he never was by war or commerce. Lapham is like Thoreau's "wearer of new clothes," the man who has worked his way out of his old clothes. However, here he is forced into being that inconstant man who must get new clothes for the latest soiree. Ironically, it is his sympathy for his more modest daughter Irene's observations about fashion that weakens his resolve, making him dress differently, forcing him to refashion himself. Finally, the passage develops the thematic critique of the Gilded Age by pointing out the extreme lengths to which even a humble family is pushed in a culture of conspicuous consumption. Clearly, dress was a key part of the material detail *and* literary approach of U.S. literary realists as they self-consciously developed a new art for a new age.

The realist attention to sartorial detail was just one part of a broader discursive attention to clothing and the social meaning of dress in American society. We see evidence of this even in this archetypal realist text. As the passage in *The Rise of Silas Lapham* continues, Silas seeks help from the public discourse on clothing in the form of etiquette books: "After he began to be afflicted about his waistcoat.... He tried to get opinion out of his family, but they were not so clear about it as they were about the frock. It ended in their buying a book of etiquette, which settled the question adversely against a white waistcoat." Silas continues to be concerned regarding the question of his cravat and the problem of gloves. "Other authors," the narrative continues, "on the same subject were equally silent, and Irene could only remember having heard, in some vague sort of way, that gentlemen did not wear gloves so much anymore." At their wits' end regarding Silas's fashion dilemma, the family releases some of its pent up anxiety by laughing heartily at Penelope's joke: "the Colonel's clothes are as much trouble as anybody's. Why don't you go to Jordan & Marsh's and order one of the imported dresses for yourself, father?" (172).

Even more important than the question of clothing itself, then, is Howells's reference to advice books *about* clothing and men's garments. Howells devotes several pages of his novel to the question of garments and to the discourse of dress and manners that was emerging in the last quarter of the nineteenth century. This discourse included advice books on how men and women should dress, but it also included social histories of costume, natural histories of dress, psychological studies, sociological analyses, and even philosophical considerations of clothing. Thus, literary references to and inclusion of material sartorial culture in fiction was part of a wider discourse. Like Howells's consideration of Silas Lapham's dress-coat and gloves, many of these studies of clothing considered the question of social class and, more broadly, social formations. But they also considered clothing as an expression (even a natural expression) of race, women's dress as a gendered expression of national identity and patriotism, and clothing in general as an expression of ethnic or immigrant identity.

The discourse on dress produces a debate between a strict essentialist conception of dress and a more fluid conception of clothing as part of historical processes of change. In the essentialist framework, social class and ethnicity, in particular, were imagined narrowly. Within these narrow limits, clothing was naturalized into race. Wilfred Mark Webb's social Darwinism of clothes is emblematic of this essentialist view — one that sees clothes as a kind of second skin, and that uses it as a marker for racial and national taxonomies and hierarchies. In a more fluid framework, garments were seen as part of broader material and historical processes marked by economic and industrial shifts. This view acknowledged structures of production as well as questions of appearance and identity. Jane Addams's writing, especially her conception of material history in the Hull House Labor Museum, is emblematic of this more fluid view. As the manufacture of clothing shifted from ready-made production on a modest scale in the 1830s to mass production by the end of the century, discourse on dress attempted either to obfuscate the material historical significance of this shift, or, as in the case of Addams, to see clothing as part of a broader change in capitalist divisions of labor. Her work is particularly important as it is keenly aware, also, of the importance of immigrants in this historical shift.

Dress and Social Darwinism

Writing for *Scribner's Magazine* in 1893, historian Edward J. Lowell traced the history of clothes from the ancient Greeks to his American contemporaries. At the two ends of this historical arc he places two orators: Demosthenes, whose statue could be found in the Vatican Museum, and Edward

Everett — professor of Greek, politician, and New England orator — whose statue stood in the Boston Public Garden. What is interesting here is that Lowell compares two orators, two masters in the use of rhetoric, but he reads them in terms of their sartorial rhetoric. For Lowell, as for most historians of dress and costume then and now, the key distinction between ancient and modern dress is that the former is draped while the latter is fitted. Elizabeth Wilson has observed, "the most fundamental distinction in dress is not, as we might suppose today, that between male and female, but the distinction between the draped and the sewn."[1] However, the relatively more naked Demosthenes — "the Athenian is less thoroughly covered than the American" — is no less dignified than the more fully clad Everett. The garment of each man is fitted to his historical, social, and cultural context.[2]

However, Lowell claims that his contemporary American context is relatively classless, a state of affairs he finds regrettable because it undermines what he calls "appropriateness." The ancient and medieval class distinctions were sacral — religious vestments being qualitatively different from secular clothes: "Clothes, then, are worn in deference to religious and moral feelings, but not the same clothes in all places" (289). In the nineteenth century, this distinction, this appropriateness, this class stratification marked by sumptuary difference is not as clearly demarcated. "In our age, as in the past," remarks Lowell,

> the chief possible merit of costume is *appropriateness*. We have seen that in Greece and Rome the citizen was dressed differently from the slave, that in the Middle Ages the king and the priest were not attired like the soldier and the peasant. Now that democracy has turned our Western world into a vast factory filled with working-men, garments that are neither flowing nor tight, colors that will not show dirt, seem to be driving out all that is beautiful and picturesque in costume.... [303, emphasis added]

For Lowell, a democracy need not give way to chaos. In a post sumptuary world, Lowell harks back to the old distinctions between strata of society. As the old distinctions have disappeared, so has beauty. Lowell seems to fear the anonymity that allowed for social mobility. For Lowell, difference produced aesthetic beauty, and the democratization of clothes threatened to turn all of American society into a plain and drab social fabric, literally and figuratively. Lowell writes,

> clothes are far cheaper and are changed far oftener than they used to be. The gain in cleanliness is enormous, the gain in beauty is not yet so apparent.... Within the last twenty-five years a relaxation has been observed in the rigidity of the laws of fashion. People of both sexes are less afraid than they formerly were to wear what they please. Let us look forward to a day when *variety* of personal taste and *appropriateness* of clothing to occupation shall be the rules of costume [303, emphasis added].

Like Lowell, art historian and President of the New York School of Fine and Applied Arts, Frank Alvah Parsons, writing in 1920, questions the democratization of dress in Europe and the United States in his book, *The Psychology of Dress*. After a three-hundred page history of the development of dress from the Medieval period to the twentieth century, Parsons concludes by considering the ways in which democracy and industrialization have tended to exacerbate the more negative aspects of fashion and the baser aspects of human nature that respond to fashion. "The term 'democracy,'" Parsons reflects,

> is fashionable now, and we find this sagaciously wedded to modern "commercial interests" and then accepted and exploited by fashion with as much finesse and success as usual, and in alliance, too, with the general uprising of those so-called lower classes who are, and always have been, determined to share the possibilities of dressing well with the classes they have learned to think are above them. How far they are right in their beliefs, or ever have been, is still problematical, but the right to be in the fashion is still the contested point among classes, and ways and means to realize and express this right are still being assiduously worked out [Parsons 332].

What is problematic for Parsons is whether the combination of democracy and commercial interests is compatible with "good taste," because "good taste never did become a general national asset overnight, and therefore we have a right to insist on waiting to be convinced that this autumn is the exception to the rule" (335). In earlier periods, good taste "was generally inherent" and "more time was allowed the individual to become acquainted with social claims and their responsibilities than is possible with a people so hard pressed as we for immediate expression on so elaborate a scale" (345–46). For Parsons, the individual's right to fashionable dress in a democratic society is an unavoidable development, but one that threatens to eliminate beauty — just as Lowell sees beauty disappear with the disappearance of distinction, variety, and appropriateness. In the final paragraph of his book, Parsons asks his reader to consider the possible results of what he terms "Utopian individualism":

> Nor is there any likelihood that the ever-increasing knowledge of the rights and privileges of the proletariat, to be as fashionable and as dressy as those whose lot has fallen among the less populous classes, will lessen the variety or the comedy of Fashion's expression, as she is represented both in the political and the social strongholds of our democracy in its onward move toward Utopian individualism. Granting all this, it still appears that man is, after all, mostly the result of his environment, and that he will certainly express, unless forced to do otherwise, precisely what he is [349].

Parsons presents the smallness of the more privileged class as a disadvantage not because he feels it is unfair to accumulate power and wealth in the hands of the few, but because the cultural capital of the privileged class is in danger of being crowded out by the mob and because a fragile standard of taste might fall prey to the lowest common denominator. The democratization of clothes threatens to pull civilization down rather than lifting the proletariat up.

Parsons's comments on environment, at the close of his book—"that man is, after all, mostly the result of his environment"— reflect a wider Darwinist influence on the discourse of dress at the turn of the century, but one that ascribed as much deterministic power to a racial essence as it did to a regional environment. Evolutionary biologist and social Darwinist Wilfred Mark Webb is a key figure. In his *The Heritage of Dress: Being Notes on the History and Evolution of Clothes* (published by the McClure Press of New York in 1908), Webb makes a direct link between dress and race, clothing and nation. A Fellow of the Linean Society of London, Webb was familiar with earlier scholarly ventures in this direction, including an essay by Charles Darwin's own son, George H. Darwin in which the latter examined the "Development of Dress" (1872). Following Darwin's lead, Webb traced the development of ornament, clothing, and fashion as part of a natural history that simply extended what others had said about skulls, skin, hair and bone: "As a matter of fact," he states early in his *Heritage*, "our artificial coverings have become so much a part of our life that one may perhaps be allowed to apply the methods of the naturalist to their consideration, and deal with them as if they were part and parcel of the creature which wears them" (2).

Webb, among others, attempted to produce a taxonomic mapping of national dress and character: "Generally speaking, however, it is not difficult to tell the nationality of a man by his clothes" (317).[3] The growing specialization of the sciences during this period makes for some interesting omissions in the service of focused analysis, as we see in this case. Webb, in leaving out the political and economic history of the development of garment crafts and industries in Europe focuses exclusively on clothes as if they were truly "part and parcel of the creature which wears them," as if dress is the outer most tissue of the ethnic body. Webb contrasts, for example, the uniformity of German dress with the flamboyance of Spanish apparel, noting the German's "lack of personality" in relation to the Spaniard's ethnic color in all senses of the term. Perhaps it is the Latin and Catholic influence upon the "Frenchman" that makes him favor "a frock coat, which he has finished off with as much ornamentation as possible in the way of silk facings, braided edges, and fantastic flaps" (319). Norwegians, Danes, and Englishmen are all "precision" and "stiffness," while for the man in the colonies doing the strenuous work of empire there is "no desire for show, and his tweed lounge suit is cut for comfort and made for strength" (320). Webb even notes the American's famous love of individual liberty, for "the American ... has his coat finished in some extraordinary way which he fancies to be original" (318). But Webb also observes that "The American's garments are usually made two sizes too large for him" (318). Clearly, the disciplinary languages of history, art history, psychology, and natural history tended to read clothes in terms of race. What Thoreau had presented as a metaphor—humans molting, shedding their clothes as snakes shed their skin—becomes quite literal in the age social Darwinism.

In *Sartor Resartus*, Carlyle writes: "Are we Opossums; have we natural pouches, like the Kangaroo? Or how, without Clothes, could we possess the master-organ, soul's-seat, and true pineal gland of the Body Social: I mean, a Purse?" (51). With this question, Carlyle's Teufelsdröckh underscores the important link between vestment and investment, between material and financial concerns. Indeed, we see a similar though less ironic link between fashion and property, between clothing and currency in Webb. Webb's social Darwinist ethnography relied on a typical separation of "primitive" peoples who remain in a simpler and "younger" stage of human development from civilized peoples who exist in a more complex and mature stage. Here, childlike attraction to decorative art in dress distinguishes the barbarous from the civilized: "Generally speaking," claims Webb, "the more simple the race, the greater is its love of ornament" (8). Interestingly, however, this distinction between the relatively innocent races and the more experienced ones leads Webb to celebrate the noble savage and to denigrate the modern conspicuous consumer and the dissipation of the powers of the race. Echoing Thorstein Veblen's famous discussion of the importance of clothes in the lives of the leisure class and of the classes who attempt to emulate them, Webb writes[4]:

> There is, however, something to be valued on behalf of savages that cannot be said for white people who bedizen themselves with the feathers of rare and beautiful birds. Uncivilized people have no pockets nor safes in which to keep their valuables, and it comes about that these take a form which permits them to be worn on the person, so that many of the objects which take the place of ornaments—such as teeth, shells, and beads—serve as the currencies of their owners.
>
> Even now there are individuals of whom it is said that they "put all their money on their backs," but, unfortunately for them, it depreciates sadly in value, and cannot be turned to account at a moment's notice [Webb 317–18].

The problem with "white" "civilized" people who wear feathers and ornaments seems to be the complicated development of investment alongside vestment. The absence of pockets and safes among "savages" leaves them innocent of the needs of any member of a modern capitalist middle class. "Savages" are exempt from the moral requirements imposed by the development of private property, of banks, and of credit and debt. This certainly explains the importance of the somber gray or brown suit of the banker who must show, clearly, that he does not "put all his money on his back." Webb seems to be saying that our attention to the cost of clothes can be a useful vestigial remainder of an earlier evolutionary stage when clothes *were* in fact a form of currency.

Clothing and Material History

In contrast to these fairly rigid histories of fashion in which race, ethnicity, gender, and class fell within nature's own sumptuary laws or within the laws of national identity, the discourses of dress found in the social/psychological theories of Jane Addams, Georg Simmel, and William James challenged the boundaries marked by cloth. For these writers — a social worker, a sociologist, and a psychologist, respectively — clothes were the symbolically *and materially* thin line that separated social formations and individual self-constructions. Writing some seventy or eighty years after these writers, Elizabeth Wilson argues that fashion is

> essential to the world of modernity, the world of spectacle and mass-communication. It is a kind of connective tissue of our cultural organism. And, although many individuals experience fashion as a form of bondage, as a punitive, compulsory way of falsely expressing an individuality that by its very gesture (in copying others) cancels itself out, the final twist to the contradiction that is fashion is that it often does successfully express the individual [12].

In this commentary, Wilson echoes what Georg Simmel writes in his essay "Fashion," published in English in the New York–based *International Quarterly* in 1904. For Simmel, fashion is a pliable screen between social belonging and individual identity. Simmel writes that "fashion represents nothing more than one of the many forms of life by the aid of which we seek to combine in uniform spheres of activity the tendency towards social equalization with the desire for individual differentiation and change" (296). His essay is concerned with how fashion allows us to negotiate the dialectic between "socialistic adaptation to society and individual departure from its demands" (294), and he outlines the ways not only that the individual can challenge the socializing dictates of fashion, but also how fashion's swift ephemeral transformations make it a powerful form of conformity and socialization.

This function of fashion as a mediating force between social equalization and individual change is a function situated at the point where materiality and consciousness meet: "We encounter here a close connection between the consciousness of personality and that of the material forms of life, a connection that runs all through history" (298). In the United States at the beginning of the twentieth century this coalescing of community and individual, and of consciousness and material, became an important place, as we shall see, for the work of assimilation. What we should note here is that disciplinary definitions of dress differed. This is not to say that historical and art historical definitions of fashion were rigid while sociological definitions of dress were more fluid. Rather, there are clear distinctions between essentialist models of the history of clothing and more materialist approaches. Simmel's work points toward a more materialist — albeit a clearly structuralist — view of cloth, fashion, and sartorial subject-formation than the "common sense" of those like Lowell, Parsons, and Webb.

Similarly, William James viewed clothes as the outermost level of what he called the empirical or material self. His theory of the tripartite self placed clothes at that outer limit of the inner self— again, the pliable screen where materiality and consciousness meet. In *Psychology: The Briefer Course*, James separates the self into three parts — the Spiritual Self, the Social Ego, and the Empirical or Material "Me." It is in this last that the self can be defined and redefined through clothes

> The *body* is the innermost part of the material me in each of us; and certain parts of the body seem more intimately ours than the rest. The clothes come next. The old saying that the human person is composed of three parts — soul, body and clothes — is more than a joke. We so appropriate our clothes and identify our selves with them that there are few of us who, if asked to choose between having a beautiful body clad in raiment perpetually shabby and unclean, and having an ugly and blemished form always spotlessly attired, would not hesitate a moment before making a decisive reply [44–45].

As if solving the debate between Madame Merle and Isabel Archer that his brother Henry presents in *Portrait of a Lady*, William James suggests that clothes are both essence and exterior. We can change our clothes and thereby, perhaps, change the self or one aspect of the self.

Clearly, at the turn of the century, the discourse of dress involved a debate between those who read clothes as a natural outgrowth of innate characteristics and identities, as opposed to those, such as Simmel and James, who attempted to historicize clothing within society and culture. Perhaps the most important commentator in this latter group is Jane Addams. We can, for example, contrast Henry Ford's well-known ceremony for the graduates of his English School with Addams's Labor Museum. John Higham describes the ceremony performed by graduates of Ford's school:

> The students acted out a pantomime which admirably symbolized the spirit of the enterprise. In this performance a great melting pot (labeled as such) occupied the middle of the stage. A long column of immigrant students descended into the pot from backstage, clad in outlandish garb and flaunting signs proclaiming their fatherlands. Simultaneously from either side of the pot another stream of men emerged, each prosperously dressed in identical suits of clothes and each carrying a little American flag. [Higham, *Strangers in the Land* 248].

What is important about this ceremony is that it is a graduation from a school that taught American English, but central to the spectacle is the adoption of new clothes; thus, literacy in the cultural practice of consumption is shown to be as important as the acquisition of English language skills. The ceremony, dramatizes the basic tenet of Fordism — that mass production leads to and requires mass consumption; trading the outlandish clothes of Russia for the ready-made clothes of America dramatizes the workers' ability to buy as well as to make. Furthermore, the spectacle of transformation performs a ritual erasure of the past, of the memories immigrants associated with their old clothes.

In contrast to Ford's pageant of assimilation, Jane Addams's Labor Museum reflects an awareness of the immigrant's agency in the processes of industrial production and material consumption. In her Museum, Addams placed the handcraft tools of pre-industrial Eastern and Southern Europe beside machines of the American garment industry. In this way, immigrants in the neighborhood of Hull House could see their work as part of a material historical narrative. Addams was aware that many immigrants came to their factory jobs with a sense of pride in their craft, a skill they had acquired through years of apprenticeship and dedication.[5] Thus, in linking Old-World needlecrafts with New World industry, Addams was merely recognizing and displaying the ways in which she believed immigrants already viewed their work. For Addams, newcomers from Eastern Europe left behind the garments of their past and also the means of producing them.

Addams wanted immigrants to see Americanization as part of a historical narrative from craft to industry, from hand- to mass-production, from old to new garments, and from use to exchange value. In recounting her initial idea of establishing a labor museum at Hull House, Addams describes a process of seeing material — specifically textiles and textile crafts — historically:

> We found in the immediate neighborhood at least four varieties of these most primitive methods of spinning and three distinct variations of the same spindle in connection with wheels. It was possible to put these seven into historic sequence and order and to connect the whole with the present method of factory spinning.... Within one room a Syrian woman, a Greek, an Italian, a Russian, and an Irishwoman enabled even the most casual observer to see that there is no break in orderly evolution if we look at history from the industrial standpoint; that industry develops similarly and peacefully year by year among the workers of each nation, heedless of differences in language, religion, and political experiences [*Hull House* 173].

For Addams, history was not to be narrated along lines of race, despite the distance between Syria and Ireland. Nor was progress merely the acquisition of skills of consumption and production as it was for Ford and the economists of his day. For Addams, there was no "outside" of material history and the history of work, and immigrants and others could come to terms with historical change if they could imagine it in terms of a narrative of material production.

Addams, along with fellow social workers Mary Simkovich and Lillian Wald, certainly recognized that learning to consume was an important step in the process of assimilation. Indeed, inspired by settlement/social work discourse, Ludmila Foxlee, as part of an attempt to help newcomers assimilate as quickly as possible, opened a clothing store at Ellis Island in 1920 in order to allow immigrants to exchange their greenhorn clothes for ready-to-wear fashion and as a consequence to begin to become consumers. However, Jane Addams saw competency in consumption as part of a wider cultural literacy, and unlike Ford, she attempted to see this fundamentally from the point of view of the immigrants themselves.[6]

In fact, these immigrants were not merely passive props in spectacles of consumerism; they actively produced their own imagery of assimilation by documenting with photographs the consumption of clothes. Newcomers from Eastern Europe often had studio photographs taken of themselves in a new suit or in a new skirt and shirtwaist. These images were not only to be sent home to show off one's wealth to relatives in the old country; they were also displayed prominently in one's home in America. While many social workers were friendly toward industry and promoted the notion that the production-consumption model was necessary for assimilation, these settlement workers tried to see this process from the point of view of the immigrants themselves, and in some cases attempted to organize social and political movements around consumption as well as labor.

Thus, the key to movement across one's own personal material history was, for Addams, the acquisition of literacy broadly defined, and often this meant a critical rather than or as well as a consuming literacy. In *Twenty Years at Hull House*, Addams describes a scene that occurs during an evening lecture on the history of the English textile industry. After hearing a lecture, held at the Labor Museum, a tailor in attendance makes a direct link between labor and literacy in his own understanding of industrial history:

...a *Russian tailor* in the audience was moved to make a speech. He suggested that whereas time had done much to alleviate the first difficulties in the transition of weaving from hand work to steam power, that in the application of steam to sewing we are still in our first stages, illustrated by the *isolated woman* who tries to support herself by hand needlework at home until driven out by starvation, as many of the hand weavers had been.

The historical analogy seemed to bring a certain comfort to the tailor.... Human progress is slow and perhaps never more cruel than in the advance of industry, but is not the worker comforted by knowing that other historical

>periods have existed similar to the one in which he finds himself, and that the readjustment may be shortened and alleviated by judicious action; and is he not entitled to the solace which an *artistic portrayal* of the situation might give him? I remember the evening of the tailor's speech that *I felt reproached* because no poet or artist has endeared the sweater's victim to us as George Eliot has made us love the belated weaver, Silas Marner [*Hull House*, 173–4, emphasis added].

It is in the light of this broader discourse on dress, characterized by the social Darwinism of Webb at one extreme and what may be called the historical materialism of Addams at the other, that we must read the literary realist representation of dress. While the following chapters deal with key figures from this period, this chapter will present a reading of others, including Mark Twain and Edith Wharton, but also Charles Chesnutt and the earlier work of Abraham Cahan, whose *Rise of David Levinsky* will be discussed at length in another chapter. These writers represented the sartorial in relation to gender, ethnicity and race, class, and money. It is clear that these writers influenced and were informed by this wider discourse on dress. The literary realist discourse on dress, itself implicated in America's culture of consumption, grappled with important questions regarding materiality and the construction of identity. As material value (the value of the thing itself) was transformed into exchange value (value in relation), clothing (along with other commodities including literary commodities) became more abstract and symbolic, taking on increasing significance and signification as a marker of identity rather than a material thing in and of itself.

Given these debates circulating among philosophers, historians, social Darwinists, art historians, psychologists, ethnographers, and social workers concerning clothing and collective/individual identity between the 1880s and the 1920s, the attempt to represent the reality of clothes within the context of a rising mass culture offered several important challenges to imaginative writers of the time. How did earlier conceptions of the clothed self in society continue to influence the contemporary literary representation of the sartorial self? How did realist writers respond to the rags-to-riches myth in the context of new disciplinary discourses of clothing that bemoaned the homogenization of American society, and regretted the disappearance of visual distinctions between classes? Also, immigrants found themselves subjected both to assimilative material processes (of work, education, and popular culture) and to discursive processes that placed their racial and ethnic identities under disciplinary control. Clothing — both materially and discursively — played a significant role in these processes of cultural assimilation and disciplinary knowledge. How did narratives written by immigrants, themselves either resist or concede to these assimilative and discursive forces? Finally, how did writers of literary fiction (both realist and "modernist") contribute to these discursive attempts to re-imagine the nation's new clothes?

Gender, Nation, and Dress in American Realism

In Edith Wharton's *The House of Mirth*, Lily Bart is caught between an ideal self—epitomized in the *tableaux vivant* of an eighteenth-century painting in which she wears a flowing white Empire dress—and her real self in American modernity encumbered not merely by clothes, but by a set of social and economic relations that bind her in her place. This complex of relations includes the cost of her clothes and the money she owes or pretends she owes her dressmaker in the opening chapter of the novel. The ideal self is embodied in a draped image that predates American modernity, though it doesn't predate European Enlightenment. Wharton's symbolic representation of the ideal Lily draws on the distinction between a pure pre-modern identity and a muddied sense of self in the Gilded Age. As Ruth Bernard Yeazell puts it, "Simply clothed in the pale flowing draperies of the Reynolds portrait, she does not so much transcend the world of conspicuous display as show off her superior refinement—a fitting emblem of the 'spiritualization of the scheme of symbolism in dress' which [Thorstein] Veblen identifies with the highest reaches of pecuniary culture."[7] Certainly, Lily falls into the traps of a culture of conspicuous consumption and invidious comparison in which she must aspire *not* to be the kind of woman a man can love, but to be, rather, the kind of woman he can show off in fine clothes. But more importantly, underneath Lily's modern clothes lies a toga-draped self. Her real identity resides "in [her] blood, that [she] got [...] from some wicked pleasure-loving ancestress" (Wharton 216). It is not nostalgia for a pagan past that Wharton points to, but, rather, an alternate modernity, one very different from that presented either by the heartless rich or by "you good people," reformers, idealists, and otherwise altruistic people like Lily's cousin Gerty. Modernity, as expressed and embodied in the draperies of a Reynolds portrait, was also a way of being true to the self in the face of fashion's superficiality.

Lily's draped figure is not just an emblem of modernity—as modernity borrows from classical models. It is also a figure for the nation, reminiscent of the Statue of Liberty, itself. In general, the female figure is often presented as the embodiment of national identity, and what that female figure wears is an important aspect of how the figure symbolizes the nation. The robed female figure is a sign of national identity, a strategy of modernity in general in which figures from classical antiquity—such as Britannia or the classically draped Lady Liberty—are invested with modern ideals. At the turn of the century in the United States, the image of Miss Columbia — a combination of Indian princess and classical goddess — came to represent national ideas such as liberty and honesty. Miss Columbia was often featured in cartoons representing the United States' imperialist expansion and the assimilation of immigrant children.[8] Thus, the modern American faith in material and moral progress could be best conveyed as *if* it came out of an archaic past, robed in the draperies of a specifically Western and eternal antiquity.

The symbolic use of the classical female figure was, in fact, one version of a modern deployment of dress to represent national identity, a relatively conservative version of modernity. By contrast progressive reform of women's clothing sought to match the material amelioration of women with their social amelioration. At the same time, however, the progressive version of modern national identity had something in common with the more conservative aims. Progressives, too, used images of the clothed female figure to represent nationalism. As early as the Bloomer controversy of the 1850s, debates over the reform of dress served as a forum for expressing concerns about the United States' national identity. Amelia Jenks Bloomer designed clothes that she hoped would rationalize women's dress, making it more comfortable, healthier and in keeping with Protestant values of restraint and decorum. However, the specific design — a loose-fitting skirt that reached below the knee and full trousers gathered with lace at the ankles — triggered a reaction against Bloomer's perceived crossing of gender boundaries, and, more surprisingly, against her perceived crossing of racialized boundaries. The common accusation was that Bloomer was infringing upon the man's right to "wear the pants" in the middle-class household.[9] However, another interesting and not infrequent response to Bloomer's design was to ridicule it in Orientalist or anti–Indian terms. Bloomer was said to be trying to get Americans to dress "à la Turk," or "à la squaw."[10] Hereafter, any attempt to reform women's dress in America was associated with inappropriate crossing of gendered, racial or class boundaries. In the 1880s, the Rational Dress movement attempted to encourage "Aesthetic costume," using designs based on Pre-Raphaelite painting. This group of activists, like Bloomer before them, was scorned and often caricatured in popular magazines. And yet, "the movement did eventually achieve its aims, as women began to lead more active lives and rigid corsets thus became unfashionable."[11]

By the 1890s the very production of women's clothing and not just its symbolism seemed to become foreignized. In the course of that decade, New York City became the hub of the women's garment industry, with clothing manufacturers comprising 47 percent of all the city's factories, and garment workers comprising almost half of its industrial labor force.[12] The final decade of the nineteenth century also saw a shift in the control of this industry away from second or third-generation German Jewish immigrants to newly arrived Jewish immigrants. Indeed, Abraham Cahan depicts this shift through fiction in *The Rise of David Levinsky*, so much so that his fictional rendering of this change in the national origin of those who worked in and had control of the industry became, between the 1860s and the 1880s, the main source for discussions of the garment industry in major histories of immigration.[13] In the 1900s and 1910s, Cahan was closely involved in the growing unionization of the workers, over 70 percent of them women by 1910, in this industry.

But despite their low wages, Jewish women workers made Grand Street, on the Lower East Side, "a sartorial marketplace and a fashion boulevard." In 1898, a *New York Tribune* reporter remarked:

> But, in the matter of dress, it is natural that the East Side should be strictly up to date[...]. If my lady wears a velvet gown, put together for her in an East Side sweatshop may not the girl whose fingers fashioned it rejoice her soul by astonishing Grand Street with a copy of it next Sunday? My lady's in velvet, and the East Side girl's is the cheapest, but it's the style that counts. In this land of equality, shall not one wear what the other wears? Shall not Fifth Avenue and Grand Street walk hand in hand?

On the one hand, the 1890s witnessed the spread of a division of labor that subordinated women to men. Married women, in particular, were recruited into a part of the industry known as "homework," taking home finishing work from the big clothing manufacturers. Thus, women were low on the ladder of the division of labor. On the other hand, as the quote above implies, immigrant women — Italians, Jews, and Germans — walked "hand in hand" with their Gentile counterparts when it came to female dress.[14]

By the 1910s, popular magazines — from *The New York Times* to *The Independent* to *The Ladies Home Journal* and *The Woman's Home Companion*— were advocating a modest and rational fashion for the American woman. Indeed, this endorsement of rational dress became one expression of American patriotism.[15] One writer in *The New York Times* wrote in 1909 that "Our national character is more reflected in *the clothes of our women* than in anything else" (Lauer and Lauer 61). Throughout the 1910s, the *NY Times* and other publications discussed the merits of producing a homespun fashion. The *Times*, for example, sponsored a contest to design a hat and dress that would be uniquely American. The response to this contest, "said the editor, reflected a protest against foreign domination of the outer expression of an inward and spiritual Americanism, an Americanism which should be distinctive in the garments of our men and women in a real revolt. It will be successful (*NY Times*, Jan 9, 1913)" (192). Institutions were also formed during this time around the perceived need to defend American national identity by producing American fashions for women. For example, the Society for American Fashions for American Women was formed in 1913. By 1918, Mary Brooks Picken — writing for the Woman's Institute of Domestic Arts and Sciences, Inc.— had composed a "A Pledge for American Women" and printed it in her book *The Secrets of Distinctive Dress: Harmonious, Becoming, and Beautiful Dress — Its Value and How to Achieve It*:

> As an American woman, I pledge myself to strive always to acquire and wear only such clothes as are appropriate and individually becoming; to avoid extremes in design and color; to respect my clothes enough to care for them to the best of my ability; and to select my clothes so that, in fairness to them, they may give back to me in service, satisfaction, and pleasure more than they cost me in money. I further pledge myself to help establish for all time, by regularly applying the rules of correct dress to myself, the fact that American women are the best dressed women in the entire land [215].

This pledge, like the pledge of allegiance to the flag — that other national cloth — affirms national belonging. These defenses of a homegrown fashion echoed calls for authentically American art forms that had been ringing throughout the land at least since the time of Emerson. Indeed, one *New York Times* article's treatment of the question of a national fashion almost paraphrases Emerson's call for a natal American culture:

> Can we do nothing for ourselves? Why should Paris and London suggest our modes? What have we — a comparative wild people, half of us yet in the woods — to do with London and Paris? We are different, a peculiar people — have necessities to which people are not subject in those great cities, and our customs should be suited to our conditions. Let us have ... a maker of modes for ourselves. Let him ask who we are — what are our occupations, our difficulties, our resources, and then determine what are the sorts of dress which we should wear [Lauer and Lauer, 179].

Here, we may return to Emerson's question: "why should we grope among the dry bones of the past, or put the living generation into masquerade out of its faded wardrobe?" Advocates for a national American dress seemed to take this quite literally.

Fashioning Race, Fabricating Ethnicity

If, according to Thoreau, clothes are the "outmost cuticle" of individual identity, and if by donning old clothes a new self shows "false colors," then clothing seems to have a great deal in common with race. If race is the supplement that anchors ethnicity to national identity, then it is similar to clothing, which is also often defined as a supplement.[16] While each of us is born with a particular skin color, hair texture and so on, these visual markers become racialized only through a kind of ideological tailoring. Race is fabricated ideologically, just as clothes are fabricated materially (*and ideologically*). Both race and clothing can be seen as the outward expression of identity.[17] Clothing can be changed in ways that race cannot be, but both set up a link between a supplement and a national identity. It is important to keep in mind that race is fixed in ways that clothing is not. But skin color is not absolutely fixed, either, and passing is precisely the destabilizing of one supplement of identity — race — through the strategic use of others — clothing, along with speech and action. Furthermore, the supplementarity of clothes is made effective *not* by the garments alone, but by the garments as they exist within a system of fashion. Similarly, the specific meanings and presumed essences associated with skin color or hair texture shift over time and space according to the discourse of race.[18] Garments signify differently in different national cultural contexts: kilts and skirts for example. So, too, does skin color signify differently in different contexts, such as the broader scope of the term "black" in England as opposed to its meaning in the United States. Still, while I am interested in how the supplementarity of clothing complicates the supplementarity of race, I want to state clearly that race cannot be chosen in the same ways that clothing can. Race can be fixed for the racializing subject who gazes upon skin color, leaving the object of that gaze relatively powerless to influence the speculation upon his identity. On the other hand, even if I dress today in traditional ethnic garb, tomorrow I can dress in jeans and a T-shirt, and to some extent, the one supplement destabilizes the other.

Thus, we would be mistaken to think of race as a saturating rather than a supplementary sign, while thinking of dress as *mere* covering. Neither one is embedded deeply in internal biological or psychological mechanisms. Both race and dress provide only ambiguous and slippery representations of identity, which is precisely what makes them interesting, especially in relation to one another. Like the supplementarity of race, dress is at once part of the body and a fabrication outside of it in the social realm.[19]

American realists, in examining the material in its regional, social, and psychological variations, also turned their attention to race, as many readers have observed. Two writers in particular dealt directly with the ways in which race and dress complicated each other. Mark Twain's *Pudd'nhead Wilson* and Charles Chesnutt's *The Marrow of Tradition* bring dress codes and blackface together in an examination of how disguise can undermine ideological underwritings of race. Twain's novel clearly depicts the way in which clothing as supplement can disrupt the "fiction of law and custom" that distinguishes black from white (9), as his characters disguise their race and gender through passing and blackface, and cross-dressing. Indeed, according to Linda Morris's reading of the novel, donning different clothes can so disrupt the social order of race and patriarchy that the order cannot be restored.[20] The character known as Chambers — the white heir to a Southern fortune — cannot return to being white after he has been raised black: "The real heir suddenly found himself rich and free, but ... his manners were the manners of a slave. Money and fine clothes could not mend these defects or cover them up, they only made them more glaring and the more pathetic" (114). The two characters whose mistaken identities propel the novel's plot (Thomas and Chambers) can be distinguished only by their clothes: "He [the black baby, Chambers] had blue eyes and flaxen curls, like his white comrade, but even the father of the white child was able to tell the children apart — little as he had commerce with them — by their clothes" (9). Not even Tom's (formerly Chambers's) mother, Roxana, who has switched their clothes, can distinguish the two without effort: "Now who would b'lieve clo'es could do de like o' dat? Dog my cats if it ain't all *I* kin do to tell t'other fum which, let alone his pappy" she reflects, and says to herself: "I got to practice and git used to 'memberin' to call you [Tom], honey, or I's gwyne to make a mistake some time en git us bofe into trouble" (14–15). The novel continues to play with disguise, both racial and gendered, as Tom (formerly Chambers), already passing (at first unwittingly) as white, dresses as a young girl in order to burgle rich people's homes so that he can pay off heavy gambling debts that threaten his inheritance. Furthermore, Tom's mother — who had swapped him with his white counterpart to save him from being sold down the river — has to disguise herself as well after Tom, ironically, sells *her* down the river, again in a bid to stave off his creditors. Tom's mother disguises herself as a black man, though she is a very fair-skinned black woman (one-sixteenth black, to be exact).

What all these disguises suggest is that neither clothing nor race is an essence or part of an unchangeable ethnic identity, that each is a supplement that can be destabilized, and that the category of gender can complicate this even further. But the disguises also show that though clothing appears on the surface, it has the same power as language, "law and custom" to determine individuals' social fates. Morris has observed that part of the genius of the novel is that its final arbiter of identity — the fingerprint — is a reliable mark of identity regardless of race *or* gender, let alone disguise (394). *Pudd'nhead Wilson* was written during the rise of Jim Crow and the backlash against reconstruction. This was also, however, a time when the discourse of dress essentialized clothing as part of ethnic and racial identities. Within this context, the novel's deconstruction of race and gender also challenges these ethnological conceptions of costume. What the novel suggests is that clothes — and the conventional expectations we associate with them — *do* influence identity. But they do so from the outside in. This is most clearly the case with Chambers (the white child raised as a slave) than it is with Tom.

Chambers, because he has dressed and lived as a black man, *becomes* one by the end of the novel. Clothing — and its associated habits — almost certainly ensures downward mobility, and only partially allows for upward mobility. Clothing and race are fictions, but fictions that do ideological work.

Charles Chesnutt's *The Marrow of Tradition* involves a similar reflection on race and disguise, and also challenges accepted notions of race by destabilizing them through disguise and mistaken identities. In the novel, Tom Delamere, the dispossessed member of a former slave-owning dynasty, and Sandy, Delamere's grandfather's "body-servant," play out a distinctly Twainian confusion of identities. Tom and Sandy are unreconstructed types in Chesnutt's novel. They represent identities of the old order afloat in a new order, or at least one in flux, and they are iconic: Chesnutt paints them broadly in relation to his other characters. Sandy is the faithful body-servant; Tom is the "Black Sheep" of a white family, the dissolute and debauched son of "gentlemen." In post-reconstruction society, the masquerade of race becomes garishly obvious in both Tom and Sandy. Tom functions as Sandy's double when later in the novel he purloins Sandy's clothes and performs a minstrel show in the costume of a black butler. The doubling of Sandy and Tom parallels another and more important doubling — that of Olivia Merkell Carteret and Janet Miller, half sisters born to the same white father but to mothers on opposite sides of the color line. These two represent the misrecognition of racialized identity, and they are divided by the natal alienation that is one of the most important legacies of the slave system. While Chesnutt's novel is set during Reconstruction, it does address the reaction against Reconstruction, a reaction that attempted to reinstall something like the slave system. As a novel that deals with the death of a child and the loss of an inheritance, both the result of racist reaction, *Marrow* exposes the attempt on the part of white supremacists to reinstall a slave society.[21] While Carteret and his cohorts attempt the natal alienation of the Miller family, they also attempt to dishonor Sandy. Thus, the doubling of Janet and Olivia on a sentimental level can be contrasted to the doubling of Tom and Sandy on tragicomic and gothic levels. As a black woman, Janet is disinherited, through trickery, from her rightful legacy (her father names her in the will that Olivia keeps hidden) and from her descendant (her child dies as a result of Major Carteret's actions). It is across this divide of natal alienation that the two women gaze upon one another: "The two women stood confronting each other across the dead child, mute witness of this first meeting between two children of the same father" (465). While the doubling of Janet and Olivia works on a sentimental level to depict the racist reaction against Reconstruction, the doubling of Tom and Sandy works on a tragicomic and gothic level to depict the absurdity of the racial masquerade. As the elder Delamere puts it, "All cats are gray in the dark,

Carteret, and moreover, nothing is easier than for a white man to black his face. God alone knows how many crimes have been done in this guise" (388). It is just such a crime — committed by the white man Tom dressed as the black man Sandy — that reveals the masquerade of race, and links the supplement of skin color to the supplement of clothing.

Tom's face is "dark almost to swarthiness;" his eyes are black and his "curly hair is of raven tint" (226). His swarthiness is matched by his behavior, which exhibits black stereotypes — laziness, insubordination, immorality and so on — that Chesnutt subverts in his novel. By contrast, Sandy, the former slave, is much more like Delamere's gentlemanly grandfather. Indeed, old Mr. Delamere says that "Sandy is a gentleman in ebony!" Tom takes offence at the favor this former slave receives, and feels repulsed by Sandy's "ridiculous air of importance, *his long blue coat, and his loud plaid trousers*" (233 emphasis added). The plot turns not only on the similarity-and-difference between Tom and Sandy, but on Sandy's best suit of clothes, the same long blue coat and loud plaid trousers that Tom ridicules. Tom steals Sandy's blue coat and plaid trousers to masquerade as Sandy and to perform a "cake walk" in blackface. This burlesque imitation may be Chesnutt's nod to Twain's *Pudd'nhead Wilson* in which an "old deformed negro bellringer straddl[es] along in [Tom's] wake tricked out in a flamboyant curtain-calico exaggeration of his finery" (24).[22] At one of these performances, Tom's uncanny appearance strikes the audience forcefully: "The newcomer was dressed strikingly, the conspicuous features of his attire being a long blue coat with brass buttons and a pair of plaid trousers" (305). Only later do we find out that the performer who seemed to be Sandy was really Tom. In a fantastic, almost Gothic scene, "Sandy sees his h'ant," and the element that produces the uncanny effect is clothing: "Sandy was quite sober enough to perceive that the figure ahead of him wore his best clothes and looked exactly like him." Again, this echoes Twain's work as haunting and a haunted house are specifically involved in the setting of racial disguise in *Pudd'nhead Wilson*. Dressed in Sandy's clothes, Tom limns out the very process by which racist stereotyping projects an exaggeration of the racist's own identity onto a fabricated racial Other. Sandy follows his double to Tom's rooms and poses a question that is as much about the ambiguity of race in general as it is about these two characters: "'Mistah Tom' asked Sandy solemnly, "ef I wuz in yo' place, an you wuz in my place, an' we wuz bofe in de same place, whar would I be?" (342). Finally, we learn that Tom has donned Sandy's duds not only to perform his cake walk, but also to murder his aunt and to steal her money to pay his gambling debts. The novel seems to show us that one of the ways in which racism oppresses is by projecting the oppressor's own crimes onto its victims.

While this storyline in *Marrow* shows how racist ideology projects the crimes of the colonizer onto the identity of the colonized, the supplements of race and clothing function as ambiguous signs of identity that can potentially subvert and expose the racist ideology of post–Reconstruction America. The supplement of clothing can cloak the supplement of race, just as the supplement of race can subvert the meanings of conventional attire. Race is so ambiguous that the supplement that is next to it, clothing, can throw the individual's identity into confusion. And Sandy's clothes embody that ambiguity. The long blue coat represents "the fashion of a former generation," while the plaid trousers are "of strikingly modern cut and pattern" (232). This contradictory presence of the outmoded with the modern suggests one of the most important ambiguities of clothing. As Thoreau noted in the nineteenth century, a new man would need new clothes. It is the shifting of identity — racial, ethnic, class, and gendered — along with changing costumes that produces cultural vertigo. It is only in a society, as Chesnutt so keenly perceives, in which unreconstructed subjects of a pre-modern South interact with subjects fashioned in modernity that Sandy and Tom's confusion can occur.

Another important text of this same period that also explores how clothing functions as the vehicle of mobility in America is Abraham Cahan's *Yekl*. Indeed, as Werner Sollors has observed, Cahan and Chesnutt are up to similar things in their work. Chesnutt's "The Wife of His Youth," and Cahan's *Yekl* are both preoccupied with clothing as a metaphor and outward sign of assimilation. In each story, a cosmopolitan husband is contrasted with a greenhorn wife, primarily through the emblem of clothes.[23] Published in 1895 with William Dean Howell's enthusiastic endorsement, *Yekl* was Cahan's first entry into American literary culture, and his first important treatment of the garment industry. In this story, the sewing machine itself functions as a vehicle of labor and of mobility. Jake/Yekl's conflict in this story is between the ways of the Old World — embodied in his wife — and the modernity of the new, embodied in his "Americanized" co-worker and lover, Mamie. Debating whether or not he should send for his wife and child, Jake first evokes "the image of a dark-eyed young woman with a babe in her lap," but is quickly shaken out of this reverie. What transports him away from it is "the sewing machine." As it "throbbed and writhed under Jake's lusty kicks, it seemed to be swiftly carrying him away from the apparition which had the effect of receding, as a wayside object does from the passenger of a flying train, until it lost itself in the misty distance, other visions emerging in its place" (*Yekl*, 9).[24] Shortly after this, the narrator tells us, "if Yekl was averse to wearing a soldier's uniform on his own person he was none the less fond of seeing it on others. [...] As a cheder boy he showed a knack at placing himself on terms of familiarity with the Jewish members of the local regiment, whose uniforms struck terror into the hearts of his schoolmates" (10). To don the uniform of the Czar's army, as these Jewish soldiers did, was to take on the mantle of gentile. Thus, Yekl discovers the mobility of modern society through both the machinery and material of non-traditional clothing. Cahan created mobile subjects in that his immigrant characters found themselves disconnected from the stationary life of their Russian Jewish past as they moved through urban space and entered a new industry as laborers, managers, and capitalists.

Conclusion

For the American realists, clothing is not merely costume — it is not solely part of a literary process of creating a detailed mise-en-scene or of limning out well-rounded characters. Writers like Howells, Twain, Chesnutt, Cahan, and Wharton contributed to and responded to a broader discourse of dress and clothing. This broader discourse was not a mere byproduct of the industrialization of clothing. Rather, as Picken's "Pledge" suggests, the discourse of dress linked clothing to national, ethnic, economic, gendered, and class conceptions of the self in society. The discourse of dress at the turn of the twentieth century was as important as any technological advance in clothing production to the development of the clothing industry.

This sartorial discourse was also important to American writers who deployed costume as a means of imagining individual identities, but also racial characteristics, class dynamics and changes, ethnic stereotypes (and their deconstruction), and what they imagined to be the very fabric of the nation — something they fashioned in their fiction. Representations of dress in the work of key figures of the time — including Howells, Twain, Wharton, Chesnutt, and Cahan — reflected and contributed to a conflicting vision of dress and its symbolic social significance: social Darwinist at one extreme, historical materialist at another. Within the broader development of American realism — in the different realist visions of Dreiser and James, in Yezierska's reshaping of literary realism's fabric into an almost sentimental urban local color, Cahan's ambiguous mix of satire and sentiment, and Cather's modernist regional romances — clothing takes on important significance for the way national identity is imagined. But while clothing was an important symbol of identity, it was also a commodity. Aware of the materiality of clothes that Thoreau and even a sentimental writer like Alger pointed to decades earlier, these later writers of the real express anxieties about national and ethnic identity, about the self and society, and, ultimately, about the literary commodities they themselves are producing through their speculations on dress.

3. Henry James's Old Clothes

TRACES OF MATERIAL THINGS, INCLUDING clothes, haunt Henry James's fiction, especially his gothic descriptions of women's dress in "The Romance of Certain Old Clothes," and the photographically mediated image of a finely dressed young woman in "Crapy Cornelia." In the first story, a haunted chest opens up to release a possessed gown seeking vengeance. In the second, a middle-aged man chooses the antique material objects he associates with a platonic female friend over and above the new money of a younger woman and potential spouse. These two stories — bookending James's oeuvre from the early tales to the late stories — show clearly how, as one critic has observed, James's career epitomizes "that extended moment in American literature ... when the claims of romance and the claims of realism were still in the balance." Moreover, this transition from romance to realism also coincides with the development of a distinctly consumerist middle-class culture in the United States.[1] Thus, an examination of James's treatment of clothing throughout his career, with a special focus on these two stories, can shed light on the development of American realism, and trace the shift from an industrializing culture of production into a commodity culture. In this shift, James moves from a gothic image of clothes possessed — both owned as property and haunted by history in "The Romance of Certain Old Clothes" — to the realist representation of clothing as the material trace and metaphorical sign of (national, cultural, and ethnic) alienation in "Crapy Cornelia." In the former story, dress is still intimately tied to older forms of materiality in which cloth and clothing transmit wealth, identity, memory, and even love from husband to wife, mother to daughter, and past to present. In the latter, clothes have become commodities, conveying abstract exchange value rather than kinship or history. However, "The Romance" already displays some of the economic and national anxieties of the later story, and "Crapy Cornelia" continues to be haunted by the fading materiality of the earlier gothic tale. In both, clothing also symbolically conveys concerns about nation and ethnicity. At the end of his career, as we shall see, James was haunted by the monstrous presence of new money and new immigrants.

James's gothic aesthetic is almost always concerned with the inability to tell the haunter from the haunted. But this ambiguity is also at work in his psychological and social observations in the late period of his work. A comparison of the more traditionally gothic tale of a possessed trousseau in "The Romance of Certain Old Clothes" and the materially haunted and haunting identity of Cornelia Rasch in "Crapy Cornelia," along with a reading of these same motifs across James's oeuvre can help us understand James's anxieties about the United States as it changed from a sartorial culture of custom-made clothing to a consumer culture of ready-made selves. More importantly, James's work expresses some of the wider anxieties of the traditional wealthy class in the United States as its own manners and fashions became antiquated while a new commodified version of American culture became increasingly available "off-the-rack."

According to Jean-Christophe Agnew, James's novels, along with his autobiographies and *The American Scene*, are guided by a "consuming vision," a "possessive outlook," that expressed "the anxieties of a middle class accustomed to affluence yet no longer secure in its proprietary powers; a class seeking to replace an older set of resources (ownership of the means of production and distribution) with another (control of the means of communication and service)."[2] For Agnew, this anxiously possessive outlook or consuming vision attempts to impart materiality where all has melted into air.[3] Similarly, Richard Adams argues that James viewed the material world through an aesthetic and economic "proprietary vision;" James "was less concerned with acquisition than with what it means to own in a culture that uses the implements of inheritance to transform proprietorship into consumption" (465). In such a culture of consumption, actual objects disintegrated into abstract exchange values. In this process, material human needs atomize into commercialized consumer desires. This process of dissolution and fragmentation produces a culture in which signs, disconnected from their material moorings, fly about in a network of symbolic exchange. In particular, the commodity of clothing suffers a significant transformation even though it continues to convey human needs and desires such as memory, identity, even love. In fact, clothing seems to resist the process by which things are reduced, dissolved, diminished, and abstracted into exchange value. In other words, dress is paradoxically the commodity par excellence, while being at the same time a *thing* that contains and conveys human memory, identity, and community — whether for progressive or relatively conservative and nostalgic ends, as is the case in James's late style.

Within the arena of American literary realism, and in that literary movement's confrontation with mass-produced identities, James's work is one of the most complex instances of reaction to the new, not because he dismisses such newness outright, but because he finds himself to be a reluctant Bohemian, in both senses of that word. Jostled by throngs of Eastern Europeans who have made themselves at home in James's native country, James found himself more alienated than the aliens — more foreign than the Bohemians. James adopted an alien identity by default, not by affirmation, as Ross Posnock has suggested.[4] At the same time, in his fiction, James expresses an affinity for that other sort of bohemianism — the fashioning of an individual identity at odds with dominant middle-class notions of taste. But while the bohemian dandy was, in the late eighteenth to early nineteenth centuries a "modern" whose self-fashioning challenged "tradition," James's bohemianism is a retro refashioning of that earlier modern ideal. Like Cornelia Rasch, James found in his return to the United States what his narrator calls "the promised land of American thrift" (229). Cornelia represents James's own sense of having effectively become antiquated, and dispossessed — no longer possessed by the spirit of the American past. Unlike his gothic ghost in "A Romance of Certain Old Clothes," both Cornelia, and perhaps James himself, are modern ghosts, haunted by the transformation of clothing from material identity to abstract desire.

"The Romance of Certain Old Clothes"

Peter Stallybrass argues that "Marx ... was mistaken in appropriating the concept of fetishism from nineteenth-century anthropology and applying it to commodities," an argument that will be discussed further and applied to Theodore Dreiser's *Sister Carrie* in Chapter 4. Stallybrass's concepts (fetishism, memory, and "the ghostly presence" of individual identity infused into clothing) offer a way of reading James's gothic representation of clothes. Stallybrass goes on to say that Marx was

> right in insisting that the commodity is a "magical" (that is, mystified) form, in which the labor processes which give it its value have been effaced. But in applying the term *fetish* to the commodity, he in turn erased the true magic by which other tribes (and, who knows, perhaps even we ourselves) inhabit and are inhabited by what they touch and love. ... for us, to love things is something of an embarrassment. Things are, after all, mere things. And to accumulate things is not to give them life. It is because things are *not* fetishized that they remain lifeless.... In a capitalist economy — an economy of new cloth, new clothes — the life of textiles takes on a ghostly existence, emerging to prominence, or even to consciousness, only at moments of crisis.[5]

Stallybrass, writing from his own personal loss and finding solace in the garments of a deceased friend and colleague, argues that the negative concept of material fetishism is misguided. The life, power, and magic of material objects and especially of clothes can have the ability to convey meaning, memory, and identity. Individuals infuse their clothes with life and continue figuratively to haunt those clothes after they die. Stallybrass means that in a capitalist economy, in which garments (like all commodities) are lifeless and abstract expressions of exchange value, the life of those objects is never completely extracted or abstracted or reduced. That life — the sweat of labor, the smell of the body, the shape of the limbs, and the memory of use — continues to haunt the garment, to invest it with an absent presence. Stallybrass also claims that "cloth *is* a kind of memory. When a person is absent or dies, cloth can absorb his or her absent presence" (38). In Renaissance Europe, according to Stallybrass, clothes given as gifts or bequeathed in wills transmitted "wealth ... genealogy ... royal connections, but also ... memory and ... the love of a mother for a daughter" (46). Even in nineteenth century New England, quilting and dressmaking were important means of social transmission and "a means of producing counter-memories," as expressed in the testimonies of *The Lowell Offering* (1845).[6]

The ghostly presence of identity in clothing, along with its full-blown emergence to consciousness, is clearly at work in "A Romance of Certain Old Clothes," in which a haunted chest contains a possessed wedding dress that reaps its former owner's vengeance on a sister who misappropriates the garment. Set in a pre-industrial colonial New England, the narrative clearly takes place within a developing capitalist economy, and at a time of personal crisis for its characters and national crisis for its historical setting (a generation before the Revolutionary War). In this narrative, the "ghostly existence" of clothes becomes literal and tangible. The narrative involves a reversal of economic fortunes, and the historical backdrop gestures towards the birth of U.S. national identity. James, writing after the establishment of ready-made clothes but before their mass production by the 1880s, looks back at American homespun society, a period when imported silk, for example, had powerful significance in terms of national identity. However, writing after the Civil War and aware, no doubt, of the cultural as well as political fallout of that conflict, namely a massive restructuring of the American economy, including the introduction of standardized measurements for ready-made garments, James was also aware of what might be called a kind of proto-consumerist desire, an early expression of consumer fetishism. These aspects of the political and economic backdrop give allegorical weight to the story of handmade garments that are meant to transmit matrilineal identity, but that become the object of a sister's proprietary vision and consuming passion. James's story exposes what Stallybrass describes as "the terror of the material trace" to be found in clothes ("Worn Worlds," 40). The coveted material turns its ghostly and terrifying presence on the proto-consumer of James's tale — the sister who longs to possess the garments.

"The Romance of Certain Old Clothes" takes place "[t]oward the middle of the eighteenth century" when "poor little New England" was "very small," and when the North American colonies allowed ample opportunity for a young man to "invest [a handsome inheritance] in trade in this country."[7] Back then, Americans waited eagerly for travelers from across the Atlantic to describe for them "the ways and means of people of fashion in European capitals" (245). Two sisters of an old New England family fall in love with a young merchant connected to a firm in England. The younger sister, Perdita, wins the affections of the young man, Lloyd, and the two are married. The older sister, Viola, is jealous not only because Lloyd favors Perdita, but also, and perhaps even more so, because Perdita gains a beautiful wedding trousseau, including a bolt of blue imported silk which Viola herself transforms into a brocade wedding gown. Perdita dies after giving birth to a daughter, and makes Lloyd promise not to give the wedding dress to Viola, if he marries her, but to save the dress for their newly-born daughter. Lloyd makes the pledge, but years later, when he has fallen on difficult financial times, he succumbs to Viola's persistent requests at least to see the trousseau. At the end of the story, Lloyd finds Viola strangled to death by a ghost that has emerged from the old chest containing the dress.

James modeled the story partly on Gothic novels, even comparing his characters directly to "the ladies in the household of the Vicar of Wakefield" to describe the way the sisters "were forever stitching and trimming their petticoats, and pressing out their muslins, and contriving washes and ointments and cosmetics" (247). The supernatural element in the tale might come, in fact, from both folk and popular sources, namely certain versions of the Cinderella myth and Charles A. Somerset's popular 1834 play, *The Mistletoe Bough; or, The Fatal Chest* (or *The Mistletoe Bough; or, Young Lovel's Bride*). As noted above, Horatio Alger's Ragged Dick is a Cinderella for the ready-made industrial age, and surprisingly like Alger, James (writing just two years after Alger published Ragged Dick) pays special attention to the importance of clothing in constructing individual identity. But James's tale focuses on a darker side of this relationship between material culture, and the making and unmaking of the self.

According to Mary Hallab, James's story, like Somerset's play, implies thematically that inheritance trumps social mobility, even lateral social mobility of one sister acquiring the fortunes of another. In the historical setting of James's story, traditional lines of propriety override modern lines of acquisition. As Hallab puts it, "the clothes of the bride represent not only an unfulfilled promise of happiness but also her *property* and *self*. ... Perdita's ghost is called up by her sister's attempt to remove the trousseau." In both James's tale and in the popular play, the ghost emerges from a chest — the repository of ancestral property — both "to avenge the betrayal of the heroine and to forestall a second betrayal involving what would have been her property. ... In James's story, Perdita's child will be [or would have been] cheated of the clothes she was intended to inherit." Similarly, James's apparent reworking of the Cinderella myth draws from versions of the Cinderella story that emphasize the claims of the past on the present and the future. Hallab points to similarities between James's tale and an early Italian version of Cinderella as told by Giambattista Basile, "The Cat Cinderella," both of which share the motif of "death by chest" and the significance of old clothes. According to Hallab, in "The Cat Cinderella," "the heroine Zezolla kills her stepmother by slamming the lid of a chest on her neck when she leans in to get the girl an old dress (more 'old clothes'). In Basile's tale, though not associated with the chest, the dead mother does operate from the grave — in the guise of a fairy — to help her child." What is interesting here is that signifiers of a propertied past (the chest, the old dress, and the intercession of a deceased parent) imply the importance of a familial past in the material desires and fears of a present generation.[8]

According to Stallybrass: "There is, indeed, a close connection between the magic of lost clothes and the fact that ghosts often step out of closets and wardrobes [and chests] to appall us, haunt us, perhaps even console us" ("Worn Worlds" 41). But, of course, there is no consolation at the end of "Old Clothes." The material inheritance seems to return with a vengeance if its claims are at all threatened by acquisition, desire, and consumption, rather than memory and inheritance. Viola's desire is a consuming desire, an acquisitive desire, and it threatens the traditional line of material transmission. In the 1860s, for Henry James and his readers, this acquisitive desire was a terrifying threat to traditional notions of kinship, economy, and polity.

In this story, Viola is associated with the fetishistic and magical qualities of cloth. Viola and Perdita's mother is "determined that her daughter should carry from home the most elegant outfit that her money could buy, or that the country could furnish," and she turns to the "sage women in the county" to bring their collective sartorial wisdom to bear on "Perdita's wardrobe" (251). But it is not this community of women who provide Perdita with the jewel of her fashion crown, but, rather, Viola who "would now fall to work and solve all their silken riddles" (252). With "her insatiable love of millinery," Viola gets to work: "Yards and yards of lovely silks and satins, of muslins, velvets, and laces, passed through her cunning hands" (252). Ironically, then, it is Perdita's jealous sister who provides her with the most beautiful elements of her wedding trousseau: "Perdita was prepared to espouse more of the vanities of any fluttering young bride who had yet challenged the sacramental blessing of a New England divine" (252). The reference to Viola's "cunning hands," and other references to her being, in the eyes of Arthur Lloyd, "a devilish fine woman," along with Perdita's suspicion of Viola practicing "insidious arts"—all these clues, in short—not only attach a fetishistic magic to the fabrics, but associate witchcraft with Viola's sartorial arts.

The story, indeed, might be read as the narrative of a curse and countercurse, but even this magic is tinged with shades of the market, as Lloyd interposes an economic element into these gothic events. When Viola congratulates her sister, Perdita, on her marriage to Arthur, Viola says, in a formulaic phrase, "I wish you every happiness, and a very long life," to which Perdita replies, "Don't speak in that tone ... I'd rather you cursed me outright. Come sister ... he couldn't marry both of us" (249). Of course, as the narrative develops, the "very long life" is an ironic foreshadowing, and precisely a curse. Similarly, on her deathbed, Perdita lays what seems to be a curse, or at least a warning, on the material inheritance she leaves for her daughter. Like later cinematic representations of cursed mummy's emerging from tombs to protect the ancestral treasures within, James's story presents the image of a cursed chest containing terrifying and vengeful textiles. Her wardrobe, except for "some dozen things [she's] left for Viola," will be "sacredly kept for this little innocent" (255). These gowns will be "wrapped in camphor and roseleaves, and [keep] their colors in the sweet-scented darkness." She extracts a promise from her husband who protests, "Are you afraid I'll sell them?" This exchange is especially instructive in that the dialogue opposes a traditional, pre-industrial notion of inheritance with a modern, capitalist notion of commerce. Perdita assures her husband: "No, but that they may get scattered." She wants to keep her material wardrobe intact, to keep it sacredly whole. And to do so, she relies on "the great chest in the attic, with the iron bands," saying that "There's no end to what it will hold" (256). This last thought, again, taps into fetishistic notions about the magic of clothes. The chest is, as it were, a magic container that can hold both the material and the material's magical power. Perdita refers not only to how much it will hold ("no end"), but also to the kind of thing ("what") it will hold: not just objects, but their essences, their life. The husband's question can be read as an expression of precisely that anxiety ("Are you afraid...") that Agnew and Richard Adams associate with James's career and with U.S. economic history: the anxiety that a traditional proprietary culture was being transformed into a consumer culture ("...I'll sell it?"). This gothic romance concerning proprietary inheritance already pre-figures James's later modern realism concerning consumerist acquisition.

James has already established the idea that Viola has a certain claim over Perdita's gown, not only because her beauty is more in keeping with the color, fabric, and cut of the dress, but also because of the fact that Viola does all the tailoring, herself. Viola is both seamstress and model. This should not be read as a Marxian critique of the commodity form, Viola's labor alienated and abstracted into the commodity. Rather, Viola's craft and labor are recruited into traditional demands of propriety. Marriage and inheritance outweigh the claims of individual beauty, the horizontal bonds of sisterhood, or the claims of labor. The resulting image — of Viola wearing Perdita's dress — is presented as a hideous, unnatural, and even terrifying reversal of the traditional economic/material order of things:

> Viola, as usual, was before the glass, but in a position which caused the other to stand still, amazed. She had dressed herself in Perdita's cast-off wedding veil and wreath, and on her neck she had hung the heavy string of pearls which the young girl had received from her husband as a wedding-gift. These things had been hastily laid aside, to await their possessor's disposal on her return from the country. Bedizened in this *unnatural garb*, Viola stood at the mirror, plunging a long look into its depths, and reading Heaven knows what audacious vision [252, emphasis added].

This mirror scene — Perdita seeing her sister as a kind of evil twin — reveals the attempt of a young woman to constitute an identity that runs counter to the claims of propriety. Even her gaze into the mirror — like that of an evil stepmother/queen asking, "Who's the fairest of them all?" — horrifies and threatens.

Thus, much of the horror of this story comes from economic, not supernatural, fears. It is precisely the *failure* of modern consumption that acts as the narrative hinge upon which this ghost story turns. Viola's consuming passion for her dead sister's wardrobe is the desire of the individual for the commodity, and this desire returns (with a vengeance) only because Lloyd loses the means by which to provide her with *new* clothes: "During the three first years of her marriage Mrs. Lloyd [Viola] failed to become a mother, and her husband on his side suffered heavy losses of money." This loss "compelled a material retrenchment in his expenditure, and Viola was perforce less of a great lady than her sister had been" (259). In response to this "material retrenchment," Viola presses her husband to open the chest. She finds it "revolting ... that these glorious fabrics should wait on the bidding of a little girl who sat in a high chair, and ate bread-and-milk with a wooden spoon" (259).

In its colonial American setting, the narrative's implications about the material and metaphysical claims of the past also take on a national significance. In addition to the economic reversal of Lloyd's material losses, the story hints at the political transformation of the American Revolution which lies twenty years in the story's future. When Arthur Lloyd and Perdita Willoughby first marry, James's narrator tells us, the "lurid clouds of revolution were as yet twenty years beneath the horizon, and that [Lloyd's] connubial felicity should take a tragic turn it was absurd, it was blasphemous, to apprehend" (250). In 1869, when the story was published, part of its horror came from the retrospective shadow cast by James's post-bellum sense of a nation whose future would be tragic, but who was living in a fairytale provincialism. The marriage is one between a colonial woman and a young Englishman — Lloyd comes into the family through his acquaintance with the brother, Bernard, at Oxford. The suggestion, here, is that average American colonists looked back to England as the cosmopolitan capital of empire. However, after Perdita's death and Lloyd's remarriage to her sister, it is the combination of Viola's infertility and Lloyd's "heavy losses of money" that provide the narrative turn that leads to the story's horrifying conclusion (259), suggesting through the image and metaphor of one family the specter that haunted New England even twenty years before the Revolution: reversals in business and in kinship. Beyond the horizon of the tale's narrative — in its implied future — Perdita's daughter will come of age precisely during the American Revolution, and despite her mother's hopes that "some fashions come back every twenty years," it is clear from the narrative that the daughter will inherit a cursed trousseau along with a financially ruined and emotionally scarred legacy, and she will live in a time of national tumult. For James's readers, the fratricidal horror of the Civil War would have resonated with the tale's horrifying version of American sibling rivalry. James continued to write fiction concerning both economic questions regarding propriety and consumption as well as national identity. And while his treatment of these issues would shift from romance to realism, he would continue to use clothing as a key material-symbolic expression of his anxieties about America's consumer culture, a culture that, James seemed to suggest, was transformed both by women and by immigrants.

Dressing the Self, Making and Selling the Nation

According to Agnew, the commodity form is the key to understanding James's oeuvre as tracing *both* the shift from romance to realism and the shift from an industrial-manufacturing culture to a commercial-consumerist culture. If so, then the specific commodity of clothing is especially instructive in understanding James's career as marking these shifts. The most famous sartorial passage in James's oeuvre, and one that falls at the end and at the pinnacle of his early phase is the conversation between Madame Merle and Isabel Archer about what constitutes the "self" in *The Portrait of a Lady* (1882/1909). In that novel, Madame Merle, a worldly American woman who has lived most of her adult life in Europe, tells Isabel:

> When you've lived as long as I you'll see that every human being has his shell and that you must take the shell into account. By the shell I mean the whole envelope of circumstances. There's no such thing as an isolated man or woman; we're each of us made up of some cluster of appurtenances. What shall we call our "self"? Where does it begin? Where does it end? It overflows into everything that belongs to us — and then it flows back again. I know a large part of myself is in the clothes I choose to wear. I've a great respect for *things*! One's self — for other people — is one's expression of one's self; and one's house, one's furniture, one's garments, the books one reads, the company one keeps — these things are all expressive.⁹

In response, Isabel herself says,

> I don't agree with you. I think just the other way. I don't know whether I succeed in expressing myself, but I know that nothing else expresses me. Nothing that belongs to me is any measure of me; everything's on the contrary a limit, a barrier, and a perfectly arbitrary one.

When Madame Merle comments on how well Isabel dresses, Isabel replies that the clothes express the dress-maker, not the dress wearer, and "it's not my choice that I wear them; they're imposed upon me by society." Isabel's innocence, her idealism, and her relatively unsophisticated response are trumped by Madame Merle, who gets the final word: "'Should you prefer to go without them?' Madame Merle enquired in a tone which virtually terminated the discussion" (175).

Clair Hughes, who writes explicitly on the question of dress in James's fiction, argues that James's novel "underwrite[s] Madame Merle's dissent from Isabel's view" (Hughes 50). This authorial endorsement of Madame Merle's materiality suggests that James, himself, was aware of the ways in which clothes function fetishistically, in the sense Stallybrass has described: conveying memory, constructing identity. However, neither Hughes, nor other commentators on this specific passage link this conversation between Madame Merle and Isabel compellingly to the figures of Casper Goodwood and Henrietta Stackpole, who can be read precisely in terms of Agnew's distinction between the two capitalist forces at work in James's fiction and in American society as a whole — a nineteenth-century industrial-manufacturing society and an emerging commercial-consumerist American culture that was taking shape in the 1880s in the form of commercial newspapers. Casper Goodwood, Isabel's young, strenuous, business-minded Bostonian suitor embodies the nineteenth-century industrialist, an American type whose enterprise and garments stand in for the nation itself. Goodwood owns a cotton-mill business in Boston. He has even developed a patent for a new way of spinning cloth. His own wardrobe, moreover, of which Isabel is so critically aware, is made up of a number of identical suits that are all-too-new looking. In the context of Madame Merle's comments, then, it would seem that the representative American businessman produces the very fabric of identity in the United States. In the context of James's oeuvre as marking the transition both from romance to realism and from industrial to consumer culture, Casper Goodwood is an important figure precisely because he is a manufacturer. He is the active agent of production, not a passive consumer. His mill and his patent suggest the vigorous making of America, and his uniform dress suggests the pragmatic making of an American.

Contrasted to this masculine embodiment of nineteenth-century industrial production, James presents Henrietta Stackpole, a feminine embodiment of late nineteenth-century commercial consumption. Earlier in the novel, after the very de-Americanized Ralph Touchett first meets the very American Henrietta Stackpole, Ralph objects to Henrietta's typically American swagger and innocence. Ralph responds to those aspects of an emerging America he finds objectionable. Henrietta's vocation as a journalist — sending society letters home for commercial consumption — places her squarely within consumer culture emerging in America by the 1880s: a culture of consumption predicated on the "control over the means of communication and service" which had replaced an older culture centered on "ownership of the means of production and distribution" (Agnew 82). But Isabel defends these qualities in her young friend, championing not so much Henrietta herself but, rather, "what masses behind her." Isabel sums up this massed quantity as "the great country stretching away beyond the rivers and across the prairies, blooming and smiling and spreading till it stops at the green Pacific! A strong, sweet, fresh odour seems to rise form it, and Henrietta — pardon my simile — has something of that odour in her *garments*" (88, emphasis added). Here, the fabric of the nation becomes both metaphorical and material. The American garments are literally infused with the essence (the odor) of the nation itself; they carry a material memory, and they *are* material memory. Henrietta's clothes carry and convey the nation because that nation permeates the fabric, just as the fabric is dispersed through and beyond the nation. Contrary to her protestations, Isabel seems very responsive to the materiality of clothes. But ultimately, she wants to have it both ways: the clothes are both materially important, and they are symbolically significant — the nation massing *behind* the clothes. If Isabel's disagreement with Madame Merle emphasizes her idealism and innocence, her defense of Henrietta registers her association with the new America.

In *The Reverberator* (1888), James would take this image of the newspaper writer even farther, presenting newspaperman George Flack as a mass-produced national commodity himself:

> He was not a particular person, but a sample ... reminding one of certain "goods" for which there is a popular steady demand. You would scarcely have expected him to have a name other than that of his class: a number, like that of the day's newspaper, would have been the most that you could count on, and you would expect vaguely to find the number high — somewhere in the millions.[10]

James gives Flack the label of "Young commercial American," and in his "light gray overcoat," itself the color of newsprint, he is indistinguishable from the other millions of his type and that "for the convenience of society he ought always to have worn something conspicuous — a green hat or a scarlet necktie" (14). This image of the commercial type extends James's critique of commercialized America already at work in his portrait of Henrietta Stackpole and her garments. In the case of Flack, the link between cloth and paper, text and textile, is even more pronounced, as the newspaperman is dressed like a newspaper. Both mass-produced materials — rags and pulp — were becoming important in an increasingly consumerist society. For James, this had significance for the nation itself.

However, in 1881 James did not realize that even if Isabel were right, by the 1890s the "dressmaker" who would express himself or herself in most women's clothes would most likely be a Russian Jewish immigrant. If Isabel is right about the link between the dress and the dressmaker, and if garments can retain the essence of a nation, then in turn-of-the-century America clothing production and consumption were increasingly guided by a new ethnic community. On the other hand, if Madame Merle is right about the self being constituted by the outward garment, then the material relations allowing for the constitution of that self were, again, increasingly guided and influenced by immigrants. Either way, American identity would be refashioned by immigrant labor and consumption, as we shall see in chapter five when we turn to Abraham Cahan's *The Rise of David Levinsky*. Henry James himself would not become completely aware of this until 1904, when he returned to the United States to find he had, in many ways, returned too late. This belatedness was the result of the disappearance of the old America that he had known as a small boy, and the emergence of a new America populated by Casper Goodwoods and also by new immigrants, an America financed by new money, represented by the hack writing of Flack and Stackpole, and populated and built, at least in part, by new immigrants. Later in his career, after the publication of *The American Scene* (1907), James's representation of clothing would be complicated by the transformation of clothing from ancestral property to ready-made commodity, much of this transformation being wrought by immigrants.[11]

"Crapy Cornelia": Materiality and Memory

"Crapy Cornelia" and "The Jolly Corner" tell a similar tale of American expatriates returning from Europe to New York to reclaim family real estate. If, as Agnew argues, the span of James's career charts an increasing social anxiety about the commodity form, then these two stories mark a moment of crisis in that curve. Both of these stories contrast material ancestral property with capital — new money and commodities — recently acquired. Written after James's return visit to the United States in 1904, the two stories look back nostalgically to old New York, the New York of the 1860s. In the new New York of the turn of the century, the memory and history of old property is eclipsed by abstract value in commodities, rental property, and cold hard cash. For James, this seems to have marked a crisis, but an ambiguous one, of course. James himself was concerned, at this point in his life, with his own finances. The journey home was, in fact, partly a financial venture. James hoped to make enough money from *The American Scene* to supplement his income.[12] The protagonists of these stories must find their place in a distinctly American economic landscape in which skyscrapers cast their shadows onto family homes from the 1830s. While "The Jolly Corner" expresses these anxieties about property and money through a ghost — the protagonist's monstrous alter ego — it is "Crapy Cornelia" that provides an even more apt bookend to James's earliest anxious exploration of materiality and money, "The Romance of Certain Old Clothes." For it is in "Crapy Cornelia" that we see something like the ghostly presence of old clothes embodied in the photographically mediated image of a young woman, the love of the protagonist's youth, dressed in the fashions of the 1860s. While "The Romance of Certain Old Clothes" presents a "real" ghost, "Crapy Cornelia" presents the "spectrally faded" photographic image of fashionable dress (839). In "The Romance of Certain Old Clothes," ghostly garments emerged from bottomless chests. In "Crapy Cornelia," sartorial specters emerge from faded photographs.

In "Crapy Cornelia," Cornelia Rasch has returned from the "economic salvation in Europe" to "the promised land of American thrift," to take possession of and manage two houses on Seventh Avenue.[13] Narrating the tale from the limited point of view of White-Mason (the friend of Rasch's youth whose hesitation on the verge of proposing marriage to the young and wealthy widower Mrs. Worthingham is the story's central plot element), James leaves ambiguous the specific catalyst of Rasch's return: to save her property from financial decline or to simply oversee its ample returns. White-Mason wonders if Cornelia is back to salvage the "shriveled interest" remaining of the estate, or, he speculates, if her "investments, decently administered, were making larger returns, so that ... rigorous thrift ... could be finally relaxed" (834). The story turns on White-Mason's decision whether to marry the young Worthingham or to live in platonic and nostalgic (though this term may be questioned) friendship with Rasch. The sibling rivalry between Viola and Perdita is here transformed into White-Mason's choice between romantic and platonic love.

But behind this decision is another: a choice between Worthingham's financial worth, and Cornelia's materiality — her ability to convey memory through materiality as Stallybrass has described the function of clothes. Worthingham's house, her property and material possessions in general, "had that gloss of new money, that glare of a piece fresh from the mint and ringing for the first time on any counter" (821). She represents for White-Mason, who seems to come from old money, "the very essence of the newness and freshness and beautiful, brave, social irresponsibility" of the new age. She has "no instinct for any old quality or quantity or identity" (829). By contrast, he sees himself as much more like Cornelia; both are "conscious, ironic, pathetic survivors together of a dead and buried society." Furthermore, while James uses the metaphor of money fresh from the mint to represent Worthingham, he uses literal descriptions of clothing, and the much more material metaphor of fabric, whether in household decoration or in garments, to describe Cornelia's historicity. For example, the very title of the story refers to Cornelia's almost ascetic habit of black crape, a wardrobe that emphasizes her symbolic function of providing shade from the blindingly bright world of money associated with Worthingham. Moreover, the first full description of Cornelia focuses on her "sparsely feathered black hat" (825). Given the importance of hats elsewhere in James's work (their significance for social class in *The Turn of the Screw*, their suggestion of knowledge or wisdom in *What Maisie Knew*, and their connection with literary signification in "The Velvet Glove" and "John Delavoy"), it is important that Cornelia leads with her hat.[14] She will be a source of nostalgia and knowledge, of history and memory, and the hat, perhaps, serves to indicate the receptacle of that important knowledge. What's more, the narrator indicates that the hat was "an ornament quite unlike those the women mostly noticed by White-Mason were now 'wearing'" (825). Thus, like so much else concerning Cornelia, the hat connects White-Mason to the past.

Moreover, even the metaphors that James's uses to describe White-Mason's perception of Cornelia tend to be metaphors of fabric or garments.

For example, he describes her as "an almost ancient and ... oddly unassertive little rotund figure whom one seemed no more obliged to address than if she had been a black satin ottoman 'treated' with buttons and gimp" (826). White-Mason's associations move from garments to fabrics to furniture to architectural materiality: he imagines Cornelia as "a massive little bundle of data," so full with historical knowledge that he wonders whether if he touches her "with a gentle though firm pressure, he would, as the fond visitor of *old houses taps* and fingers a disfeatured, over-papered wall with the conviction of a *wainscot-edge beneath*, recognize some small extrusion of history" (833 emphasis added). Materiality (Cornelia's old-fashioned hat, the metaphor of black satin on an ottoman, the image of over-papered walls) links White-Mason with the past just as money and commodities — in Worthingham's house — jar him into the present. Perhaps the most compelling metaphor James associates with Cornelia's link to the past is that of brown velvet, a metaphor that is echoed in "real" items of clothing. White-Mason sees Cornelia's "ancient reserves" of knowledge in terms of

> the old brown surface and tone as of velvet rubbed and worn, shabby, and even a bit dingy, but all soft and subtle and still velvety — which meant still dignified; whereas the angular facts of current finance were as harsh and metallic and bewildering as some stacked "exhibit" of ugly patented inventions, things his medieval mind forbade his taking in [834–5].

Clearly, Stallybrass's notion of material memory is at work here, with the rubbed and worn and shabby quality of the velvet giving it its "value" for history and memory, while the notion of the patented invention suggests the latest technical innovation and its promise of future earnings of cash. Furthermore, this use of worn brown velvet as a metaphor for historicity and the past becomes reified in Cornelia's clothing. In the story's actual (present) setting, Cornelia wears black crape, but in his memories of their youth, White-Mason remembers her as "the funniest little brown thing possible" (837). Later he recalls that Cornelia "wore brown velveteen," and, furthermore, she remembers the fashion of the 1860s to include the use of "braided velveteen" (844). Materiality and fabric — velvet, silk, crape — link Cornelia, and White-Mason through Cornelia, to the past.

The color and tint of materials is also significant in this story. Cornelia's association with black, brown, and with shade is contrasted to Worthingham's association with glare and light. When faced with the "expensive object[s]" he sees in Worthingham's house, White-Mason responds "with something of the grimace produced on persons without goggles [or sunglasses] by the passage from a shelter to a blinding light; and if he had — by a perfectly possible chance — been 'snap-shotted' on the spot, would have struck you as showing for his first tribute to the temple of Mrs. Worthingham's charming presence a scowl almost of anguish" (821). Mrs. Worthingham seems to be "lighting up his autumn afternoon of life" (823) with her "iridescent surface, the shimmering interfusion of her various aspects" which he associates with youth and pecuniary independence (824). This light, to put it bluntly, suggests conspicuousness, and implies conspicuous consumption. The relatively abstract image of light is associated with newness and with new commodities in particular, rather than history, memory, or age. In Stallybrass's dichotomy of abstract exchange value as opposed to material mnemonic value of garments, we can read Worthingham's association with light as her association with the abstract, with financial value rather than material historical value. Worthingham's social scene is marked by "Newness," and a frantic quality from which White-Mason retreats, "wounded, bleeding, blinded, from the riot of the raw — of, to put the whole experience more prettily, no doubt, from excesses of light" (822). These excesses of light require "screened observation" because her social scene "seemed to reflect as never before the luster of Mrs. Worthingham's own polished and prosperous little person — to smile, it struck him, with her smile, to twinkle not only with the gleam of her lovely teeth, but with that of all her rings and brooches and bangles and other gewgaws..." (822).

James takes this metaphor of light and shade to the extreme of comparing the contrasts between Worthingham and Cornelia to the high contrast of the new technology of cinematography. Worthingham's outlook, both literally from her house and figuratively from her shallow optimism, is "a great square sunny window that hung in assured fashion over the immensity of life" (824). She uses her "light gemmed hand, flashing on him ... [to touch] a spring, the most ingenious of recent devices for instant ease, which dropped half across the scene a soft-coloured mechanical blind, a fluttered, fringed awning of charmingly toned silk, such as would make a bath of cool shade for the favoured friend..." (825). Indeed, the introduction of this "bath of cool shade" provided by a piece of silk also introduces a different figure who we soon learn is Cornelia. Thus, she enters the excessively lighted world of Worthingham as a shade, a screen, a cloth to provide shadow. An "incongruous object" blocks White-Mason's literal and figurative view of his bright future with Worthingham, and this object "was a woman's head, crowned" with the crape hat White-Mason notices. His view of the hat "grew and grew ... came nearer and nearer, while it met his eyes, after the manner of images in the kinematograph" (825). Here, then, is one of the key figures in James's story — the dark figure of Cornelia Rasch standing out in contrast to the conspicuous glare of Mrs. Worthingham. At this moment, "everything ... altered, dropped, *darkened*, disappeared" (825, emphasis added).

Cornelia is introduced both in terms of her materiality (her hat), and within the figurative terms of the story: as benevolent shade. As a member of a social circle White-Mason sees as extinct, she appears "amid old shades once sacred" (830). Cornelia lets him dispense with the figurative eye-wear he needs to view the bright world of Worthingham. When he visits Cornelia, he finds several objects that catch his interest: material fetishes, touchstones for his and her past. These are photographs from the 1860s, and James focuses our attention on the clothes depicted in them. They provide White-Mason with "the secret for warding and easing off the perpetual imminent ache of one's protective scowl, one would verily but have to let the scowl stiffen, or to take up seriously the question of blue goggles, during what might remain of life" (839). But no such goggles or squinting against the light is necessary with Cornelia: "With you, I haven't to wear a green shade," White-Mason tells her (843). The shaded and faded quality of Cornelia and White-Mason's retrospective vision is most vividly embodied in the photographic image of Mary Cardew, White-Mason's old flame from his youth. In Cornelia's house, White-Mason notices "several objects in the room, serene and sturdy, not a bit cheap-looking, little old New York objects of '68." These turn out to be photographs, "faithfully framed but spectrally faded." The whole technological and aesthetic apparatus of photography itself functions as a kind of shade, a screen through which White-Mason can view the past, and in directing his proprietary vision towards the past he, again, focuses on garments. As in "The Romance of Certain Old Clothes," a ghost returns to haunt the protagonist, but this time the ghost is not an actual gothic spirit but rather a female figure in a "spectrally faded" photograph. Tellingly, the description of this figure, a young woman to whom White-Mason had proposed thirty years earlier, focuses on her clothes. She wears "a 'pork-pie' hat, with her hair in a net. That was so 'smart' then; especially with one's skirt looped up, and a row of very big onyx beads over one's braided velveteen sack — braided quite plain and very broad." Cornelia — full of historical data — remembers these material aspects of the past with a sense of propriety, of property ownership, not commodity fetishism: "He smiled for her extraordinary possession of these things" (844).

"Crapy Cornelia," then, divides American culture into two realms: the new concern for money, and the old interest in material. Worthingham's glaringly new commodities embody conspicuous consumption. It is as if her association with light underscores the conspicuousness of her consumption. Cornelia Rasch's objects — from her clothes to the photographic images of clothes — embody materiality, the fetishistic qualities of cloth and clothing that, according to Stallybrass, function as memory. Through Cornelia, White-Mason claims an identity that Worthingham can never provide. This attention to clothing underscores the contrast James seems to be presenting between the consumer fetishism of the present — embodied in money and machinery — and the material fetishism of the past, embodied in garments and homes.

Alien Attire

Echoing the themes of property and propriety vs. consumerism and commercialism elsewhere in James's oeuvre, "Crapy Cornelia" and "The Jolly Corner" fictionalize James's fear, which he also expresses in *The American Scene*, that all sense of history, memory, and the past has been replaced with the glare of the new and modern. James explains the dichotomy between past and present in a parable of cloth and currency in *The American Scene*:

> The slight, pale, bleeding Past, in a patched homespun suit, stands there taking the thanks of the bloated Present — having woundedly rescued from thieves and brought to his door the fat, locked pocket-book of which that personage appears the owner. The pocket-book contains, "unbeknown" to the honest youth, bank-notes of incredible figure, and what breaks our heart, if we be cursed with the historic imagination, is the grateful, wan smile with which the great guerdon of sixpence is received.[15]

As with both "Crapy Cornelia" and "The Jolly Corner," *The American Scene* suggests that the present era belongs to the abstract exchange value of commodities and rental properties, whereas the era of America's past belongs to the material aesthetic value of real things — faded photographs, ancestral homes, and worn garments.

James seems to have seen *new* Americans as also part of that broader newness allegorized in Mrs. Worthingham who shines the blinding light of conspicuous consumption in White-Mason's eyes. In James's view the new immigrants were, like new money and a new commercial culture, bringing *down* the *aesthetic* value of an older material culture. In a description of immigrants in Central Park, James pays special attention to sounds and tones of immigrant children at play. Ironically, it is only in this scene of immigrant life that costumes seem to fit into their social contexts, as if these immigrants really were more at home in America than James felt himself to be:

> The children at play, more particularly the little girls, formed the characters, as it were, in which the story was written largest; frisking about over the greenswards, grouping together in the vistas, with an affect of the exquisite in attire, of delicacies of dress and personal "keep-up," as through the shimmer of silk, the gloss of beribboned hair, the gleam of cared-for teeth, the pride of varnished shoe, that might well have created a doubt as to their "popular" affiliation. This affiliation was yet established by sufficiencies of context, and might well have been, for that matter, by every accompanying vocal or linguistic note, the swarm of queer sounds, mostly not to be interpreted, that

circled round their pretty heads as if they had been tamers of odd, outlandish, perching little birds [*The American Scene* 134].

In representing the images of immigrants in Central Park in *The American Scene*, James's attention is drawn especially to "the awful aliens [who] were flourishing there in perfections of costume and contentment. One had only to take them in as more completely, conveniently and expensively *endimanchés* than one had ever, on the whole, seen any other people, in order to feel that one was calling down upon all the elements involved the benediction of the future ..." (136). The present and the future belong to others than James, himself, who returns too late. These aliens, in their Sunday best, seem to point to the future in America.

James fictionalized the immigrants of Central Park in "Crapy Cornelia," and again he associated them with futurity:

> So, in the windless, sun-warmed air of the beautiful afternoon, the Park of the winter's end had struck White-Mason as waiting; even New York, under such an impression, was "good," good enough — for *him*: its very sounds were faint, were almost sweet, as they reached him from so seemingly far beyond the wooded horizon that formed the remoter limit of his large shallow glade. The tones of the frolic infants ceased to be nondescript and harsh, were in fact almost as fresh and decent as the frilled and puckered and ribboned garb of the little girls, which had always a way, in those parts, of so portentously flaunting the daughters of the strange native — that is of the overwhelmingly alien — populace at him [818].

In this early passage from "Crapy Cornelia," James attends to the costuming of difference — the frills and ribbons of immigrant garb are like the Sunday best of the immigrants in *The American Scene*. James sets up at once a literal and a metaphorical link between clothing and language. The "sounds" and "tone" of the immigrant children are, like their language, "almost as fresh." But the other side of this freshness is its unfamiliarity. For the protagonist, White-Mason (through whose consciousness we see these immigrants), the visual impression of the clothing and the aural register of the language are similarly uncanny — so at home yet unhomelike, strangely native.

During his return trip to the United States, James delivered a commencement address at Bryn Mawr College in 1904. In that address, aimed at America's young women and titled "The Question of Our Speech," James warns the graduating class of young women not to sleep on the job, but rather to repossess or reacquire the English language that immigrants, newspapers, and public schools seem to have acquired as a cheap commodity:

> All the while we sleep the vast contingent of aliens whom we make welcome, and whose main contention, as I say, is that, from the moment of their arrival, they have just as much property in our speech as we have, and just as good a

right to do what they choose with it — the grand right of the American being to do just what he chooses "over here" with anything and everything: all the while we sleep the innumerable aliens are sitting up (*they* never sleep!) to work their will on their new inheritance and prove to us that they are without any finer feeling or more conservative instinct of consideration for it, more fond, unutterable association with it, more hovering, caressing curiosity about it, than they may have on the subject of so many yards of freely figured oilcloth, from the shop, that they are preparing to lay down, for convenience, on kitchen floor or kitchen staircase.[16]

"Oilcloth," continues James, "is highly convenient, and our loud collective medium of intercourse doubtless strikes these *new householders* as wonderfully resisting 'wear'— with such wear as it gets!— strikes them as an excellent bargain: durable, tough, cheap" (29 emphasis added). James clearly expresses his anxiety about the penetration of "aliens" into American society and domesticity—*they* never sleep! This absence of rest in the domestic sphere transforms that domesticity itself. Indeed, James seems to hint at the social fact that many immigrant households were places not of leisure and aestheticism, but of labor. Furthermore, he equates their feeling for the language with their feeling for oilcloth — an easily produced and reproducible commodity.

For the "new householders," language is transformed into a commodity and a raw material like cloth in tenement sweatshops, tenement kitchens. And as if to underscore this commodification of language, James uses the language of commodities, the relatively new American language of advertising: "an excellent bargain: durable, tough, cheap." Furthermore, this warning against the commodification of language is spoken to the graduating class of a women's college, as if James is speaking to a group of future Cornelia Rasches and Alice Stavertons — the heroines of "Crapy Cornelia" and "The Jolly Corner," whose narrative function is to save their male counterparts from an increasingly commodified world. The capital (the English language) that James felt himself in fact to be turning into high art — the novel — is being transformed into the raw material of alien popular culture. It is the role of American women as conversationalists to honor the note of American language — its musical and exchange value.

Conclusion

A garment, or any commodity, is related to both language and money.[17] James's late work is grounded in a theory of language and literature similar, in some ways, to the Marxist notion of value as something expressed in commodity or currency. Interestingly, the commodity that James uses to explore this issue is a textile — language is like the oilcloth that the new immigrant so easily acquires and so unthinkingly uses for such common purposes. Of course, James's notions about aesthetic use value make his conception of language as currency quite different from any strict Marxian interpretation of value. However, what becomes important in examining James's theory of linguistic, literary, and artistic value is that the "newness" of American culture — including and especially its immigrants — devalues aesthetic interest accumulated over time.

James's Bryn Mawr address appeals to young American women to *save* the English language from businessmen, newspapers, progressive educators, and immigrants.[18] American women occupy a privileged linguistic and literary position in America that bears only a slight resemblance to the Victorian notion of the angel in the house. Unlike the Victorian angels in the house, James's women aesthetes are not protectors of tradition generally but the bearers of linguistic value, and they are not wives mothers and sisters, but, like Cornelia Rasch, devoted platonic friends:

> To the American common school, to the American newspaper, and to the American Dutchman and Dago, as the voice of the people describes them, we have simply handed over our property [American English] — not exactly bound hand and foot, I admit, like Andromeda awaiting her Perseus, but at least distracted, disheveled, despoiled, divested of that beautiful and becoming drapery of native atmosphere and circumstance which had, from far back, made, on its behalf, for practical protection, for a due tenderness of interest [QOS 28].

Language is the "beautiful and becoming drapery" of American culture which is subject to the monstrous combination of assimilating education, popular journalism, and the cheap commodities produced for and consumed by immigrants. But actually, in their positions within social *conversational* circles, and as teachers in the common schools — often as teachers of immigrants — women are specially situated to safe-guard the value of the language, to protect its "beautiful and becoming drapery" from being transformed into "so many yards of freely figured oilcloth" (29). Women are "torch-bearers [...] guardians of the sacred flame" (30). As White-Mason puts it in "Crapy Cornelia": "One wants a woman ... to know *for* one, to know *with* one" (842). In that story, as we have seen, the position of the female friend is to restore the past through conversation. Women, at the turn of the twentieth century, occupied an important social position. They were the keepers of old clothes — as they were the keepers of language and its aesthetic value.

4. From Clothing to Nothing: Annihilating the Self in *Sister Carrie*

HENRY JAMES AND THEODORE DREISER, along with Thorstein Veblen in his own way, noticed that things — objects, including consumer objects — can speak persuasively. Like Kate Croy in James's *The Wings of the Dove* and Caroline (Carrie) Meeber in Dreiser's *Sister Carrie,* the American consumer at the turn of the twentieth century found him or herself cajoled and seduced by the language of inanimate objects on retail racks and department store shelves, and worn by people walking down Broadway in New York or State Street in Chicago. Material objects have persuasive power both in their abstract financial value and in terms of their material appeal to the individual's sense of self. Kate Croy realizes how "material things spoke to her," and she "had an accessibility to pleasure from such sources."[1] Similarly, in Dreiser's novel, Carrie finds clothes to be "a vast persuasion," to speak to her, and to elicit desire and give pleasure. However, both Kate and Carrie also realize that clothes and other consumer products speak another language, as well, that of financial value, numbers and prices. These two related but distinguishable abilities that objects have to speak and to persuade can be described as fetishism: consumer fetishism on the one hand, and what might be called material fetishism on the other. Consumer fetishism transforms the material object into its abstract value to the point that the material object itself — its significance in or irrational appeal to the life of an individual or a group, or both — vanishes. The solid object sublimates into non-material value (the thing becoming a no-thing) within consumer fetishism. Material fetishism, on the other hand, translates the object into memory, community, and identity — it materializes the self.[2]

Sister Carrie is an especially important novel in this context. Not only are objects persuasive in *Sister Carrie*, they have power over individual characters, they have personal persuasion. As characters become consumers, they are themselves consumed by the objects they desire. In some instances — and particularly important is the image of Carrie's father in his flour-dusted miller's clothes — the clothes have a material and personal fetishistic power. They convey memory and identity. However, any such material fetishism gets gobbled up by consumer fetishism; the personal materiality of their identity is transformed into immaterial value, or into nothing. Frequently linking literal consumption of food (or starvation from lack of food) to the consumption of consumer objects — especially clothes — Dreiser shows how social existence itself in industrial commercialized America is predicated on a certain kind of measured consumption. If a character throws off this fine balance of consumption and display, he or she suffers the same fate as the object transformed from material fetishism to consumer fetishism: that character suffers annihilation, becomes nothing. In the case of Hurstwood, that annihilation is literal and physical, in the case of Carrie, it is symbolic and social.

Clothing has a set of sub-cultural functions: conveying memory, embodying the life, love, and labor of the wearer, and bearing the literal and symbolic traces of the wearer's presence. However, dress also conveys abstracted exchange value (within a political economy). Its socio-cultural function of constructing a self is caught between these two functions — a material mnemonics and an immaterial symbolism of value. In *Sister Carrie*, we see these same two functions of clothing come into conflict and also into dialogue through Carrie's desire for clothing. Clothes have this doubly fetishistic power in Dreiser's novel: both through a personal fetishism of things (which function almost as an organ of the body, at least of the social body and its very existence) and the abstract fetishism of commodities (which function as a societal organ that circulates exchange value, including the value of an individual's place within a class hierarchy). In *Sister Carrie*, the loss of clothing or its deterioration threatens to reduce characters literally to nothing. Garments have the ability to convey memory, including the very physical memory of how a garment was worn, the imprint of the body, of sweat and odor on a shirt or a coat, or the traces of work — dirt, grease, or, as in the case of *Sister Carrie*, flour in a flourmill.

As he traces the course of Marx's coat — Marx's literal, material garment — in and out of pawn, Peter Stallybrass traces the movement of human labor and memory in and out of the commodity form. In the true sense of a cloth culture, nineteenth-century English pawnshop trade involved a cycling of dress through a dialectic of currency and commodity (which embodied identity): "wages received on Friday or Saturday [were] used to get one's best clothes out of pawn. The clothes were worn on Sunday and then pawned again on Monday" (Stallybrass 194). This process, which was also at work at the turn of the century in the United States, produced an oscillation between cloth as a conveyer of memory and personal identity, and cloth as a conveyer of currency and social value. On the one hand, "Memories were thus inscribed for the poor within objects that were haunted by loss" (196). On the other, clothes were worth money, and, were read as a measure of the wearer's social worth. Cloth, in particular, is subject to this paradox. "If their things were sometimes animated by their loves, their histories, their handlings," writes Stallybrass of working-class Britons and their material possessions, "they were often animated by the workings of a marketplace that took back those things and stripped them of their loves and their histories, devalued them because they had been handled" (199). Stallybrass shows that material objects were and are important, particularly for working class people, because they convey much more and much deeper "value" than monetary value or invidious comparison. Certainly, clothes and other material objects *did* convey monetary value: "What little wealth [workers] had was stored not in *money* in *banks* but as *things* in the *house*" (202). But most importantly, they conveyed the very notion of self and subjectivity: "To have one's own coat, to wear it on one's back, was to hold on to oneself, even as one held on to one's past and one's future.... Things were the materials — the clothes, the bedding, the furniture — from which one constructed a life; they were the supplements the undoing of which was the annihilation of the self" (202–3). Stallybrass identifies a capitalist consumer fetishism and a pre- or counter-capitalist personal/communal fetishism. The latter embodies and materializes the self, the former obliterates the self.

In contrast to Stallybrass's reading of Marx and clothing, Kate Soper argues that capitalist modes of production *can* allow for much richer forms of self-production than those experienced in non- or pre-capitalist societies. Soper writes:

> Marx ... viewed the establishment of the capitalist mode of production and its generalized system of exchange-relations as having a double-edged impact on individual needs and forms of self-realization.... On the one hand, in severing the personal ties and localized dependencies of the feudal order, it destroyed the erstwhile bases of self-making and reproduction, thus denying individuals a mode of self-extension or objective dimension of being in their relationship to the land, or in their particular tasks and fixed role in their community; and in being deprived of these inorganic conditions of self-extension, individuals are rendered, as Marx puts it, "objectless" or "naked in their subjectivity." On the other hand, Marx also presents this very deprivation or loss of objective presuppositions of self-reproduction as the essential precondition of a much richer — all-around — development of the self, because it frees the individual from (in his words) "all traditional, confined, complacent, encrusted satisfactions of present needs, and reproductions of old ways of life" [29].

Soper also explains that Marx emphasized that any such self-making could never be fully realized within "capitalist relations of ownership, exchange and distribution," but she suggests that fashion could, at least partially, offer "a mode of consumption which gratifies ... the urge to escape from any fixed and presupposed existence and sense of self" (29). While Carrie's life history as a character never places her within a strictly feudal, non- or pre-capitalist context, she does make connections to material objects that emphasize memory (in Stallybrass's sense of the fetishism of the thing) and "personal ties and localized dependencies." In particular, Carrie's father's flour-dusted work clothes take on this objectified, mnemonic, personal, and localized form of materiality and identity. Furthermore, her interactions with her friends the Vances and with Ames bring her into contact with those potentially richer forms of self-making that Soper associates with fashion and more abstract forms of self making. The novel's reduction of Hurstwood to a pile of rags can be understood readily enough as a critique of the tragedy of capitalist *un*doing of the self. However, the question remains whether Carrie's disconnection from materiality (her objectlessness or her naked subjectivity) reduces her to a different kind of nothingness (her abstract value as human advertisement for the theatre and for her hotel) or whether her disconnection from such objects gives her access to that freer form of self-making Soper associates, at least potentially, with capitalism. This chapter examines how material objects function both as personal fetishes of material identity and as consumer fetishes of abstract value. When objects — clothes in particular — cease to function as personal fetishes, the material identity of the character (or person) associated with these objects vanishes. This annihilation of personal material identity can be literally fatal — as in the case of Hurstwood — or it can be a metaphor for personal loss, as in the case of Carrie. In Carrie's case, the reader is left asking, what remains of Carrie?

Without Clothes He Was Nothing: Annihilation of the Self

Critics of Dreiser's *Sister Carrie* have observed that objects make the individual in the world of that novel. Philip Fisher, for example, argues that "man is for the first time," in the late nineteenth century, "surrounded by himself [in the city]. ... Within the city anything outside the body is there only because it was projected there by will and need."[3] Amy Kaplan's gloss on Fisher's reading suggests that "identity is conferred on the self by things around one" (Kaplan 150). Along with Fisher and Kaplan, Walter Benn Michaels also identifies and critiques a significant relationship in Dreiser between material things and the imagined self. Michaels argues that Hurstwood "is described through the oxymorons of an 'active manner' and 'solid, substantial air,' which create an image of solidity composed of the objects with which he adorns himself" which include references to clothing, clean linen, and jewelry.[4] Ultimately, those "things" that most intimately surround the self (that is, garments) are the most important in giving that self a material and social solidity.[5] To lose those things, is to risk annihilating that self.

Dreiser introduces this logic of clothing-or-nothing very early in the novel when, in describing Charles Drouet, Dreiser's narrator states: "Good clothes, of course, were the first essential, the things without which he was nothing."[6] The idea here is that without fine clothing, social existence, let alone social mobility, is not even possible. Without the right clothes he cannot drum up any business, without drumming up business he cannot wear the right clothes, and so on in a tautology of fashion, suggesting that there is no other form of existence for Drouet. The novel invites the reader to apply this measure of identity to Hurstwood and Carrie, as well as to Drouet. If Drouet is *nothing* without his clothes, then Hurstwood certainly follows this same fate. Even after losing his social position in Chicago, "Hurstwood was nothing" (205), and his physical and financial decline, and his death are all described with great attention to sartorial detail. His decline can be measured in cloth. However, in Carrie's case, things are different. While she gains clothes — a full wardrobe — she gains them only to become an abstract value herself. She becomes the fetish object of men who go to the theatre. In comparing herself to other actresses on the stage, she sees "that they were privileged and deferred to. She was nothing — absolutely nothing at all" (271). While she gains a great deal of privilege and receives the deference of a good many people, she is, in a sense, reduced to "nothing" in that her value is often immaterial: she is an advertisement for the theatre, a name for the hotel where she stays. Since Philip Fisher's work on *Sister Carrie*, critics have assumed that the novel presents Hurstwood's decline while tracing Carrie's rise. However, both decline and rise lead to the same end — annihilation of the material self, of what Stallybrass associates with the material, mnemonic, personal, and communal fetishistic power of clothes.

Hurstwood's Annihilation

George Hurstwood is caught within a professional and a domestic economy both of which require expenditure on clothing, and in which such clothing establishes one's identity, and even secures the person's social existence. But Hurstwood controls *neither* his professional position *nor* his household economy. He is not a partner with Messrs. Fitzgerald and Moy, but is a paid operative who runs their leisure establishment: he "lacked financial control" even though his "stewardship ... was imposing" (32). Nor has he complete control of his domestic economy: Mrs. Hurstwood is "pleased by the fact that much of her husband's property was in her name, a precaution which Hurstwood had taken when his home interests were somewhat more alluring than at present" (80). Hurstwood's *value*, in both private and public life, has little to do with financial worth, capital, or assets. His value is bound up in his personal appeal and his material show of wealth, including his clothing and the wardrobes of his wife and daughter. As a manager, his "grace, tact, and *ornate appearance* gave the place an air which was most essential..." (88).

Hurstwood is a robust, well-dressed, middle-class manager with a family and a house in Chicago's upwardly mobile North Side. He is, in a sense, a function of his material surroundings rather than those material surroundings being an expression of his identity. He has "a good, stout constitution, an active manner, and a solid, substantial air, which was composed in part of his fine clothes, his clean linen, his jewels, and, above all, his own sense of importance" (31). Hurstwood's domestic economy is guided by conspicuous consumption, and as Amy Kaplan has observed, functions as a rehearsal and at the same time a critique of sentimental fiction in which home, hearth, and family establish the subject's refuge from the world: "Hurstwood's residence could scarcely be said to be infused with this home spirit. It lacked that toleration and regard without which the home is nothing" (60).[7] Hurstwood's daughter Jessica becomes the vehicle of the family's mobility: "Through Jessica [Mrs. Hurstwood] might rise a little" (61). The few scenes set in the Hurstwood household involve conversations about purchasing clothes. When attending the races, for example, Mrs. Hurstwood "wished to exhibit Jessica, who was gaining in maturity and beauty, and whom she hoped to marry to a man of means;" and "Her own desire to be about in such things and parade among her acquaintances and the common throng was as much an incentive as anything" (99).

Hurstwood's eventual annihilation begins when he starts to imagine an identity for himself outside of either his professional or his domestic reality, when he begins to imagine an identity for himself through Carrie's eyes which repeatedly focus on Hurstwood's clothes. It is through his wardrobe that Hurstwood first appeals to Carrie, and it is in contrast to Drouet's cheap flamboyance that Hurstwood's solid and sober appearance touches Carrie's sympathies. He appeals to her as a "man of money and affairs": "Behold, he had ease and comfort, his strength was great, his position high, *his clothes rich*..." (92, emphasis added). In contrast to Drouet's flashiness, Hurstwood's clothes convey stability:

> His clothes were particularly new and rich in appearance. The coat lapels stood out in the medium stiffness which excellent clothes possess. The vest was of a rich Scotch plaid, set with a double row of round mother-of-pearl buttons. His cravat was a shiny combination of silken threads, not loud, not inconspicuous. What he wore did not strike the eye so forcibly as that which Drouet had on, but Carrie could see the elegance of the material. Hurstwood's shoes were of soft, black calf, polished only to a dull shine. Drouet wore patent leather, but Carrie could not help feeling that there was a distinction in favor of the soft leather, where all else was so rich [69].

Carrie's point of view situates the reader's sense of Hurstwood, *and Hurstwood's sense of himself*: "When he looked at his fine clothes, he saw them with her eyes — and her eyes were young" (99). Hurstwood begins to believe in a different version of himself, one not pinned down either to his work — where he holds no financial stakes — nor to his home, where he has no emotional investment and lacks full economic control.

Dreiser presents Hurstwood's decline not only through the observations of his journalistic narrator, but also through Carrie's keen eye for fashion: Hurstwood's reduction to "nothing" can be read through Carrie's increasing revulsion at Hurstwood's ragged clothes. One of the key narrative moments in Hurstwood's decline occurs when the morally attuned narrator observes that "A man's fortune or material progress is very much the same as his bodily growth. Either he is growing stronger, healthier, wiser as the youth approaching manhood, or he is growing weaker, older, less incisive mentally as the man approaching old age" (230). Hurstwood, according to the narrator, is suspended at that midpoint, age forty-three, caught between his successful life in Chicago and his decline towards failure and death. Philip Fisher has observed that Dreiser's talk of the "body" is really much more deeply connected to material objects, including those that cover and adorn the body, than to organic physiology:

> This life history is that of products and objects which are best when new or fresh and then become worn out and discarded. The life history of a shirt is one continual decline. All goods are used up and replaced. Within *Sister Carrie* relationships, houses, cities, and especially living situations are discarded in the way clothing might be. Hurstwood himself is worn out rather than captured and submitted to moral or legal defeat. He is obsolete like a pair of shoes rather than aged like a man.... By the end of the novel he is not so much dead as extinct" [175].

For Fisher, the deterioration of clothing is not just one among a number of material forms of decline, but, rather, the material measure par excellence of all other forms of material and physical decline.[8] Hurstwood gains a sense of renewed youth and vitality because, as noted above, he sees himself through Carrie's eyes. Thus, the most significant moments at which the reader observes Hurstwood's fall are those moments when Carrie in particular becomes aware of how "worn out" Hurstwood's clothes and the man himself have become.

For example, after an evening out with the Vances and their cousin, Ames, Carrie comes home to find Hurstwood at home: "Hurstwood had returned, and was already in bed. His clothes were scattered loosely about" (229). This may be the first image in the novel in which Hurstwood is separated from his clothes. He is in bed, his clothes scattered, as if his body is itself fragmented, dismembered, robbed of its integrity. This image is at once intensely material and profoundly metaphorical. It foreshadows a pattern of references to Hurstwood's declining and deteriorating wardrobe, a decline viewed at least in part through Carrie's eyes. For example, when Hurstwood finally confesses that his business efforts in New York were falling well short of success, she responds by taking note of his sartorial state: "There came a night when he confessed to Carrie that the business was not doing as well this month as it had the month before. This was in lieu of certain suggestions she had made concerning little things she wanted to buy. She had not failed to notice that he did not seem to consult her about buying *clothes for himself*" (232, emphasis added). Viewing his decline through Carrie's eyes, the reader is alerted to the material and specifically sartorial consequences of financial decline. When he falls ill, Carrie notices how poorly dressed he is: "He was feverish until morning, and sat about the next day while Carrie waited on him. He was a helpless creature in sickness, not very handsome in a dull-coloured bath gown and his hair uncombed" (248). Again, according to Fisher's reading, the decline of the body is linked closely to the decline of clothing, and here Carrie witnesses Hurstwood's feverish body, his uncombed hair, and his drab bath robe. His clothes continue to show wear because he is reduced to fewer of them and his conspicuous consumption of them takes on a new meaning — they are conspicuously worn and worn out: "he decided to wear some old clothes he had." And, again, it is not just for himself that this matters, but for Carrie: "This came first with the bad days. Only once he apologized in the very beginning.... Eventually these became the permanent thing.... Of course, as his own self-respect vanished, it perished for him in Carrie" (250). She knows that "he was not bad looking when dressed up," but she notices that he is rarely if ever dressed up any more. His brief moments of adorning himself in fine feather have little purpose, and seem to be aimless: "he would occasionally dress up, go for a shave, and, putting on his gloves, sally forth quite actively. *Not with any definite aim*" (253, emphasis added). While in Chicago his clothes had a very specific social function, in New York that social function seems to have all but vanished.

However, Carrie is aware that Hurstwood's clothes reflect on her standing. In fact, what seems to have occurred is a reversal of the gendered relationship of Thorstein Veblen's notion of a woman's clothes as a sign of her husband's wealth and social standing. Carrie is increasingly fearful that *his* poor clothes will reflect poorly on *her*. Carrie's response to Hurstwood's declining wardrobe is framed through her association with the Vance household. Her anxiety about Hurstwood's clothing has more to do with her growing awareness of what Veblen called standards of pecuniary taste than with any concern for Hurstwood, himself:[9]

> Remembering Mrs. Vance's promise to call, Carrie made one other mild protest. It was concerning Hurstwood's appearance. This very day, coming home, he changed his clothes to the old togs he sat around in.
> "What makes you always put on those old clothes?" asked Carrie.
> "What's the use wearing my good ones around here?" he asked.
> "Well, I should think you'd feel better." Then she added: "Some one might call" [255].

And, indeed, someone does: Mrs. Vance. What is interesting here is that Hurstwood himself feels the shame after greeting Mrs. Vance at the door and telling her that Carrie is out: "He was so ashamed that he folded his hands weakly, as he sat in the chair afterwards, and thought" (255). This decline in his sartorial worth pushes him further into inaction, and closer to social annihilation or what Fisher calls extinction.[10] Added to his own shame is the scolding he receives from Carrie: "I've asked you a dozen times to wear your other clothes. Oh, I think this is just terrible" (256). Hurstwood himself becomes increasingly aware of the state of his wardrobe. "Now that his money was so low, he began to observe his clothes and feel that even his best ones were beginning to look commonplace. This was a bitter thought" (267). Most importantly, perhaps, the very sight of Hurstwood's rags drives Carrie away; she is literally repulsed by his attire: "The sight of him always around in his untidy clothes and gloomy appearance drove Carrie to seek relief in other places" (277).

If Carrie and Hurstwood's relationship is a reversal of Veblen's notion of conspicuous consumption—in which the woman's clothing advertises her own freedom from labor and her husband's ability to afford a fine livery for her—then it is one that Carrie realizes cannot be upheld, that *she* cannot be the one to spend money on *his* wardrobe, to keep him in finery while she works. Hurstwood's decline accelerates not only because of his own inaction, but also because both he and Carrie understand that she is in no position socially (even if she might be financial) to provide him with a wardrobe. She first recognizes this fact shortly after her repulsion from his ragged clothes. After finding out that she would be earning eighteen and not twelve dollars a week: "Her first move was to buy a shirt waist, and in studying these she found how little her money would buy—how much, if she could only use all. She forgot that if she were alone she would have to pay for a room and board, and imagined that every cent of her eighteen could be spent for clothes and things that she liked" (279).

This course in home economics also involves a lesson about the two forms of consumption that Dreiser so often juxtaposes: food and clothing. When Hurstwood reminds Carrie that they owe money to the grocer and the milkman, Carrie resists giving her money out for anything other than clothing: "That's always the way. It takes more than I can earn to pay for things. I don't see what I'm going to do" (279). She resolves to spend her money on clothing, though reluctantly pays for some of these bills. Later, when Carrie is making even more money, the crisis also becomes more severe, but Carrie becomes all the more resolved to spend on her wardrobe rather than to save a sinking household. And at this moment, she becomes aware of Hurstwood's clothes yet again, though this time with a tinge of sympathy and pity rather than revulsion. When Hurstwood suggests that they find a smaller apartment, she resists: "Who would furnish the money to move?" she asks herself. The narrator goes on to explain:

> To think of being in two rooms with him! She resolved *to spend her money for clothes quickly*, before something terrible happened. That very day she did it.... Hurstwood rose and took the money, slipping on his overcoat and getting his hat. Carrie noticed that both of these articles of apparel were old and poor looking in appearance. It was plain enough before, but now it came home with peculiar force. Perhaps he couldn't help it, after all. He had done well in Chicago. She remembered his fine appearance the days he had met her in the park. Then he was so sprightly, so clean [305, emphasis added].

In her farewell letter to Hurstwood, she explicitly explains that she needs her money for clothing, a duty that he has not met: "I wouldn't mind helping you, if I could, but I can't support us both, and pay the rent. *I need what little I make to pay for my clothes*" (307, emphasis added). Hurstwood's isolation is brought home for the reader, again, not in Carrie's physical absence but, rather, her "material" or sartorial absence. He notes her absence from dresser and wardrobe: "From the chiffonier had gone the knick-knacks of silver and plate. From the table-top, the lace coverings. He opened the wardrobe: none of her clothes. He opened the drawers: nothing of hers. Her trunk was gone from its accustomed place. Back in his own room hung his old clothes, just as he had left them. Nothing else was gone" (308). Her clothes are gone, his remain. More striking and forceful than Hurstwood's aloneness his the isolation of "his old clothes," the image of a shabby suit hanging alone in a closet.

In contrast to Hurstwood's empty suit hanging in his closet is the ideologically full uniform of a policeman sent to protect strikebreakers during the Brooklyn engine-driver strike in which Hurstwood participates toward the end of the novel. The entire episode is important in the ways it describes the annihilation of Hurstwood's identity. This annihilation of self becomes clear through the contrast between Hurstwood's attire and that of the policeman, in Hurstwood's night at the Brooklyn station where he sleeps under a dirty blanket and a pile of rags, and the increasing identification between Hurstwood's worn clothes and his worn body.

Part of Hurstwood's transformation involves a complete loss of socially sanctioned identity or authority, and this is nowhere more evident than in the contrast between Hurstwood and a uniformed policeman sent to defend the strike-breakers. The description of this uniformed functionary of state power draws attention to how he is, in fact, situated in his social position and authority by his clothes, his blue uniform, without which he ceases socially to exist. When Hurstwood arrives on the scene of the strike, he asks this policeman where he can go to find work.

> "The offices are up those steps," said the bluecoat. His face was a very natural thing to contemplate. In his heart of hearts, he sympathized with the strikers and hated this "scab." In his heart of hearts, also, he felt the dignity and use of the police force, which commanded order. Of its true social significance, he never dreamed. His was not the mind for that. The two feelings blended in him — neutralized one another and him. He would have fought for this man as determinedly as for himself, and yet only so far as commanded. Strip him of his uniform, and he would have soon picked his side [288].[11]

This passage speaks volumes about the importance of clothing in social and ideological formations, and in suturing individuals into ideological roles. More than the "dignity" of the police force, it is the uniform that embodies and reifies the policeman's social and political position. More importantly, the uniform further signals Hurstwood's symbolic and material annihilation, because Hurstwood has no such fabric holding him in place within the society. For one thing, when the policeman asks if Hurstwood is a motorman or what, Hurstwood replies, "No; I'm not anything," further emphasizing the various ways in which Hurstwood, along with Drouet and Carrie, too, is associated with the idea of being "nothing" (288). Furthermore, shortly after this passage, the narrator tells us that strikers and bystanders "gazed at the broken windows and at Hurstwood in his *plain clothes*" (297, emphasis added). In contrast to the policeman's uniform, Hurstwood's "clothing was not intended for this sort of work" (298). The Brooklyn motorman strike episode, then, emphasizes how Hurstwood's once significant clothing — his self-adornment in his role as a functionary of a leisure establishment — has now been stripped away, and in contrast to a man *identified*, in fact, by the very term *bluecoat*, Hurstwood has no sartorial social designation at all. He's "not anything."

Through the course of his career as a strike-breaker, Hurstwood is further reduced in his material existence: falling into a pile of rags under a dirty blanket. Lacking enough money for both food and for his car fair home, Hurstwood spends the night in the train yards, and is reduced to a stark image characterized by an amorphous bundle of cloth rather than a stylishly cut suit of clothes, as he is earlier in the novel: "Rising, he went to one of the cots and stretched himself, removing only his shoes, and pulling the one blanket and dirty old comforter over him in a sort of bundle. The sight disgusted Hurstwood, but he did not dwell on it..." (292). More compelling than the image of a dirty blanket and Hurstwood's own bundle-like shape is the fact that he is growing accustomed to these rags. "Hurstwood made the best of a bad lot by keeping on his clothes and pushing away the dirty covering from his head, but at last he dozed in sheer weariness. *The covering became more and more comfortable, its character was forgotten*, and he pulled it about his neck and slept (293, emphasis added). Here, Hurstwood seems to grow accustomed to rags and dirty clothes, despite his initial repulsion from them.

Hurstwood suffers social annihilation through a gradual assimilation of clothing to the body, as if the two are one and the same. This begins to happen in the strike-breaking scene when Hurstwood crumples into a bundle of rags, but also the next morning when he is attacked by the striking motormen. When the strikers attack Hurstwood's train, "A man grabbed him by the coat" (299). This phrase — using an article (the) rather than a pronoun (his) — equates the coat with a part of the body: not something he has (*his* coat) that is separate from him but part of what he *is* (*the* coat as in "grabbed him by the throat" or "the arm"). Later, the equivalence of clothing and body becomes even more pronounced when Hurstwood falls ill and recovers only after losing a great deal of weight. "His stoutness had gone. With it, even the semblance of a fit in his clothes" (324). That stoutness which he had before was not separate from his overall appearance and attire. If conspicuous consumption and conspicuous leisure imply an absence of physical activity and an abundance of food, then his current state means that Hurstwood has lost those signs of leisure that had identified him with a particular class. Furthermore, the "fit" of the clothes that is now gone suggests a kind of ghostly presence of Hurstwood's former self. After three weeks at Bellevue, where he is known by one of his pseudonyms (Wheeler) — further suggesting his social disappearance, at least in terms of his primary identity as "Hurstwood"— he emerges radically changed both physiologically and sartorially: "No more weakly looking object ever strolled out into the spring sunshine than the once hale, lusty manager. All his corpulency had fled. His face was thin and pale, his hands white, his body flabby. *Clothes and all,* he weighed but one hundred and thirty-five pounds. Some old garments had been given him — a cheap brown coat and misfit pair of trousers" (326, emphasis added). Again, as with the earlier reference to his stoutness, his "corpulency" is presented as a sign not only of his formerly "hale" and "lusty" physique, but also of his having been a "manager." Furthermore, his own clothes seem to have vanished along with his corpulence — his physiological surplus value. By the time Carrie sees him again, he is almost anonymous, a "shabby, baggy figure" (338); Hurstwood is characterized entirely by the unfitness of his clothes (baggy and shabby). He is reduced to seeking charity, and by this point he declines even further to mere clothes, and clothes that are characteristic of him not as an individual, but as part of a mass: "*several such as he* had shambled forward out of Sixth Avenue, their thin clothes flapping and fluttering in the wind" (344, emphasis added). The clothes flapping in the wind metonymically stand in not for Hurstwood alone but for a group of which he is an almost undifferentiated part. This link between body and clothing, and the body of a mass and their clothing, continues through Hurstwood's further decline at the end of the novel when he "was beginning to find, in his wretched clothing and meagre state of body, that people took him for a chronic type of bum and beggar.... He found it more and more difficult to get anything from anybody" (346). He is no longer recognized as an individual with a name, but as a "type."

We last see Hurstwood once again as part of an undifferentiated mass characterized by the rags they wear: "They had on faded derby hats with dents in them. Their misfit coats were heavy with melted snow and turned up at the collars. Their trousers were mere bags, frayed at the bottom and wobbling over big, soppy shoes, torn at the sides and worn almost to threads." Their emaciated bodies accentuate the shabbiness of the clothes and vice versa: their "frames so lean that clothes only flapped about them," and "There were wrists, unprotected by coat or pocket, which were red with cold. There were ears, half covered by every conceivable semblance of a hat, which still looked stiff and bitten" (351). Finally, Hurstwood's coat and vest play an important role in his suicide: "Now he began leisurely to take off his clothes, but stopped first with his coat, and tucked it along the crack under the door. His vest he arranged in the same place. His old wet, cracked hat he laid softly upon the table. Then he pulled of his shoes and lay down" (352). Note that Dreiser does not write "he lied down" but rather "lay down," as if Hurstwood's body is another item of clothing, receiving the action of what should be a transitive verb. As the gas fumes fill the room, it is Hurstwood's coat that traps those fumes. Hurstwood finally becomes literally nothing.

As Stallybrass suggests, the loss of one's material possessions can have a far greater meaning than their abstract financial value within a circuit of exchange. Rather, as a material fetishism of the *thing* rather than its immaterial monetary value, such loss can be a loss or annihilation of self. What we witness in Hurstwood's decline is both. His clothes had a kind of exchange value — they were part of his professional position and mobility. However, they also became valuable in another way in Carrie's eyes. When Carrie looked at Hurstwood's clothes, they embodied, at one and the same time, his desire for and his appeal to her. This was a self that Hurstwood had constructed outside the economic and moral orders of work and home. Thus, it rested on nothing else — only on the emotions invested into the clothes and materials themselves. However, even this emotional investment seems to follow the logic of other forms of investment (financial as well as social investment — Hurstwood's limited though undeniable power as a manager). Once the clothes begin to decline, the emotional investment in them vanishes as well. Ironically, in seeking an emotional investment that is free of economic or moral value (in the abstract notions of professional and domestic identity), Hurstwood finds an investment that is, in fact, governed by an even more relentless relationship between material reality and imagined identity. As Carrie's view of and her own emotional investment in Hurstwood's clothing declines, his sense of self declines, eventually vanishing into nothing.

Carrie's Clothes

In *The Gold Standard and the Logic of Naturalism,* Walter Benn Michaels argues that Hurstwood's decline results from his inability to desire intensely enough: "Wanting less, needing less, he finds himself not, like [Silas] Lapham, saved from the indignities of capitalist 'truckle' but condemned instead to the breadline and the flophouse. Old age is a failure not of ability but of desire" (44). By contrast, Carrie is able to succeed because, as Michaels argues, her desire is insatiable: "Carrie ... embodies insatiability. Carrie's body, infinitely incomplete, is — literary and economic, immaterial and material — the body of desire in capitalism" (56). This is a convincing and tidy contrast, and anticipates Michael Tratner's argument about the 1920s, when the nineteenth-century economic and sexual ideal of saving up energy gave way to the twentieth-century privileging of expenditure and debt: desire on credit.[12] However, to read Carrie as the embodiment of capitalist desire overlooks the ways in which her desire for materiality — for clothes in particular — is not always, or not only, contained within the abstract fetishism of capitalism but is, rather, often expressed in the material fetishism of the intimate thing: its ability to embody personal experience and local memory. Linking the *imma-*

terial to the literary and the *material* to the economic, as Michaels does, overlooks the ways in which the literary can be material, and the economic can be immaterial. To use Stallybrass's terms, her fetishizing of objects is abstracted into a fetishism of commodities; her relationship to things is turned into a relationship with values. However, at key moments, such as her recollection of her father's flour-dusted work clothes (which will be discussed later), Carrie resists capitalist desire.

Early in the novel, then, the physical objects (especially clothes) that surround Carrie, seem to have an animate life and even a pleading voice. For example, Drouet's ostentatious clothing and adornment appeal to Carrie as magical objects. As is often the case in this narrative, the conspicuous consumption of fine clothes is juxtaposed with the literal consumption of food. In one of these scenes, where Drouet buys a meal for Carrie, she observes his clothing: "As he cut the meat his rings almost spoke. His new suit creaked as he stretched to reach the plates, break the bread, and pour the coffee" (43). Dreiser integrates his description of the consumption of food with his description of clothes. Furthermore, the aesthetics of food (the touch and smell and taste) mingles with the sound of a new suit, its materiality made audible. Amidst all this sartorial and gastronomical sensuality, Dreiser explicitly points to the fetishistic magic of materiality, the rings seeming to have a voice of their own.

In addition to buying her a meal, of course, Drouet buys Carrie new clothes. While they're shopping at Partridge's on State Street in Chicago, Carrie again responds to the material appeal, rather than the value, of clothes: "Together they went. In the store they found that shine and rustle of new things which immediately laid hold of Carrie's heart" (51). Throughout this stage of the narrative, as Drouet introduces her to the material pleasures of the city, inanimate objects speak to her, and she responds in a physical and visceral way, with little or no thought to the value of the clothes either in terms of their cost in dollars or as signs of pecuniary taste. "Fine clothes to her were a vast persuasion; they spoke tenderly and Jesuitically *for themselves*. When she came within earshot of their pleading, desire in her bent a willing ear. The voice of the so-called inanimate! Who shall translate for us the language of the stones?" The clothes speak "for themselves," not for their abstract value. They speak Jesuitically to the soul of the observer, not Puritanically to the "values" or morality of the observer. They speak their own language, and require translation. Dreiser's narrator offers such translation, literally giving voice to these objects: "'My dear,' said the lace collar she secured from Partridge's, 'I fit you beautifully; don't give me up'" and "'Ah, such little feet,' said the leather of the soft new shoes; 'how effectively I cover them. What a pity they should ever want my aid'" (72). Here, the language of the clothes addresses the body. This is not the abstract language of exchange — clothing and other consumer objects as mere signs exchanged for other signs in the form of money. This is a bodily language, and the magical language of extra-capitalist fetishism, material fetishism (not commodity fetishism).

Increasingly, however, in Carrie's consciousness this visceral experience of personal fetishism concedes ground to the abstract value of clothes as part of an elaborate process of exchange. The urban space of the newly developing department stores of the United States is a particularly apt setting for Carrie's position between material value and abstract value, between clothing and nothingness, between self-construction through fashion and self-annihilation through consumer fetishism. On her first day searching for work in the city, Carrie makes her way to Chicago's burgeoning retail district where the Midwest's first department stores, such as Marshall Field's, were being established. Fashion historians suggest that the rise of the department store in England, France, and the United States marked an ambiguous shift in the place of women as consumers in the public sphere. According to Elaine Abelson, for example, "a good shop provided the context for diverse forms of public and even cultural life, yet it was sanctioned by the demands of the private sphere."[13] This paradox of public life and private roles of women was further complicated by the status of the consumer object in department stores where women "had to walk a tightrope between real needs, defined by practical use, and stimulated wants created by a suggestive ambience, lavish display, and often manipulated prices."[14] However, despite these pitfalls, "identity was to be found in the things one possessed. Consumption itself became a substitute for being bourgeois."[15] Recounting her own immigrant experience in Boston, Mary Antin, for example, writes in *The Promised Land*: "A fairy godmother to us children was she who led us to a wonderful country called 'uptown,' where, in a dazzlingly beautiful palace called a 'department store,' we exchanged our hateful homemade European costumes, which point us out as 'greenhorns' to the children on the street, for real American machine-made garments, and issued forth glorified in each other's eyes." In short, the department store presented an ambiguous space where a young woman like Carrie walked a fine line between claiming agency through or being annihilated by consumption.[16]

Here, Dreiser's narrator indulges in one of those editorial asides that make *Sister Carrie* both bulky and interesting. This aside provides a journalistic gloss (a first draft of history, even) regarding the development of department stores:

> The nature of these vast retail combinations, should they ever permanently disappear, will form an interesting chapter in the commercial history of our nation. Such a flowering out of a modest trade principle the world had never

witnessed up to that time. They were along the line of the most effective retail organization, with hundreds of stores coordinated into one and laid out upon the most imposing and economic basis. They were handsome, bustling, successful affairs, with a host of clerks and a swarm of patrons. Carrie passed along the busy aisles, much affected by the remarkable displays of trinkets, dress goods, stationery, and jewelry. Each separate counter was a show place of dazzling interest and attraction.

On the one hand, this commentary distances the narrator from Carrie's point of view. On the other, it situates her in a context that helps explain the forces that impinge upon her sense of identity and memory. In this setting, Carrie becomes aware of how clothes, seemingly simple objects of desire for her (the material fetishism of *things*), are subject to an abstract system of exchange value (the abstract fetishism of commodities). Secondly, the urban retail district setting also forces Carrie into a position she has already taken in her interaction with Drouet: the object of evaluation and judgment for well-dressed men:

> She could not help feeling the claim of each trinket and valuable upon her personally, and yet she did not stop. There was nothing there which she could not have used — nothing which she did not long to own. The dainty slippers and stockings, the delicately frilled skirts and petticoats, the laces, ribbons, hair-combs, purses, all touched her with individual desire, and she felt keenly the fact that not any of these things were in the range of her purchase. She was a work-seeker, an outcast without employment, one whom the average employee could tell at a glance was poor and in need of a situation [16].

Carrie's longing gaze upon these objects has no power over them, but the "glance" of the average worker reduces Carrie herself to an object of valuation. Her role as consumer places upon her the burden of self-making. She is caught between agency and abjection, subjectivity and objectification.

As Carrie becomes more aware of the value of objects, she becomes increasingly aware that she, herself, can be transformed into value. In this novel, characters take on the qualities and fulfill the value-carrying function of the objects around them. Carrie moves through other spaces of the city as the embodiment of capitalist desire, and as she does so her connection to objects begins to shift from the personal fetishism of things intimately linked to her past (or as objects of self-production) to the abstract fetishism of commodities or values. The personal fetishism of intimate objects is embodied most vividly in her father's flour-dusted coat which she recalls and uses as a talisman of identity and a mnemonic device recalling her past. This image, however, is increasingly displaced by Carrie's desire for department store clothes that embody both their financial exchange value as well as the value of social status — the value of invidious comparison.

One of the first times this shift begins to occur is when Carrie finds work in a shoe factory. Here, the magical power of clothing to speak and persuade is reduced to the industrial reality of producing it, of "punching eye-holes in one piece of the upper, by the aid of a machine," fastening a "piece of leather, which was eventually to form the right half of the upper of a man's shoe, by little adjustable clamps" (26). In contrast to the "fantastic and otherworldly" space of the department store, Carrie finds herself in the workaday world of the factory (Breward 167). Carrie takes her place in the machinery of clothing production: "The pieces of leather came from the girl at the machine to her right, and were passed on to the girl at her left. Carrie saw at once that an average speed was necessary or the work would pile up on her and all those below would be delayed" (26). In addition to taking her place in the factory, her sensory response to clothes shifts. No longer a sensual response to material rich with memory (as in her memory of her father's coat), but, rather, an awareness of how *dead* the material resources of production are: "the room was not very light. It had a thick odour of fresh leather...." (27), and "The place smelled of the oil of the machines and the new leather — a combination which, added to the stale odours of the building, was not pleasant even in cold weather" (28). Furthermore, Dreiser underscores the conditions of this sweatshop: "As the morning wore on the room became hotter. She felt the need of a breath of fresh air and a drink of water.... Her neck and shoulders ached in bending over" (27). She begins to feel and understand what it takes to produce clothing: "Her hands began to ache at the wrists and then in the fingers, and towards the last she seemed one mass of dull, complaining muscles, fixed in an eternal position and performing a single mechanical movement which became more and more distasteful, until at last it was absolutely nauseating" (28).

Also contrasted to the potentially liberating world of the department store is the domestic and patriarchal space of Carrie's sister's home. Just as Hurstwood had no claims on either his domestic economy or his place of employment, so Carrie is caught between the oppressiveness of industrial labor and the ugliness of her sister's domestic economy, embodied in her sister's sewing. When she wakes up after her first night with Minnie and Hanson, she sees her sister "busy in the dining-room, which was also the sitting room, sewing" (10), and later after working in the shoe factory, she comes home to see Minnie "sewing by a lamp at the table" (38). In this home, she is confronted with a number of images of sartorial ugliness, including her brother-in-law, embodied in Hanson's "pair of yellow carpet slippers which he enjoyed wearing" (21). And when Minnie offers Carrie her "worn and faded" umbrella on the first cold and rainy day of the season, Carrie rejects it for aesthetic reasons: "There was a kind of vanity in Carrie that troubled at this. She went to one of the great department stores and bought herself one, using a dollar and a quarter of her small store to pay for it" (39). Not even the umbrella's simple use value of keeping rain off her head is worth its ugliness and its worn-out aspect.

Thus, between the modern nausea of industrial labor and the aesthetic nausea of a domestic economy, Carrie recognizes a third option offered by Drouet who gives her money, clothing, and a furnished flat. Ironically, it is here, in the comfort and ease of conspicuous leisure, that Carrie is forcefully struck by the idea that people, as surely as the objects they produce and consume, can be reduced to value. Dreiser carefully describes Carrie's growing awareness of a set of social and economic relations in which people, along with their clothes, are measured in a system of values and comparisons. Dreiser further underscores Carrie's realization by contrasting Carrie's relative finery with the "poor" clothing of one of those same shoe-factory girls who trained Carrie to make men's leather shoes. Walking on Adams Street with Drouet, Carrie notices "a pair of eyes" that meet hers

> in recognition. They were looking out from a group of poorly dressed girls. Their clothes were faded and loose-hanging, their jackets old, their general make-up shabby. Carrie recognized the glance and the girl. She was one of those who worked at the machines in the shoe factory. The latter looked, not quite sure, and then turned her head and looked. Carrie felt as if some great tide had rolled between them. The old dress and the old machine came back. She actually started [56–7].

This shock of recognition suggests that Carrie is alert to the social value of clothes, not just her desire for them, and her longing for clothes gradually begins to take on a new dimension: her sense that clothes have a social value, and that this social value attaches itself to the wearer.

Thorstein Veblen provided what he called a "technical" definition of invidious comparison in 1899: "a comparison of persons with a view to rating and grading them in respect to relative worth or value" (34). Within what he called pecuniary standards of taste, invidious comparison reduced the person to nothing more than the *value* of the clothes he or she wore. Carrie's acquaintanceship with her neighbor Mrs. Vance, the contrast between Carrie's and Hurstwood's clothes and those of Mrs. Vance, and especially the walk the two women take down Broadway show Carrie's growing awareness of the social value of dress and the value it attaches to the wearer. Her desire for the clothes themselves begins to translate into a desire for the social capital they convey. Carrie and Mrs. Vance strike up a friendship that revolves around fashion and finery. They discuss hats, gloves, and shoes "with thick soles and patent-leather tips" which "are all the rage this fall;" Mrs. Vance encourages Carrie to buy the right kind of cloths, such as "new shirtwaists at Altman's" or "those nice serge skirts ... at Lord and Taylor's" (221–22). Mrs. Vance also instructs by example, wearing her "dark-blue walking dress, with a nobby hat to match" when the two women walk down Broadway between Fourteenth and Thirty-fourth streets (217). Carrie begins to use her keen sense of sartorial observation to compare her own attire to that of Mrs. Vance, and takes note especially of how some of Hurstwood's old charm is reignited by Mrs. Vance's glamour: "He now turned his attention to Mrs. Vance, and in a flash Carrie saw again what she for some time had sub-consciously missed in Hurstwood — the adroitness and flattery of which he was capable. She also saw that she was not well dressed — not nearly as well dressed — as Mrs. Vance" (216). Invidious comparison is clearly at work here, with Carrie not simply reflecting that her attire is less appealing than Mrs. Vance's but realizing that this difference in dress is apparent also to Hurstwood. This is an important point: Carrie's awareness both of the consumer objects with which her friend adorns herself and of Hurstwood's attraction to them. Ultimately, it becomes clear that those items are more important to Carrie than Hurstwood's desire for her. She takes note of every detail in Mrs. Vance's wardrobe: "She seemed to have so many dainty little things which Carrie had not. There were trinkets of gold, an elegant green leather purse set with her initials, a fancy handkerchief, exceedingly rich in design, and the like. Carrie felt that she needed more and better clothes to compare with this woman, and that any one looking at the two would pick Mrs. Vance for her raiment alone" (217). Here is a textbook illustration of Veblen's invidious comparison — Carrie notes the objects and the attention they attract. She "needed" these clothes, as if without them, she would be reduced to nothing.

This kind of invidious comparison continues and is reinforced with a display of conspicuous consumption as the two women walk down Broadway:

> The walk down Broadway then as now, was one of the remarkable features of the city. There gathered, before the matinee and afterwards, not only all the pretty women who love a showy parade, but the men who love to gaze upon and admire them. It was a very imposing procession of pretty faces and fine clothes. Women appeared in their very best hats, shoes, and gloves, and walked arm in arm on their way to the fine shops or theatres strung along from Fourteenth to Thirty-fourth streets. Equally the men paraded with the very latest they could afford. A tailor might have secured hints on suit measurements, a shoemaker on proper lasts and colours, a hatter on hats. It was literally true that if a lover of fine clothes secured a new suit, it was sure to have its first airing on Broadway [217].

In this display of dresses and draperies, "To stare seemed the proper and natural thing," and Carrie finds "herself stared at and ogled," and realizes that she "was in fashion's crowd, on parade in a show place." Noting the men's "flawless top-coats, high hats, and silver-headed walking sticks," as well as the ladies' "dresses of stiff cloth," Carrie begins to compare herself to Mrs. Vance: "She could only imagine that it must be evident to many that she was the less handsomely dressed of the two. It cut her to the quick, and she resolved that she would not come here again until she looked better. At the same time she longed to feel the delight of parading here as an equal. Ah, then she would be happy!" The allure of clothes, up to this point, had been seductive and magical. They have either been expressions of desire or markers of memory, not quite yet measures of money or of status. In this passage, allure turns into value. Carrie measures herself by the yardstick of invidious comparison.

Critics have discussed Ames in a number of ways, but generally focused on his worldview as the antithesis to the notion of conspicuous consumption.[17] He is a man of science and technology whose knowledge and education allow him to appreciate the more abstract forms of pleasure to be derived from capitalist society, such as literature, and "serious" drama in particular. First of all, he voices the novel's critique of conspicuous consumption, saying at one point to Carrie: "Look at that woman's dress over there.... Do you see that brooch?" He criticizes the wasteful ostentation, and Dreiser contrasts this wastefulness with Ames's own identity: a "strong young man ... [with] his clear, natural look" (227). But beyond this, he is also a "cultured" man who appreciates literary drama, as opposed to the popular comic musicals in which Carrie plays. Much later in the novel, leading up to its tragic end for Hurstwood, Ames expresses what Soper describes as that "richer" form of self-fashioning available within capitalist modes of production, despite their destruction of more material and objective forms of self-fashioning in non-capitalist social relations. He does so, in particular, by explaining to Carrie that she has a natural, an inborn, quality that cannot be bought or sold: her face. He tells her that she should act in more dramatic rather than comic roles because her face and her sensitive nature allow her to play roles that touch the audience deeply: "Most people are not capable of voicing their feelings. They depend on others. That is what genius is for. One man expresses their desires for them in music; another one in poetry; another one in a play. Sometimes nature does it in a face — it makes the face representative of all desire. That's what has happened in your case" (341–2).

Then, Ames puts an even finer point on this idea by telling Carrie, explicitly, that this artistic gift falls completely outside relations of economic exchange or pecuniary culture: "That puts a burden of duty on you. It so happens that you have this *thing*. It is no *credit* to you — that is, I mean, you might not have had it. *You paid nothing to get it*. But now that you have it, you must do something with it" (342, emphasis added). Even though he describes a "thing," literally part of Carrie's body, he describes it in the abstract, as helping to express the ineffable, to embody emotions. But the novel leaves Carrie at this particular threshold. She has been turned into an abstraction — an expression of entertainment value, of exchange value, and even of social value — but has her material identity vanished in the process? Has her materially constructed self been annihilated as surely as Hurstwood's was, even though she is physically alive and financially sound?

The answer to this question may be that she neither holds on to her earlier material construction of self which allowed her to recall her father's presence, nor does she achieve Ames's conception of art and its potential for self production. If, as Seguin and others have claimed, Carrie is often at a threshold, then this threshold reduces her to nothing, results in the annihilation of identity. In fact, Carrie's entry into the world of the theatre, and rise to its commercial heights involves a gradual transformation of her physical and material presence into an abstract value. Carrie is turned into currency. Carrie is caught in this bind at least partly because she mistakes the glamour of clothing for the appeal of art. Dreiser seems to place her between an inarticulate longing for the aesthetic, for artistic expression, and a passionate desire for material adornment. On the one hand, she observes "the airy grace of the *ingénue* in several well-constructed plays," and begins to imitate these actresses: "[M]any were the little movements and expressions of the body in which she indulged from time to time in the privacy of her chamber. On several occasions, when Drouet had caught her admiring herself, as he imagined, in the mirror, she was doing nothing more than recalling some little grace of the mouth or the eyes which she had witnessed in another." And Dreiser's narrator describes Carrie's play-acting as "nothing more than the first subtle outcropping of an artistic nature." According to Dreiser's narrator, this kind of imitation is the essence of art: "In such feeble tendencies, be it known, such outworking of desire to reproduce life, lies the basis of all dramatic art." However, Dreiser also describes this first attraction to the theatre as an attraction to the costumes of the actresses as much as, if not more than, to their dramatic artistic genius: "How often had she looked at the well-dressed actresses on the stage and wondered how she would look, how delightful she would feel if only she were in their place" (112). Carrie is drawn by "the nameless paraphernalia of disguise," the "beauty of the dresses upon the stage" (123). Again, she is at a threshold: "Here was an open door to see all of that. She had come upon it as one who stumbles upon a secret passage, and, behold, she was in the chamber of diamonds and delight!" (123), and "Frequently she had considered the stage as a door through which she might enter that gilded state which she had so much craved" (260).

Conclusion: Bread and Clothing, Flour and Fabric

An oft-quoted passage in *Sister Carrie* describes Carrie's observations of the working poor, a social category she has already begun to leave behind, and this passage is significant in how it represents clothing.[18] Clothing becomes memory and identity. The scene explains that her sympathies lie with "the under-world of toil," and touches on one of the novel's central themes: Carrie's emotional intelligence, to use more recent terminology. While the passage may show the fine line between sentimentalism and realism, its description of clothing offers a powerful critique of consumer fetishism.[19] Having just described Hurstwood's growing dissatisfaction with his middle-class domestic life—steeped in conspicuous consumption and feminized power (all of Hurstwood's property is in his wife's name)—the narrator turns to Carrie. The narrator emphasizes Carrie's "spiritual side," her richness of feeling, the "upwelling of grief" she experiences for the "weak and the helpless" (102). But Dreiser focuses Carrie's sentimental gaze on clothing in particular: "She was constantly pained by the sight of the white-faced, *ragged* men who *slopped* desperately by her in a sort of wretched stupor" (102–3 emphasis added). Here the terms "ragged" and "slop" suggest the men's clothes, as in rags bought from what was called a slop shop in the nineteenth century: a store selling remnants and second hand clothes. Then the passage focuses more directly on clothing: "The poorly clad girls who went blowing by her window evenings, hurrying home from some of the shops of the West Side, she pitied from the depths of her heart." And, most vividly: "It was so sad to be ragged and poor. The hang of faded clothes pained her eyes" (103). Here, the physical quality of the material—hanging loosely and faded in color or vibrancy—has a physiological, not a mental, effect: these images "pained her eyes," not her heart. What seems "sentimental" is steeped in a material reality, and the response is visceral not cerebral.

The passage continues, focusing (as Fisher, Kaplan, and Seguin have observed) Carrie's gaze through the architectural and formal literary threshold of windows, emphasizing her sentimental distance from the working class figures she describes. However, the passage also highlights the materiality of clothing, and, most importantly, the relationship between *memory* and *materiality*, a key relationship in what Stallybrass describes as the fetishism of things rather than the fetishism of consumer values, the fetishism that functions as an embodiment of the memory of work and of human connection beyond the abstract value of commodities:

> Toil, now that she was free of it, seemed even a more desolate thing than when she was part of it. She saw it through a mist of fancy—a pale, somber half-light, which was the essence of poetic feelings. *Her old father, in his flour-*

dusted miller's suit, sometimes returned to her memory, revived by a face in a window. A *shoemaker* pegging at his last, a blastman seen through a narrow window in some basement where iron was being melted, a benchworker seen high aloft in some window, *his coat off, his sleeves rolled up*; these *took her back in fancy* to the details of the mill. She felt, though she seldom expressed them, sad thoughts upon this score. Her sympathies were ever with that under-world of toil from which she had so recently sprung, and which she best understood [103, emphasis added].

The open windows at the end of the work day, as earlier readings of *Sister Carrie* have shown, emphasize Carrie's proximity to, but disconnection from toil.[20] Clearly, she is "free" from toil; she has recently sprung from it. Furthermore, she imagines work through "poetic feeling." However, these observations only present half the story. What complicates this reading of Carrie as being close to but free from labor is the combination of memory and cloth that weave her into the texture of the working-class culture she observes and, more importantly, that she remembers. There is, first, the work of the shoemaker. Carrie's own first job in Chicago is to work at a shoe manufacturer. But what she sees here is a shoemaker working at his craft, not in a production line. Like Jane Addams's Labor Museum at Chicago's Hull House, this passage reminds the reader that industrial production has a history, and an awareness of that history is necessary to resisting the alienation of industrial capitalism. Secondly, Carrie notices the details of dress when she looks at the bench-worker, and looking at the man's rolled up sleeves and observing that he has cast off his coat takes her back, causes her to remember her father's mill. Finally, it is in her memory of that family mill that Carrie recalls the most important sartorial image in this passage: her father's flour-dusted suit. As noted above, Dreiser often describes the consumption of food alongside the conspicuous consumption of clothing, but here we see clothing literally covered with the ingredients for bread, and those same clothes bearing the physical traces of work, both from the father's weary body and from the resources required for that labor.

Most importantly, Carrie's connection with the very material existence of her father's labor is a mnemonic not a fantastic connection: she does not imagine a fanciful and sentimental vision of work; she *remembers* the very real and material work of her father. Elsewhere, Dreiser depicts the consumption of food alongside the commodity fetishism of clothes. Here, through Carrie's consciousness, the narrator depicts the pastoral (rather than industrial) production of food. It is not Drouet's rings shining as he cuts the steak nor is it the spectacle of finery and food that Carrie gawks at in the restaurant with the Vance's, but, rather, her father's clothes infused with flour. Thus, any reading of this passage that focuses solely on the ways in which windows present a boundary or threshold between "toil" and Carrie's freedom from it misses the significance of memory triggered by materiality in Dreiser's depictions of dress.

However, once at this threshold, Carrie must also consider the price of entry, for like the theatre that she so desires to enter, her own sartorial satisfaction forces her to come to terms with various calculations — how much she can spend on clothes, how much she should give to Hurstwood. Here, again, Dreiser juxtaposes the consumption of food with the consumption of clothing, but with an increasing awareness on Carrie's part that social mobility through this or that door of opportunity requires abstract financial and social transactions. For example, Dreiser describes the final "parting of worlds" between Carrie and Hurstwood "the beginning of the new order" (273–4). Carrie "scarcely noticed" the changes in her household economy as part of this new order (274), but clearly she begins to make the kind of calculations that require her to walk through that door. In a key scene in which Hurstwood and Carrie discuss and negotiate a grocery list, they focus in on precisely the item that Carrie associated with her father: flour. Recall that one of the most important material mnemonic fetishes in Carrie's view of the world was her father's flour-dusted work clothes. In that image, work, personal identity, memory, and the materiality of the self predominated. That image of the flour-dusted work clothes fell outside the abstract fetishism of commodities and within the material fetishism of things. Here, however, flour appears as part of a series of abstract exchanges and calculations. Carrie, however, remains sensitive to the material importance of flour simply as food: "There was something sad in realizing that, after all, all that he wanted of her was something to eat" (274). But her sympathies for Hurstwood and his basic need for food are eclipsed by her own social need for clothes as a means of mobility: "That very evening, however, on going into the theatre, one of the chorus girls passed her all newly arrayed in a pretty mottled tweed, which took Carrie's eye. The young woman wore a fine bunch of violets and seemed in high spirits.... 'She can afford to dress well,' thought Carrie, 'and so could I, if I could only keep my money. I haven't a decent tie of any kind'" (274). After looking down at her shoes she reflects further "I'll get a pair of shoes Saturday, anyway; I don't care what happens" (274). So, here, Carrie chooses clothes over flour. The narrative here suggests that the image she had of her father in a flour-dusted coat has been displaced by the image of herself in fine dress. Furthermore, she no longer covets the material object itself, but becomes increasingly aware of the relations of that material object to a whole circuit of abstract values, whether in the form of financial or cultural capital.

While she does not decline financially, and lives on to continue desiring at the end of the novel, she is reduced to the immaterial, if not to nothing.

She is turned into an exchange value when she becomes a living advertisement for the Wellington Hotel whose agent tells her "your name is worth something to us" (316). However, *things* are not so simple in *Sister Carrie*. Here, the line between material and immaterial is thin. In the literal fabric of clothes this boundary between the physical thing and its value becomes even more flimsy. Her pursuit of career, clothing, and costume turns her into value. She becomes immaterial. The unresolved question at the end of the novel is whether Carrie's transformation into value gives her access to what Ames describes. Ames, whose intellectual comments on society echo Veblen's cultural critique and, perhaps, Dreiser's own aesthetics, endorses abstract aesthetic values of high culture in a capitalist society: what Kate Soper, in discussing fashion, calls that "much richer — all-around — development of the self" that capitalism *potentially* allows (Soper 29). In short, Carrie changes; her material self becomes an immaterial value. If Hurstwood is reduced to "nothing" both physically and metaphorically, then Carrie, too, is reduced to nothingness, at least in terms of her identity. She loses any sense of a self expressed in things, despite having invested much of her money and all of her professional identity in them. By the end of the novel, she has entered into an abstract system of exchange. Where once she saw a suit dusted with flour as a material expression of personal and familial history, she now sees a new dress or a serge skirt as a commodified expression of abstract value. She now sees a set of financial equations in which a finite amount of money must be used to pay *either* for flour or for clothes. Flour might be used to bake bread, but it is clothing that makes the self.

5. Dress and Mobility in *The Rise of David Levinsky*

HORATIO ALGER, JR. FABRICATED THE American myth of upward mobility. Both Henry James and Theodore Dreiser responded to this myth. James was anxious about how the upwardly mobile transformed property into commodity, proprietorship into acquisition, material aesthetic value into abstract exchange value. And, as we have seen, Theodore Dreiser charted the American reality of downward mobility. This chapter argues that Abraham Cahan examines mobility up, down, across, and through American society and culture. Rather than espousing Alger's romantic celebration of the upwardly mobile young man, or expressing a Jamesian social anxiety or a Dreiserian political critique, Cahan offered a re-valorization of mobility not understood as financial rise but as nomadic movement.

Cahan's *The Rise of David Levinsky* shows how a mobile subject — the individual disconnected from national, ethnic, and even familial home — has the potential to re-imagine and transform not only his or her own identity, but the identity of a nation, or at least to contribute to its transformation. In this case, as a mobile or homeless subject, David Levinsky is in a position — or moving across many positions — to redesign American fashion. In an age of assimilation, Cahan writes the story of how an immigrant was transformed by migration, but also of how that immigrant transformed America. While clothing is, of course, central to this novel's narrative trajectory, it is shelter — or the lack of it in expulsion from domestic space — that becomes another key trope for understanding how immigrants changed the United States.

If the higher spiritual need for clothing, according to Thorstein Veblen, was part of American culture generally, it was a special need for European immigrants whose mode of dress, along with their "physiognomy," was the first and most striking ethnic distinction they wore and bore upon their bodies. Veblen saw clothing as the most insistent social measure of personal worth or value. He writes, "expenditure on dress has this advantage over most other methods [of conspicuous consumption], that our apparel is always in evidence and affords an indication of our pecuniary standing to all observers at the first glance."[1] Thus, to speak of American fabric and clothing during the Gilded Age is to speak not only of material culture, but also of financial and personal value. When newly arrived immigrants bought clothes in America, they were making a cultural and ethnic investment. However, they were investing not in the abstract and relative values of the stock market, but, instead, in the cultural capital of sartorial identity. It can be argued, in fact, that they were investing in a new self. Many immigrants worked in the garment industry; many of them sold second-hand clothes on the streets of Boston, Chicago, and New York, and many realized that wearing a ready-made or even a modern tailored suit would always put "in evidence" and afford an indication both of pecuniary standing *and* ethnic (or de-ethnicized) identity. Often, immigrants (and the working class more generally) wore clothes that indicated the pecuniary standing and assimilated ethnic identity to which they aspired.

At the same time, Georg Simmel, whose sociological work on fashion remains a touchstone for contemporary fashion historians, argued that it "is peculiarly characteristic of fashion that it renders possible a social obedience, which at the same time is a form of individual differentiation."[2] Simmel argued that fashion allowed individual members of a society to balance their adherence to group demands with their desire for differentiation. However, given the differences in religious and ethnic practice that immigrants brought with them to the United States, something more than such a balance was required. As Andrew Heinze puts it: "For Jewish newcomers, American dress represented something more than a means of asserting social respectability. The new suit of clothes gave physical form to the essentially spiritual undertaking of aliens striving for membership in a new society." Thus, what Veblen described as a spiritual need and Simmel explained in terms of socio-psychological demands, Heinze explains in terms of what he calls "transformation": "It became a means of cultural transformation. Only the concept of *transformation* adequately conveys the impact of new material standards on these eastern Europeans." Furthermore, Heinze suggests that the "idea of transforming one's self-image" was a central theme in the Yiddish press, including the *Jewish Daily Forward* which Abraham Cahan edited, and Cahan's novels. However, while Heinze refers to Levinsky as a key example, he does not offer a detailed analysis of that novel in the context of these comments on sartorial self-transformation.[3] Heinze, applying the models of Veblen and Simmel to the situation of ethnic immigrants, argues that clothing "was the simplest and most obvious way for newcomers to announce that they were settling into American society and gaining an appreciation of the modern urban lifestyle" (98). Because they worked in the garment industry itself, because of an emphasis on individual attainment, because of a vibrant Yiddish press, and because of "a passionate commitment to American society," Jews viewed "clothing as an important symbol of cultural transformation" (90).

This chapter traces David Levinsky's narrative of cultural self-transformation on three levels. First, Levinsky's transformation can be traced through his frequent and pivotal changes in costume or clothing. These changes in clothing tend to replace the sacred vestments of the young Hebrew school boy with the modern attire of an American businessman. However, Cahan underscores a kind of existential sartorial dissonance in Levinsky's attempts to reconstruct his identity through dress. Levinsky's change of clothes echoes but also complicates Henry David Thoreau's notion that a change in clothes comes with a change, or even crisis, in life. Secondly, Levinsky's self-fashioning embraces homelessness and rootlessness. The more he changes his clothes, the more they become his only real home. Despite mastering the language and dress of a New World, Levinsky does not belong to that world; it is not his "home," yet neither is Antomir, where he was born. As a homeless subject, Levinsky represents the movement from modernity as a way of being to modernism as a style of life. Thirdly, we can read the story as a transformation of America. Despite being an outsider, Levinsky transforms the very world that excludes him. Levinsky becomes iconic, an emblem of how Jewish immigrants tailored a new American identity. The key trope for this transformation is the Jewish couturier's design of a woman's dress specifically for a white, and interestingly, Irish immigrant model. In the first and third of these trajectories clothing functions as the key metaphor for change and mobility. In the second, home is the important signifier. In terms of Levinsky's own transformation, David's clothing, of course, changes as he acquires a new language, a new faith, and a new identity. Levinsky, as the first-person narrator, is ever aware of these changes as he sees them through his own changing wardrobe. In the second narrative trajectory, shelter, or its lack, becomes as important as clothing. As other readers of Cahan have observed, Levinsky finds himself on the margin of a number of domestic scenes. However, while this homelessness, this exile, may be lamentable in some ways, it, nevertheless, offers the occasion for the final trajectory: it is *as* homeless subject that Levinsky can transform America.

Clothing as a Language of Cultural Identity

According to Heinze's analysis of the cultural transformation of Jewish immigrants in America, "Like language, appearance must be understood in order to be meaningful. When a person's dress registers in other people the same associations that are intended by the wearer, then it has functioned as a mode of communication" (90). The link between language and dress is complex, especially in its psychological implications. Like language, the psychosocial function of clothing can be divided into two realms: the imaginary and the symbolic. At the imaginary level, clothing can set up an ideal ego. We wear clothes and imagine ourselves in these clothes as a way of expressing who we want to be, not necessarily who we are. The imaginary function of clothing and fashion is, at bottom, fantasy. It is a pre-linguistic function in which clothing reflects identity rather than communicating identity in a highly socialized system of exchange. Clothing can help the subject to construct a kind of ideal self, as if the clothes help to hold together an otherwise fragmented image of the body. We might think of this as a pre-linguistic or pre-communicative function of dress. Fashion anthropologists Dani Cavallaro and Alexandra Warwick describe the difference between the imaginary and symbolic realms on which dress registers. In its imaginary function, "dress represents a projection of the ideal egos which we seek to embody and with which we wish to identify." On this imaginary register, clothing allows for "the subject's rejoicing in the phantasmatic plenitude of its own misrecognized mirror image."[4] On the symbolic level, clothes are part of a general system of signs: a language. As signs and symbols in the codes and conventions of normative society, garments fasten us into place in social discourse — into what Simmel calls social obedience. Clothing, in fact, is one of the first, most visible and, at the same time, most intimate ways in which we become socialized into culture. According to Cavallaro and Warwick, in its symbolic function, "dress is symptomatic of our introjection of sartorial and vestimentary codes and conventions, as instances of a broader network of intersubjective values designed to guarantee the socialization and institutionalization of personal identity and thus secure the cultural grooming of vision" (xvii). What does this mean in term of Heinze's discussion of Jewish immigrants' adoption of American urban fashion? One could argue that if our initial socialization into society involves the appropriate adoption of clothes as a form of communicating the self, immigrants, then, must learn a second sartorial language.

Immigrants can be thought of as deterritorialized.[5] If, as Eva Hoffman puts it, deterritorialization is "the detachment of knowledge, action, information, and identity from specific place or physical source," then it might be the case that exiles and immigrants are also desartorialized — detached from the epistemological and even practical grounding of dress in a national, religious, or ethnic system of meaning and action. While Hoffman emphasizes the loss and alienation of exile (both in her own autobiography, *Lost in Trans-*

lation, and in her essay "The New Nomads") she nevertheless suggests that by acquiring a new language, the exile or immigrant can turn adversity into advantage. By living in two or more languages simultaneously, the "nomad" exploits the "advantages of defamiliarization" ("New Nomads," 52). Centering her discussion of exile on the question of language, Hoffman advocates a model of exile and migration "in which the force of our first legacy can be transposed or brought into dialogue with our later experiences, in which we can build new meanings as valid as the first" (62).[6] If these contrapuntal, dialectic, and defamiliarizing qualities of *language* become available to the deterritorialized subject through the experience of exile, and if dress and fashion comprise a language, then the desartorialized subject, to coin a term, can refashion existing communicative functions of clothing and fashion. Desartorialization can produce new material meanings.

Heinze argues that dress is a "flexible form of silent communication" that conveys a host of psychological and social, individual and collective attitudes, moods, and even identities. Moving from the sacred vestments of the past into fashion's urban and secular system of signs, Jewish immigrants saw "American dress" as "something more than a means of asserting social respectability." Heinze singles out "stylish dress" as "the foremost symbol of Jewish transformation in the American city" (104). Heinze's point can be taken further to suggest that Jewish newcomers not only transformed themselves but also the very codes of dress they adopted. Caught between the codes and conventions of two different cultures, immigrants can operate in different symbolic realms, and deploy conflicting sumptuary codes, even if unintentionally; they can, potentially, develop a meta-sartorial perspective on clothing as one deeply experienced dress code clashes with another. The transnational subject—in this case the *shtetl* Jew in an American city—can turn to the vestments of the old country and the fashions of the New World, and thereby draw on more than one "flexible form of silent communication."

David Levinsky's New Clothes

Cahan's *The Rise of David Levinsky* pays close attention to clothes both as vestments of the *shtetl* and fashions of the American city. The images Cahan provides of clothes within Eastern Europe seem ghostly and spectral, almost immaterial rather than material manifestations of identity. Two of David's memories, in particular, suggest a kind of sartorial imaginary of the old country. In one, David recalls a pre-linguistic connection with his father in which his father's coat becomes a talisman, a fetish object that recalls a distant past and a deeply felt connection to the material culture of that past. In another

5. Dress and Mobility in The Rise of David Levinsky   113

image, this time a highly sexualized one, an airy and diaphanous kimono represents David's entry into sexual consciousness.

David's recollections of his childhood in Antomir focus his connection with sacred rituals and religious knowledge. However, these recollections also connect David with both his mother and the material trace of his dead father. David recalls his father through the mnemonic device of a coat:

> When I ... would no longer sleep with my mother, *a rusty old coat of my deceased father's* served me as a quilt. At night, before falling asleep, I would pull it over my head, shut my eyes tight, and evoke a flow of fantastic shapes, bright, beautifully tinted and incessantly changing form and color. While the play of these figures was going on before me, I would see all sorts of bizarre visions, which at times seemed to have something to do with my father's spirit.[7]

This "flow of fantastic shapes" and "bizarre visions" that Levinsky conjures up through the use of his father's coat-as-quilt work clearly at the level of the imaginary, of an irretrievable past, a childhood from which the protagonist is completely cut off, but which he can recall through the memory of a coat. The coat contains David the child and brings him into pre-linguistic relation with his "father's spirit." A childhood in another country makes the mnemonic function of clothing all the more complex, and that much more tenuous than a childhood in one's native land. If the past is another country, then David is reaching back into a doubly displaced region of his consciousness. The father's coat becomes a fetish object, a talisman with which David conjures up the plenitude of his childhood connection with both mother and father. This constitutes the imaginary psychological function of dress. It is not so much David's communication of identity to others, but, rather, his own idealized identification with his father, an ideal ego. Like everyone else, David must separate from this ideal and construct a self.

Thus, even before the displacement of migration and exile, David goes through the universal experience of deracination from familial connection, and this displacement is presented as a distinctly psycho-sexual experience, and, moreover, one experienced, again, through cloth. Cahan centers his description of David's first real sexual experience on another material object: Matilda Minsker's kimono. After his mother is murdered by an anti–Semitic mob, David becomes a Talmud student in order to replace what his mother would have provided. Thus, despite his physical disconnection from both parents, this orphan is connected to the world of his progenitors through the practices and structures of the sacred. However, a secular and sexualized world uproots him from this safe and sacred space. A charitable and "modern" Jewish woman, Shiphra Minsker, learns of his plight, and takes him in as one of her adopted young scholarly Talmudists who "eat days" with her. Matilda, the woman's equally modern daughter, teases David about his Orthodox ways, calls him a hypocrite because he harbors secret desires for her. As teasing turns into flirtation, a flimsy kimono becomes a central image in this remembered liaison. Indeed, like a fetish object the kimono stands in for the person desired: "her white kimono was all I could see of her." The kimono becomes an almost immaterial material, a vanishing screen that links rather than separates: "her indistinct kimono vanished in the darkness" (78). However, this disappearing kimono does not suggest Matilda's nakedness so much as it suggests the absence of any mediating social codes between self and other, an imagined plenitude of sexual union. "[O]ne did not have to stand on ceremony with a fellow [David himself] who did not even wear a stiff collar and a necktie. Nor did I know enough to resent her costume," i.e., the flimsy kimono (69). Like all clothing this kimono is an ambiguous boundary. More importantly, however, the kimono functions as a historical and cultural signifier of modernity and its reliance on Orientalism to construct itself as modern. Only modernized Russian Jews would own kimonos, not only because of their wealth, but also because of their adoption of Western European discourses about the East and its exotic appeal. Thus, the kimono links Matilda to the modern by giving her access to the discourse of Orientalism, but it also makes her primitive because of its draped rather than fitted design. The item of clothing is an ambiguous signifier of modern and primitive identities. However, *both* the modern and the primitive challenge the abstract notions of the sacred, or the strict formal requirements of "the stiff collar and necktie." These symbols of his religious orthodoxy become meaningless in contrast to the vanishing kimono. David's secularization (his sartorial transformation) begins in Russia, and is completed in America. This brush with the secular/modern Jews of Russia begins to tear David away from his fantastic memories of his father and from his Talmudic vestments. The flimsy white kimono becomes the fetish object of this transformation, a veil between the past and the future.

Upon arriving in America, one of David's first realizations is that he can lose his "greenhorn" status by learning English and by wearing the right clothes. According to Andrew Heinze, "Jews spoke of the initial period of learning American ways as a time of 'purificaiton' and they looked approvingly on a person who had turned from 'green' to 'yellow,' a vital transition in the making of an American" (Heinze 98). Part of this transition involved gaining an understanding of new forms of authority and their social and sartorial signs. As signs of authority (or social hierarchy) and authenticity (or cultural identity) translate across the Atlantic, David must redefine his notions of society and self. Language and clothing, the language of clothing, *and* the adornment and cover provided by language, offer a complex matrix of self-transformation. For example, after meeting a young tailor named Gitelson,

5. Dress and Mobility in The Rise of David Levinsky 115

who is dressed in "tatters," and upon entering New York through Castle Garden, David describes the New York police as "uniformed noblemen," and he notices the "well-dressed trim-looking crowds" (90, 91). Immediately, then, David has noticed the contrast between a Jewish tailor in tatters, and the uniformed noblemen who represent authority in this New World. This contrast between the week and the powerful is developed further as a contrast between modern and traditional, the term "trim-looking" suggesting the all-important development of form-fitting clothing in the evolution of modern dress. The "cut" of a suit was one of the clearest markers of modernity. Already, then, it is clear that authority has shifted from a sacred and familial social order to a secular, modern, industrialized, and bureaucratic one. While there was, of course, the modern and bureaucratic world order of gentile Russia in Antomir, David's world was insulated to a degree by the inner circle of *shtetl* life, at least culturally speaking. In urban America, the mediating function of the sacred is lost, or at least shifted.

Instead of insulating David from the goy world, the transplanted sacred structures of Jewish culture function in this case to facilitate David's transition, at least insofar as he is male, and thereby privileged as a member of official sacred agencies such as the synagogue. As Heinze argues, "Jewish individualism contrasted with the comparative collectivism of other immigrants" (96). This emphasis on individualism arose, at least in part, from what was seemingly the center of collective cohesion: religion. "As authority within the community sprang from knowledge of the Torah and the Talmud, anyone who was versed in these sources could challenge the opinions of rabbis and officials" (Heinze 95–6). In a Lower East Side temple, David meets a rich and pious man — Mr. Even — who takes an interest in him, as if David is a Ragged Dick and Even is his rich Algeresque benefactor, Mr. Whitney, who gives Dick his son Frank's suit.[8] David recalls that Even "took me to store after store, buying me a suit of clothes, a hat, some underclothes, handkerchiefs (the first white handkerchiefs I ever possessed), collars, shoes, and a necktie." Mr. Even tells him, "Now you won't look green," or "That will make you look American." This kind and pious benefactor also tells his barber to "Give [David] a hair-cut and a bath.... Cut off his side-locks while you are at it. One may go without them and yet be a good Jew" (101). David's reaction to all this is divided. On the one hand he feels that the new clothes, the hair-cut and the shave in particular rob him of his faith:

> If you are a Jew of the type to which I belonged when I came to New York and you attempt to bend your religion to the spirit of your surroundings, it breaks. It falls to pieces. The very clothes I wore and the very food I ate had a fatal effect on my religious habits. *A whole book could be written on the influence of a starched collar and a necktie on a man who was brought up as I*

was. It was inevitable that, sooner or later, I should let a barber shave my sprouting beard [110, emphasis added].

After his hair cut and in his new wardrobe, David feels he is now cut from a different cloth, cut off from his religious past. And yet he realizes that wearing American clothes is an investment in his future: "I was quick to realize that to be 'stylishly' dressed was a good investment, but," and what follows is consistent with the idea that clothing and language are parallel if not linked elements of identity, "I realized, too, that to use the Yiddish word for 'collar' or 'clean' instead of their English correlatives was worse than to wear a dirty collar" (105). Levinsky is caught between loss and gain, between lamenting the vanishing past and celebrating economic futures, between the clearly sacred function of the synagogue in Antomir and its apparent openness to the secular in the Lower East Side. It is not so much that the synagogue itself endorses the assimilation that Mr. Even encourages, but rather that it can function as a homo-social space, a space of male bonding and camaraderie, and this masculine social milieu can facilitate self-transformation. David gives up religious vestments for cultural investments.

Linguistic and sartorial transformations went hand in hand at the turn of the century. According to Heinze, "Along with American speech, American ways of consumption constituted a powerful symbol of social status for most Jewish newcomers" (98). The cultural investment is especially interesting as a combination of language and clothing: the language of clothing speaks to Levinsky's class and ethnicity; the clothing of language covers up his racialized and religious past. Levinsky uses language as clothing to fashion his new self. "One of the first things I did was to make up a list of the English words and phrases which our people in this country had adopted as part and parcel of their native tongue. This, I felt, was an essential step toward *shedding one's 'greenhornhood,'* an *operation* every immigrant is anxious to dispose of without delay" (104, emphasis added). The terms *shedding* and *operation* suggest a bodily change, and *shedding* has the secondary connotation of disrobing. Both terms use a bodily metaphor to describe a change in language. In short, Cahan uses clothing as a kind of language of self, and he uses language as a kind of clothing of self. In observing the personal style of other characters, Levinsky notes their attire through metaphors of language, but also notes their discourse through metaphors of dress. Observing his former night-school teacher, Levinsky notes Bender's use of President Grover Cleveland's phrase "offensive partisanship," and relates this affectation in speech to the fashion in clothing of the times: "He dwelt on the civil-service reform of President Cleveland, charging the Republicans with 'offensive partisanship,' a Cleveland phrase then as new as four-in-hand neckties" (313). Language can be as fashionable as the latest style in men's "furnishings." His rhetoric becomes raiment. Bender's idiomatic phrase covers, perhaps, a lack of real knowledge, while Levinsky's adoption of English disguises and eventually transforms identity.

However, any transformation involves moments of instability, moments when the self is neither the old identity nor yet the new, or is both at the same time. While earlier in the novel we witness vanishing clothes (the kimono), as Levinsky begins to change we see vanishing individuals, characters seen *only* through their clothes, or depicted as ghostly reflections of themselves. What vanishes now is the subject that the attire cloaks. One figure in particular, occurring later in the novel, can be used to contrast vanishing clothes with vanishing subjects. On their walk along the docks, David and Gussie — a woman employed in the same cloak shop as David — see lovers embracing. This assignation is really a business meeting; David is trying to talk Gussie into marrying him so that he can use her dowry for his business scheme: to start a cloak manufacturing business with Chaikin, a fellow worker and the best designer at the German firm where all three of them work. However, unlike his earlier experience with Matilda, in which the kimono vanishes, and all that is left is the object of desire, in this scene, the only thing that is visible is the clothing, not the body: "A little further off and nearer to the water I could discern *a white shirt-waist in the embrace of a dark coat*" (198, emphasis added). In this metonymic use of clothing to stand in for lovers, we can find a telling commentary on how David's identity is becoming alienated. In light of his conversation with Gussie — a homely looking woman whom he views merely as a source of income — the embrace of clothes rather than people suggests the classic Marxist account of commodity fetishism, that relations between people is expressed as relations between commodities.[9]

There are, however, pitfalls in becoming a modern. In relation to Levinsky, modernity can be defined as a desire to dismantle an earlier framework for experience and to establish a new point of departure.[10] To a certain extent, as in his memory of his father's coat, Levinsky wants to recall the past. But this desire to restore the past conflicts with another motivation for him: the desire to break with the past entirely, even if this desire is mere disguise at first. Levinsky destroys his past and fails in his present identity. What is modern about the novel is that Levinsky's ambiguous relation to the past results in a kind of "self-estrangement." Taking up this notion of modern self-estrangement in relation to clothing, we can see that what happens to Levinsky is similar to what happens to an object when it becomes a commodity.[11] One scene clearly shows how David's modernization is a kind of alienation that he shares with the objects and labor he exploits. Cahan presents this idea of identity-as-commodity when he shows David admiring his new outfit reflected in a store window. "I was ever conscious of my modern garb, and as I walked through the streets I would repeatedly throw glances at store windows, trying to catch my reflection in them" (106). In this amazingly vivid and concise image, we see David transformed from a Jewish Talmud student into an American commodity as opposed to an American citizen, as he appears, so to speak, in a shop window. The reflection in the window is like David's emerging identity, his materializing self, his investment in the future. It also suggests the gradual disappearance of his old self. Like the vanishing kimono, David himself becomes a kind of apparition, a reflection. This ghostly reflection suggests the indeterminacy of the narrating subject. David is indeterminate because it is not clear if he is selling himself or his product. His spectral image is reflected, after all, in the shop window, and thus sums up his indeterminacy: is he the salesman or the item for sale?

Later, in another reflected image of himself, David sees the discrepancy between the unassimilated greenhorn and the assimilated dandy. In his passage across the Atlantic, David has met a young tailor named Gitelson. On board ship, Gitelson is the epitome of the naïve greenhorn. Not only is his cap blown off his head, but the one that he obtains to replace it is too small (88). But once on shore, Gitelson, because of his talent as a tailor, is picked up by a garment manufacturer and put to work. Months later, David runs into him again, and is amazed by the transformation. He wears a "jaunty straw hat" without a forelock to distract the eye. His hair, on the contrary, is "freshly trimmed and dudishly dressed." Even Gitelson himself "could not get over the magic transformation that had come over him. [...] He felt like a peasant suddenly turned to a prince" (148). After they enter a "candy-store" and sit down at "marble-topped tables," David not only observes the difference between the old Gitelson and the new, but also, alas, between Gitelson and himself: "The contrast between his flashy clothes and my frowsy, wretched looking appearance, as I saw ourselves *in the mirrors* on either side of me, made me sorely ill at ease" (149, emphasis added). Like the store window that offered David his own reflection, so do the candy-store mirrors offer him another angle of vision. Like Peter in Marx's footnote on commodities as men, David "sees and recognizes himself in another man," Gitelson. As if the genus homo in the Gitelson-ness before him isn't enough, David is offered a double reflection — the mirrors as well as the human mirror.

Rather than simply and unselfconsciously wearing clothes, David is always aware of his own difference from what he once was, but also from what he now wears. He tells his reader, "I was mentally parading my 'modern' make-up before Matilda" (101). On one level, Matilda represents David's past. She is, he believes, his first "real" love, her kimono-clad body his first object of desire. On another level, she represents modernity itself—the fact that her family lived like Gentiles and were reformed Jews, spoke Russian and traveled all over Europe. The kimono, for instance—in its cosmopolitan European context—is no longer traditional, but modern, a sign of European wealth and imperialistic reach. After all, it was she who said to David, "Look at *the way you are dressed*, the way you live generally.... Why don't you try to study Russian, geography, history? Why don't you try to become an educated man?" (71). This trio—Russian, geography, and history—can be read as the requisites for modernity: a modern language, a non-sacred sense of space, and a chronological rather than mythic sense of the past. What Matilda really means, then, is "Why don't you become a modern man?" And it is Matilda who tells David, "Good clothes would make another man of you," and playfully dresses him up in her brother's *gymnasium* uniform (75).[12] Thus, mentally parading himself in front of Matilda is a way of showing off his modernity to someone who can appreciate it.

Now, David *does* ultimately master the dress codes of American business, just as he masters its jargon. But he remains so self-conscious of them that they feel alien to him. At a certain point in his economic rise, he seems to have perfected the look. "I sought to dress like a genteel [or Gentile] American, my favorite color for clothes and hats being (and still is) dark brown." The subdued tones of the dark brown or gray suit have been, since the time of Carlyle at least, the preferred color for clothing that communicates self-restraint and the pursuit of success. David uses his acquired style as a badge of his Americanization: "Now, Dora seemed to notice these things in me, and to like them. So I would parade my newly acquired manners before her as I did my neckties or my English vocabulary" (260). This self-consciousness is matched by a need to erase identity.

It is also in this exchange that Cahan refers again to a thematically intricate relationship between clothing and language. While Gitelson is the better dressed of the two, it is David who has a better command of the English language. When David writes down his address for Gitelson, the latter remarks: "Writing English already! There is a mind for you. If I could write like that I could be a designer" (150). Not only is language acquisition as important a marker of assimilation as clothing—more important in fact—it also points to the ability to control one's future: to "be a designer," both literally a designer of clothes and figuratively a designer of one's own destiny. Gitelson also inspires David to pursue his dream of becoming a modern educated man: "The image of that cloak-operator reading books and laying by money for a college education haunted me. Why could I not do the same? I pictured myself working and studying and saving money for the kind of education which Matilda had dinned into my ears" (150). However, this dream is soon displaced. Soon he realizes that "American education [is] a cheap machine-made product," like the ready-to-wear clothes he is producing (167), and a new image takes the place of the studious machine-operator: "I visioned myself a rich man" (189). When Gitelson and Levinsky meet again, one last time, David can hardly recognize either his old friend, or even himself. Gitelson, who had struck him on their second encounter as an "American dandy," now seemed broken: "He was quite neatly dressed, as trained tailors will be, even when they are poor, and at some distance I might have failed to perceive any change in him. At close range, however, his appearance broke my heart" (514). Their old connection is completely severed, and in trying to be friendly and revive their old friendship, David is struck by the in-authenticity of his own voice. "There was something forced, studied, in the way I uttered these words. I was disgusted with my own voice" (515). Again, David is so self-conscious that he seems divided. His listening to his own alien sounding voice echoes the fragmentation of self that occurs in the reflections David sees in the shop window and at the candy store. The reflected image divides David into seer and seen; the sound of his own voice divides him into speaker and listener.

By the time he meets Gitelson for the last time, David has adopted not the studious style of Gitelson, but the flashy dandyism of another young man, Jake Mindels. Jake is an effeminate, intellectual dandy that David attempts to emulate in his aesthetic tastes, his fluent English, and, above all, his personal style and clothing. While David sees Jake as a sham-intellectual — all looks, no rigor — he cannot help admiring him, and even having a slight crush on this young man, a crush expressed indirectly through their mutual admiration, what David calls "loving jointly," for a Yiddish theatre diva. David and Jake share a love for the Yiddish theatre and for one of its divas — Madame Klesmer. Truly a love between men, their adoration of Madame Klesmer points to a homosocial if not homoerotic intimacy: "And so we went on loving jointly, Jake and I, the companionship of our passion apparently stimulating our romance as companionship at a meal stimulates the appetite of the diners" (160).[13]

"Loving jointly" comes to mean loving each other. Jake's "soft-blue eyes" are "too soft and too blue" and his "masculine exterior contained an effeminate psychology" (158). And the "chastity" of this effeminate young companion "bothered" Levinsky so much that the "idea of breaking it down became an interesting temptation" (162). Even after he becomes a successful business man, David admires the young dapper medical student that Jake has become: "His studiously dignified carriage, his Prince Albert coat, the way he wore his soft hat, the way he held his open umbrella, and above all, the beard he was growing, betrayed a desire to look his new part. ... He was handsomer than ever, and there was a new air of quiet, though conscious, intellectual importance about him" (348). In part, this is simply Cahan's fictionalized commentary on a phenomenon that was well known in the Yiddish American press: the figure of the Jewish dandy — characterized as a coquette or "dude," whose conspicuous consumption of fine fashion was matched by his womanizing.[14]

However, beyond the sexual ambiguity and the caricature of the dandy, Jake further develops the idea that Levinsky knows himself and constructs himself only as he is reflected in others, and that this reflected identity focuses especially on consumption and clothing. Levinsky's desire *for* Jake Mindels is part of his desire *to be* Jake Mindels. David sees himself in the other, specifically in the costume of the other. The Prince Albert coat, soft hat, the umbrella, and the beard — all of these give us the desired identity in iconic form, like a caricature that sketches the most distinctive features of a figure. In this case, those features are clothes. In Russia, David had striven to be the smartest student in his Yeshiva; in America, he strives to be the smartest looking man about town. This "queer moment" in the novel, as Magdalena Zaborowska has called it, allows Cahan to both narrate as well as "debunk" the rags-to-riches formula of economic success. As simultaneously a "failed ethnic and an unfulfilled American," Levinsky is a narrative subject "devoid of significance."[15]

On the last page of the novel, David Levinsky again refers to his clothing as an ambiguous sign of his identity — or a sign of his enigmatic self, of subjective instability. He reflects that despite material success, he is unhappy. He recounts — in the pages leading up to this finale — his failed familial and matrimonial relationships. He recalls his childhood, and that other David, the one that he has not ceased to be, but who seems so far away. He points to the new David Levinsky — the one he pretends to be — as a representative of the success of Jews in general: the builders of sky scrapers and the composers of popular songs. It is in this measuring up of his past and present that he again, one last time, refers to his clothes: "I am always more or less conscious of my good clothes, of the high quality of my office furniture, of the power I wield over the men in my pay" (531). This self-consciousness is an indication of the degree to which Levinsky remains an outsider. Despite David's control over commerce, culture stands aloof from him, does not let him in. One vivid sign of this outsider status is Levinsky's reaction to waiters in restaurants. The uniforms of these men make them seem like the cultural police guarding the places of Gentile patronage from the Jewish outsider. "Charles Eaton, a full-blooded Anglo-Saxon of New England origin," gives Levinsky his "first baptism of dismay as a patron of a high-class restaurant." As he enters the restaurant with Charles, David is struck forcefully by the imposing figures of uniformed waiters: "the imposing black-and-white figures of the waiters struck terror into my Antomir heart" (259). And later, again in the last pages, David continues to feel intimidated by waiters, a further sign of his exclusion from America: "Their white *shirt-fronts*, reticence, and pompous bows make me feel as if they saw through me and ridiculed my ways. They make me feel as if my expensive *clothes* and ways ill become me" (515, emphasis added). As experts in the language of clothing and manners, waiters make David feel like an imposter, as if he is performing a masquerade and will soon be found out. And this feeling of being an imposter in expensive clothes follows David to the very last page of the novel where he says: "As I have said in another connection, I still have a lurking fear of restaurant waiters" (530). While he has mastered American customs and the English language, he still fears that he wears these accoutrements of assimilation like ill-fitting garments. The seams show. However, the instability of his sartorial self—the ambiguity of his cultural transformation—can be read as a way of claiming agency rather than as a way of closing it off.[16] Indeed, as will be clear, David's instability can be read as mobility, and this mobility challenges the existing dichotomy of upward or downward mobility allowing not only for a transformation of self, but for agency in the transformation of American culture itself.[17]

From Clothing to Shelter: David's Modern and Modernist Homelessness

In *Kafka's Clothes,* Mark Anderson examines the importance of sartorial signification and substance in European modernism through a reading of Franz Kafka's writings, and through an analysis of Austro-Hungarian material culture at the turn of the twentieth century. The lessons of this study are useful in looking at similar circumstances in the United States, especially where Anderson examines Kafka's conception of the homeless subject in the American metropolis in Kafka's *Amerika*. The instability of his subjective position can become an advantage, but only through the pain of loss. Like Kafka's Karl in *Amerika*, Cahan's David is a mobile subject in America, his mobility expressed most explicitly when he becomes a drummer (like Drouet in *Sister Carrie*) for his own garment-manufacturing firm, and goes "On the Road," the title of Book Ten. Because of his refashioning of his own identity to fit into industrial America David, like Karl, "remains *underwergs*, always on the outside."[18] Like Karl, David is allowed to enter into familial relations only to be expelled "into another set of foreign circumstances." Kafka imagines America (a place he never saw firsthand)—and New York City in particular—as a space of mobility and instability. In Anderson's reading, *Amerika* is a traveling text. "A travelling text works to destabilize the identity of the protagonist as well as the genealogical structures through which this identity is normally presented. The protagonist has no property, is always on the road, never knows what is about to happen, and never asks why he is there at all" (114). Clearly, given Levinsky's trafficking in clothes and sexuality, given his instability, and given his homelessness and mobility, as will be clear, *The Rise of David Levinsky* can also be read as a traveling text or traveling narrative.

Clothing becomes a central metaphor in Kafka's creation of a fictional world, and the relation of that fictional world to Kafka's own realities. As a contemporary of Kafka, Cahan uses clothing in similar ways, not because of any direct or traceable influence between the two writers but because both wrote in a historical moment when clothing was a vehicle of and an emblem for movement, for the traveling and mobile subject. In their mobility and the importance of clothing in that mobility, Cahan's David Levinsky, Kafka's Karl Rossman, along with Dreiser's Charles Drouet, are characteristic of their time. These characters' detailed wardrobes exist alongside and, in some ways signal their homelessness.

Homelessness, exile, nomadism, and diaspora, according to John Durham Peters, are central to the Western canon, and comprise an important aspect of the "fantasy life and social repertory of the West."[19] Peters argues that "concepts of mobility lie at the heart of the Western canon; otherness wanders through its center" (17). Tracing the fantasy of mobility from *The Odyssey* through Jewish and Christian scripture down to the films of Luis Buñuel and to contemporary critical debates in cultural studies, Peters concludes that "Diaspora teaches the perpetual postponement of homecoming and the necessity, in the meanwhile, of living among strange lands and peoples" (39). It is no surprise, then, that in adopting and adapting American realist literary discourse, Abraham Cahan — himself a Jewish immigrant from Russia involved in transnational socialist movements such as the Jewish Workers' Bund — would draw on and contribute to this rich literary history and socio-historic fantasy of perpetual postponement of homecoming.[20] As Daniel and Jonathan Boyarin have observed, in "Eastern Europe at the turn of the [last] century, The Jewish Workers' Bund, a mass socialist organization, had developed a model of national-cultural autonomy not based on territorial ethnic states." Rather, they were guided by a notion of identity closer to what the Boyarins privilege, a mobile subjectivity, an identity disaggregated from any notion of a primordially sacred and promised "Land." There was a distinct split between Hebraist Zionist Jews — like the fictitious Hebrew revivalist poet and Zionist, Abraham Tevkin, in *David Levinsky*— and Yiddishkeit Bundist Jews more sympathetic to socialist internationalism. While later in life, by the mid 1920s, Cahan became sympathetic to the Jewish community in Palestine — if not to Zionism itself as an ideology — he remained more committed to Yiddishkeit as a diasporic modernizing culture based around Yiddish than to revivalist and nationalist ideologies that linked a people and a language to a particular geographic space. The Boyarins define "Diaspora" as "a dissociation of ethnicities and political hegemonies" and offer their definition of it as "the only social structure that even begins to make possible a maintenance of cultural identity in a world grown thoroughly and inextricably interdependent." In the United States, where "mobility" was either upward or downward, and assimilation meant Anglicization, Cahan imagined a version of "mobility" that cut across these categories and hierarchies. While his American David falls prey to the ideological claims of both assimilation and hierarchy — especially economic hierarchy — he, nevertheless, remains "homeless," familially, ethnically, and nationally. The terms that Peters emphasizes — diaspora and, even more importantly, "mobility" — are apt characterizations of David Levinsky as a key figure in the literary re-imagining of American "national" identity at the turn of the last century.[21]

Amerika "begins with Karl's sudden expulsion from his own family ... by severing its protagonist from the network of familial, social, and linguistic relations that in more traditional novels customarily situates characters and events in a distinct milieu" (Anderson 105). This initial expulsion is repeated through the novel as various characters "momentarily allow Karl into their world only to expel him from it into another set of foreign circumstances" (106). Similarly, the death of Levinsky's mother sends him out of the family circle and this expulsion is repeated, like Karl's, when David is momentarily allowed into a series of "American" households only to be expelled. He enters the homes of the Minskers, Mrs. Levinsky (his American landlady whose name is accidentally the same as David's), the Nodelmans, one Irish family, the Kaplans (with whose daughter David breaks an engagement), the Tevkins, and the Margolises. Furthermore, these expulsions usually, though not always, result from David's untoward advances upon a woman of the household (again, echoing Karl's narrative in Kafka's *America*). Finally, the novel ends with David living alone, ironically, in a family hotel, a paradoxical architectural urban space that combines public consumption (hotel culture) with private life (domesticity). Clearly, Levinsky remains outside the nation-state's construction of identity because he does not continue his schooling in America — as expressed by the title of Book 8, "The Destruction of My Temple," the "temple" being New York's City College — nor does he enter and remain in any family situations.

Each failed relationship underscores David's position as a boarder or transient. David's exclusion from domestic space contrasts Mary Antin's search for new domesticity in *The Promised Land*, in which Antin laments the deterioration of the immigrant home where the young modern child feels disconnected from her traditional parents, but celebrates the possibility of a modern secular home in America. The parents' desire that their children becoming American through any means available leads to "that laxity of domestic organization, that inversion of normal relations which makes for friction, and which sometimes ends in breaking up a family that was formerly united and happy." However, this "sad process of disintegration of home life ... is part of the process of Americanization; an upheaval preceding the state of repose." As noted above, immigrant self-transformation involves a period of instability, of "upheaval" leading, in Antin's case, to a "state of repose." For Antin, ideally "the bent and heart-sore immigrant forgets exile and homesickness ... when he beholds his sons and daughters moving as Americans among Americans" (*The Promised Land*, 213). Ultimately, the disruption of domestic space leads to a new sense of belonging in the adopted land of promise. Note, however, that even in Antin's celebration of a new American "repose," she divides the experience between the first and second generation, with the first generation finally at rest and the second "moving."

However, ultimately, rather than remain homeless, Antin enters at least two new spaces of public and private belonging. In her meeting with her teacher Miss Dillingham, Antin enters the expansive space of Boston common, and in this space she feels a sense of belonging to America.[22] Unlike David, who is locked out of the new temple of American intellectual life (the urban university), Antin feels welcomed into the public/private space of modern assimilative education. Secondly, in her encounter with the family of Edward Everett Hale, Antin enters the private intellectual space of the Hale home as well as the institutional space of Hale House, the Boston settlement house that introduces Antin to modern ideas like social Darwinism. Though short-lived, these instances of both public and private belonging clearly show Antin *at home* in an American middle-class intellectual culture.

Try as he might, on the other hand, Levinsky never feels at home *either* in Anglo-America or in the homes of assimilated immigrants. This sense of his not belonging in private space is matched by Levinsky's mobility across the American landscape — not just through the cityscape of New York, but across the American Midwest by train. Levinsky's profound sense of vagrancy suggests a kind of modern alienation. However, and more importantly, it shows the kinds of social transformation that the homeless subject can produce in American culture. Looking at some of David's failed relationships more closely can help explain the nature of David's homelessness, his mobility, and his ability to view American society and culture critically.

When David first moves in as a boarder in Dora Margulis's tenement apartment, his "room appealed to [him] as a compartment in the nest of a family of which [he] was a member. [His] lonely soul had a sense of home and domestic comfort..." (251). He and Dora, the wife of his fellow street peddler Max Margulis, enter into a romantic liaison, making love to each other while David's friend is out peddling. Eventually, Dora, fearing that the affair will be found out, and disgrace her in the eyes of her daughter Lucy, breaks off the relationship, effectively evicting David. As a result, he moves into a furnished room on East Nineteenth Street. Though this street is a slightly more affluent part of town, near the park, it lacks the sense of domestic comfort David felt in the flat of a poor Jewish family. He finds himself expelled from home and domesticity into what seems like a prison: "I moved out according to her program. I came home at 10 the first evening. My double room, with its great arm-chair, carpets, bookcase, imposing lace curtains, and the genteel silence of the street outside, was a prison to me" (305). For the sake of argument, imagine Mary Antin's autobiographical persona in this same room. One can almost hear her say how much the bookcase, lace curtains, and genteel silence appeal to her sense of self. For Levinsky, all that he feels is a lack of homely comfort. More importantly, this absence of material domesticity is linked to a sense of emotional disjuncture. "It was as though I were two men at once, one being in the toils of hopeless love and the other filled with the joy of loving, all injunctions and barriers notwithstanding" (312). His lack of a physical home parallels his lack of an emotional home. David begins to develop a vagrant subjectivity. This divided self, in fact, recalls the notion of the uncanny as un-home-like. Like those reflections of himself that seemed so other, Levinsky's homelessness (or un-homeliness) splits him in two. This doubling of identity is not, however, a reinforcement of ego, but a shattering of a sense of self at home in the world.[23]

Levinsky's growing sense of homelessness leads him in search of reminders of his home in the Old World. Drawn to laborers and prostitutes (like Argentine Rachel) from his home-village of Antomir, David eventually decides to marry a woman from that same town. David's brief engagement to Fanny Kaplan, the daughter of an orthodox father, is meant to cure his "homesickness." For the immigrant eastern European Jewish experience, courtship was a key process of cultural transformation and one that involved consumption.[24] A cantor from Antomir, Fanny's father seems as good as a father to David. And when he attends a Passover ceremony with the Kaplans, David feels "memories and images [take] possession of [him]" turning "[his] present life into a dream and [his] Russian past into reality" (389). As the service comes to a close, he says, "I beheld myself in [my mother's] arms, a boy of four, on our way to synagogue, where I was taught to parrot the very words that I was now saying for her spirit" (392). In marrying Fanny, David hopes to come home. However, the secondary reason for David's engagement to Fanny is anything *but* a need for domesticity and community belonging:

> Another motive that led me to matrimonial aspirations of this kind lay in my new ideas of respectability as a necessary accompaniment to success. Marrying into a well-to-do orthodox family meant respectability and solidity. It implied law and order, the antithesis of anarchism and socialism, trade-unionism, strikes [379].

In reacting against trade-unionism, Levinsky ironically shuns one of the prime formations of community belonging among immigrants, the community of workers. Furthermore, this motivation to use matrimony as an "accompaniment to success" undercuts the whole idea of marriage as a way to get back home — spiritually speaking. Indeed, David soon realizes that becoming the Kaplans' son-in-law is no homecoming at all. Their house "was drearily too large for the habits of the East Side of my time, depressingly out of keeping with its sense of home" (394). And his potential brother-in-law strikes him as a burlesque of Jewish identity: "That an American school-boy should read Talmud seemed a joke to me" (397). Again, it is the divided self that leads Levinsky astray. On the one hand he wants to marry Fanny to heal his homesickness, on the other, he sees the marriage as a way of advancing his business, a business that feels more and more alien to him.

What precipitates Levinsky's self-imposed exile from the Kaplan household is his encounter with a more desirable woman during his visit to, appropriately enough, a vacation resort. In his observation of the various bevies of young Jewish girls at the Rigi Kulm, an exclusive Jewish resort in the Catskills, Levinsky feels displaced. The very site of his sights — a vacation resort — suggests the unsettled and mobile nature of his narrative position. At the same time, as an all–Jewish establishment, it might also suggest a cultural home for the culturally dislocated. But it is here that David decides to give up on his plans to marry Fanny Kaplan and where he meets Anna Tevkin, another lover beyond his reach. Later, when he meets her father, he realizes that his love for Anna is ambiguously tied up with his love of the father's poetry: "To be sure, every word I read in his three little volumes was tinged with the fact that the author was the father of the girl who had cast her spell over me. But then the thought that she had grown up in the house of the man who had written these lines intensified the glow of her nimbus" (452). But despite efforts on both David's and the father's side, David never quite feels at home in the Tevkins' place. The father himself feels estranged from his Americanized, Socialist children, a feeling he expresses in one of his poems which includes the line, "I am homesick for them even when I clasp them to my bosom" (451). Expressing what many first-generation immigrants feel toward their assimilated children, Abraham Tevkin's sentiments also suggests a more general homelessness that this poet shares with Levinsky. In their relationship, home — like almost everything else in David's life — is turned into commodity, ancestral estate becomes real estate. David enters into a real estate scheme with Tevkin, but he does so only because of the possibility that this investment will bring him closer to Anna: "But the great point was that I was literally intoxicated by my new interests, and the fact that they were intimately associated with the atmosphere of Anna's home had much — perhaps everything — to do with it" (482). Here, David confuses investment in real estate, with domesticity itself.

Before going further, it is important to note that Levinsky's knowledge of the Tevkin family goes back to his life in Antomir, and, more importantly for us, to the first part of Cahan's novel. We first hear of Anna's father from David's childhood friend, Naphtali, who tells David about Abraham Tevkin who writes "little books written in the holy tongue on any but holy topics." We also learn that Tevkin has published "a long series of passionate letters addressed, not to his lady-love, but to her father" (57). More than twenty years later, David meets Tevkin under unusual circumstances — through his obsession with Tevkin's daughter. Like Tevkin himself, then, David finds his love for a woman mediated by the woman's father. The title of the penultimate book in the novel suggests how David's desire for women underscores his homelessness rather than pointing to any kind of sexual neurosis. Book 13 is titled, "At Her Father's House." The preposition "at" rather than "in" suggests the tentative nature of David's entry. Where he might expect to reconnect to the ethnic community from which he feels dislocated, David finds only the anti-home of Wall Street. Levinsky's entry into the Tevkin family suggests not a circular structure to the novel, but, rather, traces one of its spirals into modernity. Levinsky's early encounter with the Tevkins represents modernity as romance, even utopia. That two young people entered into a chosen rather than arranged marriage, that the man was a poet, and that his poems were written in the sacred tongue but about secular subjects — all of these suggest an ideal modernity. When Levinsky encounters them in New York, he sees modernity as the pretense of the younger generation, and as the father's artificial return to tradition. The father, now a devoted Zionist, turns his talent to a new kind of patriotism.

What Levinsky finds as he enters this household that he dreads is the transformation of Jewish identity into modern Socialism, and the transformation of a Diasporic identity into the nationalist identity of Zionism. Levinsky learns that Tevkin, a Hebrew poet whom he respects, has turned the language and rituals of Judaism into a national ideology. Tevkin expresses a linguistic nationalism when he says that Hebrew is "the living tongue of the Zionist colonists in Palestine," and that this "tongue of our fathers spoke from the grave to us. Now, however, it has come to life again" (463). Tevkin is a poet who used the sacred Hebrew language for profane purposes — to write love poetry — and also for ideological purposes of nationalism. He sees the language as a way of inventing a new Jewish nationalism.

The roots of the Yiddish/Hebrew split in Eastern European culture is an important historical backdrop to the themes Cahan explores in *David Levinsky*. The Mendelsohnian strand of Jewish modernity — based around the writings of philosopher Moses Mendelsohn in the eighteenth century — was a relatively elite movement that took the German language as its medium of "Enlightenment," and grew out of the German Jewish ghettoes. This movement of Jewish cultural and philosophical modernity came to influence the Eastern European strand of the Enlightenment known as the "Haskalah." The Eastern European *maskilim* (men of the haskalah) chose Hebrew as the medium of enlightenment, and thus the haskalah was, ironically, a *revivalist* modernity that took a sacred language and used it to broaden religious ideas into a broader rationalism.[25]

In contrast to Tevkin's linguistic nationalism within Hebrew and Zionism, Levinsky (and, it can be argued, Cahan) embraces what might be called *yiddishkeit*. Though more generally referring "to that phase of Jewish history during the past two centuries which is marked by the prevalence of Yiddish as the language of the east European Jews and by the growth among them of a culture resting mainly on that language," the term can refer also more specifically to a third version of Jewish modernity.[26] As Irving Howe defines it in his classic *World of Our Fathers*, *yiddishkeit* attempted to reconcile dichotomies. It is a paradoxical position that attempts to build identity without nationality, embraces secularism while retaining elements of the sacred, and is political without being ideological. For this chapter's discussion of David Levinsky's homelessness, *yiddishkeit* is the most apt cultural-historical designation. As Howe suggests, *yiddishkeit* is "at home neither entirely with its past nor entirely with the surrounding nations. Out of its marginality it made a premise for humaneness" (17) Howe also points to Simon Dubnow as a key late nineteenth-century historian of *yiddishkeit*. According to Howe, Dubnow "saw the Jewish people as a spiritual community held together by historical, cultural, and religious ties, despite *the absence of a common homeland or territory,* and he urged the Jews to struggle for cultural and religious autonomy in whichever country they happened to find themselves. In opposition to the Bundists, he stressed the unity of the Jewish people, and in opposition to the Zionists, *he desired the preservation of the Jewish identity in the Diaspora*" (Howe 18, emphasis added). Like Diaspora, itself, *yiddishkeit* seems to embody a way of embracing race in a non-racist way and without linking race to an autochthonous homeland.[27] David Levinsky was Cahan's expression of a homeless cultural identity in contrast to Tevkin's landlocked Zionism. *Yiddishkeit* is an important expression of this ideological homelessness.

Thus, religious rites are transformed into rituals for imagining a national community: "[R]eligious faith never had been known in their [the Tevkins'] house. Of late years, however — that is, since Tevkin had espoused the cause of Zionism or nationalism — he had insisted on the Passover feast every year" (493). Tevkin calls the Passover ceremony "the Fourth of July of our unhappy people" (495). But Levinsky, and Tevkin's own children see this re-invention of tradition as a sham, a sham expressed most clearly, again, through clothing: "He was now bent upon having a Passover feast service precisely like the one he had seen his father conduct, not omitting even the *white shroud* which his father had worn on the occasion. As a consequence, several of these details were a novel sight to his children. A white shroud lay ready for him on his sofa, and as he slipped it on, with smiles and blushes, there was an outburst of mirth" (494–95, emphasis added). The shroud becomes the emperor's new clothes. Levinsky is disconnected from his Antomir home; he is an interloper in Jewish domesticity in America; and he cannot see Palestine as a new homeland the way Tevkin does. Just as his commerce in the world of clothes suggests a mobile subject position, so does his exclusion from domesticity suggest a homeless subjectivity.

At the close of the novel, David considers marrying a Gentile woman. However, the "chasm of race" ultimately separates him from this woman (528). This chasm of race also separates David from what this woman would have given him in terms of cultural capital. She was "a woman of high character," and she tells him "something of the good novels she had read" (527–28). In fact, she introduces him to "good, modern fiction" (528). Considering that at the beginning of his own economic success he obsessively read Victorian novels (especially *Vanity Fair* and *Dombey and Son*), his relationship with this Gentile woman promises to be of "intellectual interest" or an investment in his own cultural growth (529). The ultimate irony is that he meets this woman in a "family hotel." Like his use of the term "house" to refer to his business, the combination of family and hotel suggest the homelessness that is central to David's narrative voice. And it is from this displaced narrative point of view that David delivers his most biting critique, and perhaps Cahan's as well, of the United States' culture of invidious comparison, a comparison that measures ethnic identity along with class standing:

> Most of the people of my hotel are German-American Jews. I know other Jews of this class. I contribute to their charity institutions. Though an atheist, I belong to one of their synagogues. Nor can I plead the special feeling which had partly accounted for my visits at the synagogue of the Sons of Antomir while I was engaged to Kaplan's daughter. I am a member of that synagogue

chiefly because it is a fashionable synagogue. I often convict myself of currying favor with German Jews. But then German-American Jews curry favor with Portuguese-American Jews, just as we all curry favor with Gentiles and as American Gentiles curry favor with the aristocracy of Europe [528].

When a synagogue becomes fashionable, the sacred has been converted into a commodity. But the selling of religion is not, as some critics have argued, a sign of Cahan's stereotyping of Jewishness.[28] Rather, the fashionable synagogue is part of a wider American — Jewish and Gentile — ideology of conspicuous waste. This comment is not an indictment of Jews, but a clear critique of a national American ideology. In a time when distancing American identity from European identity was central to constructions of national identity in the U.S., Cahan — through the homeless voice of David Levinsky — convicts American Gentiles of wanting to emulate aristocratic European culture. Levinsky's exclusion from the wealth he has created, from any home life, and from a mixed race marriage — all of these mark the occasion of his exposing America's own masquerade behind its homespun identity, a masquerade that hides an affiliation with the most inequitable elements of the Old World.

Despite his homelessness, perhaps even facilitated by it, David Levinsky transforms America. Indeed, it may be because of his homeless subjectivity that Levinsky is able to transform the place where he finds himself a resident alien. In addition to his remaining on the periphery of domestic scenes, Levinsky is an interloper in other ways as well. Soon after establishing his cloak-manufacturing business in New York, he becomes a drummer for his own outfit, traveling throughout New England and eventually across the Midwest. However, rather than using costume to colonize the West as Cather does in her novels, Cahan presents Levinsky's business traveling as a remaking of America without its containment. As a traveling manufacturer of clothing, Levinsky represents the transformation of American culture through a combination of mobility and performance, traveling and tailoring.

Tailor-Made Girls, Tailor-Made America

The Rise of David Levinsky was first published as an ethnological fiction in the pages of *McClure's Magazine* in 1913 under the title, "The Autobiography of an American Jew," and later expanded to the much longer novel. Later that same year, Willa Cather would ghostwrite S. S. McClure's *Autobiography*.[29] *McClure's* placed two very different frames around these two ostensibly autobiographical texts. With the McClure autobiography, Cather's authorial presence is completely erased. *McClure's* presented it as an authentic narrative of individual triumph over traditional limits and barriers. On the other hand, the same magazine framed Cahan's authorship as ethnology, even though the narrative was a fiction. Cahan's work appeared as a study of a race rather than the narrative of an individual. While both pieces could be considered "fictional," both are given different qualities of "truth." McClure's is an individual, personal, and admirable truth. Levinsky's is an ethnic, impersonal spectacle of the social. By the early twentieth century, McClure's Irish identity could be presented as becoming white; Cahan's Jewishness could not.

This early and shorter "Autobiography of an American Jew" was framed by another editorial choice, the publication of Burton J. Hendrick's essay "The Jewish Invasion of America" in the March issue of the magazine, a month before "The Autobiography" began to appear.[30] The first page of Hendrick's essay features the illustration of "A pure type of Arabian Jew."[31] "This boy of eighteen," Hendrick's caption continues, "a tailor by trade, traveled alone to this country from Jerusalem. He arrived here December 28, 1912." The boy wears a fez and a collarless shirt, much stained. By contrast, an illustration of "the successful, aggressive Jew" features a middle-aged man with full proportions, hatless, wearing a starched shirt, tie, and formal suit. The caption tells us that this Jewish type "dominates the clothing business and kindred enterprises." These two images set up the narrative structure that Cahan's "Autobiography of an American Jew" will follow, the gradual "metamorphosis" from a young Jewish tailor into an American clothing tycoon. In the closing comments of his article, Hendrick introduces Cahan not as a novelist, but as an "ethnologist":

> Mr. Cahan will show ... the minute workings of that wonderful machine, the Jewish brain. His article will make clear why it is that the Jews so easily surpass or crowd out, at least in business and finance, the other great immigrating races, — Irish, Germans, Scandinavians, and Italians, — and why, in the next hundred years, the Semitic influence is likely to be almost preponderating in the United States.[32]

The basic narrative of *The Rise of David Levinsky*, then, first appeared in a particular social context: the public space of the literary journal during a time when the autobiographical form was an important genre of American identity construction (given the work of Henry Adams on the one hand and Mary Antin on the other), and when that form functioned differently for different ethnic groups. For Irish-Americans, autobiography — albeit a stylistically if not substantively fictional, ghost-written one — could represent the process of an individual becoming an American. For Jewish-Americans, the autobiographical form was primarily ethnological, showing the type, and the workings of the machine-like brain of the ethnic other.

The first installment of Cahan's "Levinsky" opens with a full two-page spread. Across the top of both pages we see the skyline of the Lower East Side. On the far left of the two-page spread, we have an illustration of David Levinsky — in a long coat, one bundle under his left arm and another in his right hand. He wears a hat and looks lost. The caption reads, "With twenty-nine cents in my pocket, I set forth in the direction of East Broadway." On the facing page at the far right we have an illustration of Abraham Cahan, presumably at his desk as founding editor of the *Jewish Daily Forward*, a publication that would become the largest Yiddish-language newspaper in the world. This visual contrast between Levinsky the young immigrant, and Cahan the "editor, author, and general counselor of the Jewish East Side of New York" echoes the contrast presented in Hendrick's article between the "pure Arabian Jew" and the "successful, aggressive Jew." In both pairs of images, the contrast between different identities is illustrated most vividly through contrasts in clothing and physiognomy. These editorial frames through which Cahan's work is presented function, in effect, as alterations of his text just as assimilation is seen as an alteration of the Levantine boy's rags into the Jewish capitalist's riches. But Cahan was, himself, aware of the ways in which text could be altered like textile, how identity could be refashioned. By 1917, he had turned his series of "articles" for *McClure's* into *The Rise of David Levinsky*, a text that was not only an alteration of the earlier article, but that went on to depict the alteration of identity, and the alteration of America. What the Hendrick article presented as a frightening and lamentable "invasion" of New York, becomes, in *The Rise of David Levinsky* a cultural transformation. Assimilation means not only the transformation of the immigrant, but the immigrant's effects upon the nation.

Cahan's own story is one of a rise to prominence but in the text rather than the textile trade. As the editor of the *Jewish Daily Forward*, he had risen from obscurity to the leading Jewish writer and publicist in the United States. Furthermore, his involvement in the cloak and suit industry strikes of 1913 made him keenly aware of the plight of the immigrant working class. Two recent events, preceding the publication of "The Autobiography of an American Jew," would have been familiar to Cahan's readers: the Triangle shirtwaist factory fire of 1911, and the strikes of 1913. The *Forward*, with Cahan's leadership and writing, endorsed the strikes of 1913, but also endorsed the relatively weak compromise gained by the unions involved: the United Garment Workers, the International Ladies Garment Workers' Union, and the Brotherhood of Tailors. Thus, by the time he decided to re-write "The Autobiography of an American Jew" into a fuller fiction, he had reflected on the competing interests and problems associated with the lives of garment workers. His critical view of all involved is reflected in *The Rise of David Levin-*

sky.³³ However, rather than write either an ethnography or a political tract, Cahan wrote a novel. As a protégé of William Dean Howells and a contemporary of writers like Frank Norris and Theodore Dreiser, Cahan was aware that the realist novel could be used as a tool in building class coalition. However, *The Rise of David Levinsky* is, at times, a satirical and comic text. Cahan, like his protagonist, transforms American culture. If, towards the end of *David Levinsky*, its protagonist alters the fashion and fabric of American society, then Cahan also transforms the novel of social critique. Unlike Theodore Dreiser, for example, Cahan re-tailors the novel of social critique, emphasizing themes of transformation, homelessness, and comic incongruities of identity. In part, Cahan was responding to ways in which he and his work were being framed by a literary and popular culture that viewed him as picturesque, at best, or alien and inferior, at worst. Along with Mary Antin and Anzia Yezierska, Cahan attempted to re-fashion American popular culture itself.

One of the illustrations that accompanied *McClure's* publication of "The Autobiography of an American Jew" in 1913, depicted the putative sexual danger Jews posed to white American women — the threat of miscegenation. This image appeared in the final installment of "Autobiography of an American Jew" in July 1913, and bore the caption: "Many a time, when I see a well dressed American woman in the street, I follow her for blocks." This caption is taken out of context from Cahan's text itself, which should read: "I follow her for blocks, *scanning the make-up of her cloak, jacket or suit*. I never weary of studying the trend of the American woman's taste. The subject has become a veritable *idée fixe* with me."³⁴ Within its appropriate context, this reads as the musings of a clothing designer, a craftsman, an entrepreneur. Out of context, it reads like the male Jew's illicit desire for the Gentile woman.³⁵ This construction of Cahan as a sexually perverse Jew was in keeping with a common stereotype of Jewish identity, one made infamous in the lynching of Leo Frank in 1915. Frank had been falsely accused of raping a young white woman in his pencil factory in Atlanta, Georgia in 1913. First convicted of the crime, Frank's sentence was commuted in 1915, and in response to this commutation, a mob attacked the prison, took Frank by force and lynched him. The popular-press coverage of the case presented Frank's Jewish "physiognomy" as evidence of his racial perversity.³⁶

The *McClure's* version of *David Levinsky* was published at the time of Frank's trial but before his being murdered. As a separate volume, *David Levinsky* was published in 1917, after Frank's lynching. In the later version, Cahan — as a journalist — would surely have heard about and followed the case, and would probably have been aware of any connotations of "perverse" interracial desire in his own representation of Levinsky. However, rather than making Levinsky less threatening to women and to white women in particular, in the 1917 version of his novel, Cahan makes Levinsky more threatening, at least in some ways, to white American womanhood. He does so in order to parody and critique any such suggestion of Jewish perversity.

Levinsky's "Oriental blood" is one factor in his threat — or, I want to argue, the parody of such a threat — to masculinity. The Jew of the "pure Arabian type" was a stock stereotype that various nativists trotted out as their evidence for the alien invasion of Nordic America. This anti–Semitic stereotype had distinct "sexual" and "national" connotations. He was an effeminate, wily degenerate whose racial identity could be traced to a "remote Oriental origin." One of the most threatening predilections of this effeminate and unscrupulous type was his "penchant for cross-racial perversions — sparing the Jewess but pursuing the Gentile."[37] Thus, "it was the charge of perversion that crystallized [Leo Frank's] Jewishness as race in public discussion" of the case (Jacobson, 65). Both the stereotype of effeminacy and of cross-racial "perversion" might be attached to Levinsky.

Levinsky tells his reader about his own Oriental origin: "There is a streak of sadness in the blood of my race. Very likely it is of Oriental origin" (4). And David's emulation of his friend Jake Mindels might serve as further illustration of Cahan's manipulation of the effeminate Jew stereotype. But rather than being a sign of Cahan's acceptance of stereotypes or a sign of Levinsky's misogyny and miscegenation, Levinsky's "queer" identity and his interest in women's clothing are really signs of Cahan's broad critique of the American ideology of invidious comparison — a measuring of people's value and worth on the bases of class, gender, sexuality, nation, race and ethnicity.

Racist anxieties about perverse Jewish masculine sexuality made Cahan's thematizing of Levinsky's attention to the gentile female body a risky narrative move. But Levinsky's gaze upon the female frame reveals the ideological work done by clothes in constructing national identity. In particular, his attention to the Anglo female identity underscores the racial and ethnic component of conspicuous consumption. Two outsiders who make up the clothing industry — women and Jews — were integral to refashioning American national identity. Cahan brings these two together in dangerous business liaisons.

At the height of Levinsky's material success, Cahan, through the voice of his first-person narrator, gives us a journalistic discussion of how "the" Russian Jew has, indeed, invaded the New York clothing industry.

> Foreigners ourselves, and mostly unable to speak English, we had Americanized the system of providing clothes for the American woman of moderate or humble means. The ingenuity and unyielding tenacity of our managers, foremen, and operatives had introduced a thousand and one devices for making by

machine garments that used to be considered possible only as the product of hand work. This — added to a vastly increased division of labor, the invention, at our instance, of all sorts of machinery for the manufacture of trimmings, and the enormous scale upon which production was carried on by us — had the effect of cheapening the better class of garments prodigiously. We had done away with prohibitive prices and greatly improved the popular taste. Indeed, the Russian Jew has made the average American girl a "tailor-made" girl.[38]

This passage appears in both versions of the novel. In the 1913 *McClure's* version, of course, this language serves to endorse the magazine's framing of Cahan as ethnologist. However, the full length, 1917, version makes an even clearer reference to the ethnic identity of this "tailor-made" American girl as the white figure upon whose frame Levinsky fashions American dress. By having Levinsky specify the ethnic identity of the tailor-made American girl, Cahan makes his hero a cipher through which the reader can understand the racial, ethnic, and gendered ideologies surrounding conspicuous consumption and invidious comparison. It was not simply a matter of wearing the most expensive clothes that made conspicuous consumption an important marker of class and passport of caste. We must not forget that white skin and good grammar — those qualities that distinguish the native-born white from swarthy foreigners — constituted the basis upon which other qualities were built. Especially the reference to the Irish shop-girl as model underscores the importance of ethnic transformation in America. Cahan, a keen observer of group characteristics, would have noticed what cultural historian Andrew Heinze has documented: that "young Irish women were more able than their men to advance socially in America," thus "they, in particular, strove for style" (Heinze 93). Thus, the Irish model becomes emblematic of American national identity itself. Like the "Pledge for American Women" to dress well (discussed in Chapter 2 of the present study), Cahan's image of the white American female fashion model implies the symbolic significance of the well-heeled female figure for national identity.

Levinsky's salesmanship makes the significance of race and ethnicity in commerce and advertising abundantly clear:

> I employed a large staff of trained bookkeepers, stenographers, clerks, and cloak models. These models were all American girls of Anglo-Saxon origin, since a young woman of other stock is not likely to be built on American lines — with the exception of Scandinavian and Irish girls, who have the American figure. But the figure alone was not enough, I thought. In selecting my model-girls, I preferred a good-looking face and good manners, and, if possible, good grammar. Experience had taught me that refinement in a model was helpful in making a sale, even in the case of the least refined customers. Indeed, often it is even more effectual than a tempting complexion [444].

If we recall Veblen's notion that a culture of conspicuous consumption fosters the "rating and grading" of a person's worth and value through their property and especially through their dress, then Levinsky's insistence upon his models' white racial physiognomy and middle class literacy tells us more about his customers than about himself. Levinsky insists on white models because he is interested in "making a sale." Thus, his criteria are simply a reflection of the market he is serving — middle class Americans, including assimilated Jews. But Cahan is not condemning Levinsky for his use of Gentile models. Indeed, Levinsky's self-conscious decision to choose these models distances him from the code he is using. He makes ethnicity a sort of costume decision.

Conclusion

Cahan's extensive and wide-ranging use of clothing and shelter as tropes of materiality in *The Rise of David Levinsky* suggests his awareness of the ideological function of dress in a cloth culture. Clothing was a central emblem in the culture of consumption in turn-of-the-century North America. It was also central to invidious comparison, but not only in the strictly economic sense that Veblen suggested, but also in terms of ethnicity. In a sense, Cahan undresses American society. He exposes contradictions by showing how an immigrant community reaps America's favors while imitating its faults. This critique of both host culture and exile community is possible because of the narrator's homeless voice, and this homelessness is itself expressed through the culture of clothing — the immigrant tailor, the traveling salesman, the dandified bachelor, even the ethnic flaneur. Caught between the imaginary of the homeland and the symbolic realm of the host culture, David Levinsky is an important example of a nomadic narrator. Even though he puts on Gentile vestments and makes American investments, Levinsky has no vested moral interest in the New World, and only a fetishized link to the Old. Without clothing or capital, a "man" was nothing in the Gilded Age. However, even with the suit and the checkbook, he continued to be nothing if he was not of the right ethnic identity. David is as close to nothing as a millionaire garment-industry tycoon can get. He is nothing because he is no place: no longer home, but not at home in America. However, paradoxically this indeterminacy of cultural location makes Levinsky's a perfect narrative voice for cultural critique, and a challenge to stable notions of ethnic identity in the United States, and, most importantly, allows him to be an emblem of the transformation (or alteration or refashioning) of American culture. As Daniel and Jonathan Boyarin put it, "Diasporic cultural identity teaches us that cultures are not preserved by being protected from 'mixing' but probably can only continue to exist as a product of such mixing. Cultures, as well as identities, are constantly being remade. While this is true of all cultures, diasporic Jewish culture lays it bare because of the impossibility of a natural association between this people and a particular land — thus the impossibility of seeing Jewish culture as a self-enclosed, bounded phenomenon" (108). To imagine identity in terms of garments rather than in terms of "Land" is central to the narrative trajectories in *David Levinsky* analyzed above. To imagine identity in this way — as a mobile identity disconnected from a homeland — constitutes a "threat to cultural nativisms" (108). In Chapter 7 it will be clear how one writer, Willa Cather, distilled and expressed American anxieties about this threat, a threat that, as we shall see in Chapter 6, was elaborated upon further by Anzia Yezierska. It was this challenge to a unified, uniform, ready-made national identity that Willa Cather responded to in her extensive use of clothing as signifier of national identity in her novels of the American West in the years following Cahan's publication of the Levinsky narrative in the nineteen teens. However, while Levinsky disconnected a mobile sartorial identity from any notion of "homeland," and while Yezierska attempted to invest a Jewish cultural past into an American future, Cather imposed certain imperial designs on national identity, using a unified notion of *the* American fabric to consolidate a romantic conception of homeland.

6. The Financial and Sartorial Fictions of Anzia Yezierska

IN ANZIA YEZIERSKA'S FICTION, A CHARACTER named Muhmenkeh appears in two different novels—*Bread Givers* and *Arrogant Beggar*. Yezierska used these two versions of the same character to represent the struggles of Eastern European women to unite a socialist conception of memory and history with the capitalist spirit of the Gilded Age in the United States. These two Muhmenkehs are really the same character: Yezierska's archetype for union between the spiritual wealth of the past and the material wealth of an American future. Yezierska, documenting in part her own dilemma over identity, also presents failed investments—both emotional and financial. Time and again her characters in these two novels and in her other fiction invest their love in the wrong person, pawn family heirlooms for mere financial gain, or sell their birthright for the empty promises of a host culture. It is through these two Muhmenkehs that Yezierska resolves her dilemma.[1]

In much of Yezierska's fiction, clothing and money together function to present the idea of investment as opposed to speculation. Speculation involves a wager, and even when its gains are great, they do not reflect or embody what was invested: labor or material, for instance.[2] Investment, on the other hand, suggests the notion of a *vested* interest, of measurable input into the system, especially in the form of money, but also, symbolically in the form of identity in the case of Yezierska's work. Yezierska's novels present an idealized economy in which her protagonists invest the American future with tangible and intangible labor and "capital" from the European past. Physical labor, cloth, and clothing organized around communal ideals from Russia constitute the wealth that is invested in a new life in urban America. But most of Yezierska's characters fail in this effort to invest the future with the past. Rather, most of them end up speculating on that future and losing. They liquidate, as it were, the assets of the Old World but never quite achieving meaningful gains from the New.

In the classic rags-to-riches story, no such bargain was necessary: Ragged Dick has no family to speak of, and his past is a generic American past embodied in his George Washington coat.[3] His speculation on the future requires only direct and personal investment: hard work, honesty, and the generosity of the morally correct members of the upper classes. Even in Dreiser's reversal of the rags-to-riches myth, the past has little value: Carrie's family has no real hold on her; her sister's life seems to be a dead end, and, in the case of Hurstwood, his past has no value for his future. In Abraham Cahan's ethic rewriting of the rags-to-riches narrative, however, speculation on a middle-class American future does involve the past, but requires the liquidation of sacred assets from that past: religious education, a father's coat, a mother's labor, the loyalty of Levinsky's townsfolk who end up working under him as wage laborers. Social mobility involves a net loss of moral and emotional capital from the past. However, Yezierska attempts to secure the best of both worlds: a middle-class American future invested with the communal culture of a Russian Jewish past. In most of her novels and stories, Yezierska shows how much immigrant Jews gave up in order to assimilate and climb up social and economic ladders. However, some of her protagonists, especially Adele in *Arrogant Beggar*, succeed in investing their Jewish past into their American future. In what is basically a sentimental ending, *Arrogant Beggar* culminates in Adele's honoring Muhmenkeh, an old woman she has met whose Old-World ways first repel Adele but then inspire her to reconnect with her Russian past.

Sara Makes a Profit: Vestments and Investments in Bread Givers

Bread Givers begins with a chapter on "Hester Street" which introduces us to the Smolinsky family, whose youngest member, Sara, narrates her gradual alienation from her father but also her ultimate reconciliation, by the final chapter of the novel, with the past that the father represents, with "the generations who made" him.[4] This first chapter focuses more specifically on certain dilemmas within the immigrant family: "empty-head" Mashah's inordinate love of Fifth Avenue clothing, Reb Smolinsky's oppressive and obsessive concern with books and faith as central to the household, Fania and Bessie's struggles to marry well and take care of the Smolinsky household as well, and, most importantly, Sara Smolinsky's venture into the world of capitalistic entrepreneurship. Mashah pursues fashion like a religion or a duty: "she lived in the pleasure she got from her beautiful face, as Father lived in his Holy Torah" (4), and "nobody touched Mashah's things, no more than they dared touch Father's Hebrew books, or Mother's precious jar of jelly which she always kept ready for company" (5). Apparently, clothing answers Mashah's material and spiritual needs, as physically nourishing as her Mother's cuisine and as spiritually rewarding as her father's religious texts. Mashah purchases lace for her hat; she keeps "her clothes in a soapbox under the bed;" she spends her wages at the five-and-dime, and comes home with pink roses in her hat: "to match out my pink calico — just like the picture on the magazine cover," she tells her sisters (4, 3). This expenditure on her beauty is much like her Father's attitude toward religion: just as the Holy Torah keeps Reb Smolinsky from the active pursuit of productive labor, so too does the dogma of fashion keep Mashah from working and earning. The reader sees these things through Sara's eyes, so that the father's religious devotion becomes rigid orthodoxy that hurts the family economy, and, at the other extreme, Mashah's irrational love of clothes becomes speculation on assimilation and social mobility, at best a risky investment in the future. In contrast to Reb Smolinsky and Mashah, Sara attempts to negotiate between the sacred world of the Jewish past and the material world of American assimilation. Sara's negotiation of the assimilation process centers on clothing and money, vestment and investment.

In her sartorial negotiation of assimilation, Sara ultimately fails in weaving the past into her American future, giving up the sacred function of clothes in Jewish funereal rites for the social function of clothes in professional advancement in the United States.[5] Towards the end of the novel Sara refuses to follow the Jewish funeral ritual of having a hole cut into her clothes — in this case, a new dress that represents her new identity as a *teacherin* and is, in fact, both a vestment and an investment: it opens doors of opportunity for her. Her new dress embodies her new self— a college graduate, a teacher in the public schools, a new woman living on her own. Her refusal expresses the more general ambivalence she and her real-life counterparts felt in being caught between urban American culture, and the culture of the Polish or Russian *shtetl*. However, the new dress — a simple serge indicative of the intellectual East Side — is not just a sartorial signifier, but also an investment. It is certainly a financial investment because it secures her a teaching position. As Yezierska's narrator suggests in the story "Soap and Water" in *Hungry Hearts*, teaching positions went first to the best-dressed candidate. However, the dress is an investment also in identity. It works as an installment, both situating (or installing) the wearer in a professional place and advancing payment towards an identity that the wearer builds over time. Most importantly, it is investment in assimilation, paying both social and financial returns.

In fact, the dress is only one example of failed or successful investments in the novel. Mashah, for example, as the frivolous and fashion-obsessed "empty-head" of the family, constantly invests her money in clothing that has no professional function, as Sara's clothes do. Fania is the most pragmatic of the sisters, as her marriage to a wealthy garment industry tycoon suggests later in the novel, but her marriage is more speculation than investment — ultimately not integrating Fania into the *work* of producing wealth. Bessie is the bearer of family burdens, and never breaks away long enough to enter into anything other than an old-world domestic economy. Mother is one of the links to the past, but also a believer in the American future, if only her husband, Reb Smolinsky would work for a living. The father, Reb Smolinsky, wants American wealth along with the traditional division of labor for *shtetl* households in which the father is a religious scholar: the best of both worlds for him, the worst for the women who have to earn a living *and* take care of the home.[6] Furthermore, his speculation on a business interest is a financial disaster for the family. In the midst of all this, Sara, with the help of an old woman named Muhmenkeh, is the only member of the family to figure out American culture through her successful venture as a ten-year-old merchant. Her financial negotiation with Muhmenkeh is also an emotional negotiation of the past with the future.

Sara goes to Muhmenkeh for "a loan of a featherbed" (14). The featherbed is itself a signifier of the culture and traditions of the Old World, an indispensable item in a bride's trousseau, expressing and conveying materially the matrilineal link in the *shtetl* family. Sara and Muhmenkeh negotiate tradition, and reinvent notions of labor, capital investment, and profit. For one thing, Muhmenkeh's work ethic is decidedly not the Protestant work ethic of the adopted nation, but rather, the work ethic of eastern European women who were expected, often more than their husbands, to earn a living for the family. Their work was not in the service of accumulating wealth, but of facilitating sacred worship. However, at the same time, the expectation that Jewish women be breadwinners for the devout husbands endorsed the very idea of women working outside the home.[7] Thus, Muhmenkeh's independence and her use of her labor are emblematic of a certain type of immigrant Jewish woman in urban America at the turn of the last century. "Muhmenkeh worked as hard for her pennies as anybody on the block." Furthermore, she has brought with her the communal sense of property that also complicates any American notions of labor or capital: "her heart was big with giving all the time from the little she had" (14). When she loans Sara the featherbed, she also lets Sara borrow two quarters, giving her financial credit as well as sharing her material possessions. Muhmenkeh is a poor woman with the spirit of an aristocrat or millionaire: "She didn't have the scared, worried look that pinched and squeezed the blood out of the faces of the poor. It breathed from her the feeling of plenty, as if she had Rockefeller's millions to give away" (14). When Muhmenkeh comes to visit them, "Even mother forgot for a while her worries, so like a healing medicine was Muhmenkeh's sunshine!" (15). Giving as she is, Muhmenkeh does not make any of the beneficiaries of her charity feel guilty, as Anglo-American benefactors make Adele Lindner feel in *Arrogant Beggar*. Muhmenkeh instructs and inspires Sara to use the 50-cent loan, a credit that becomes both a financial and emotional, both an economic and social, investment.

The money and the featherbed constitute loans from Russia and America. Yezierska seems to be balancing American speculation in the future with ethnic investment in the past. Before Mashah can snatch the two quarters that Muhmenkeh has given, Sara takes one of them and makes the first investment of her life. Going back to Muhmenkeh, who is the "herring woman" on Hester Street, Sara buys some squashed but not spoiled herrings and sells them for a profit. She tells Muhmenkeh, "I'm no beggar! ... I want to go into business like a person" (21). She begins with 25c and ends up with 50, a profit of 100 percent, but a profit made from negotiation with a feminine link to the past, a profit from selling one of the staples of Old-World and East Side meals. When she counts her profits she thinks, "Richer than Rockefeller, I felt" (22). Beyond this, she experiences a feeling of ecstasy and elation that is unmatched anywhere else in the novel, even after her success at College and her landing a job as a teacher.

> I was always saying to myself, if I ever had a quarter or a half dollar in my hand, I'd run away from home and never look on our dirty house again. But now I was so happy with my money, I didn't think of running away, I only wanted to show them what I could do and give it away.
> It began singing in my heart, the music of the whole Hester Street. The pushcart peddlers yelling their goods, the noisy playing of children in the gutter, the women pushing and shoving each other with their market baskets — all that was only hollering noise before melted over me like a new beautiful song.
> It began dancing before my eyes, the twenty-five herring that earned me twenty-five cents. It lifted me in the air, my happiness. I couldn't help it. It began dancing under my feet. And I couldn't stop myself. I danced into our kitchen. And throwing the fifty pennies, like a shower of gold, into my mother's lap, I cried, "Now, will you yet call me crazy-head? Give only a look what 'Blood-and-iron' has done" [23].

Thus concludes the first chapter of *Bread Givers*, with Sara throwing back in English, the same words her father had used against her before in Yiddish — *blut-und-eisen*. Her use of English, her role as capitalist and not laborer, her view of herself as Rockefeller — all of these suggest that part of her elation comes from having mastered the American game, having successfully assimilated to the point of being an American merchant and entrepreneur.

However, her elation comes as much, if not more, from her community, her family, and her past. Her elation is based on the "music of Hester Street." She looks around her ethnic place and embraces it. This space enriches her literally and figuratively. The "beautiful song" of her neighborhood makes her dance, and gives her visions of herring and quarters — stock and profit, Old-World substance and American value. She channels this dance of capitalist euphoria into a dance of giving — "I only wanted to show them what I could do, and give it away." Finally, her profit falls like a shower of gold into her mother's lap — the site of maternal nurturing and symbolic signifier of the motherland.

The first chapter of *Bread Givers*, then, sets up important relationships between commodities, capital, and credit. First, the father embodies the traditional religious and scholastic vestments of the Old World. He is robed in the garments of and invested spiritually in Old World religious belief and custom. These are not commodities, but sacred materials.[8] He has cultural, not financial, capital. Secondly, Mashah fetishizes the commodity. At best, her interest in fashion is a kind of speculation on the future: if she dresses well, she thinks, she will get a good husband. This is very much an empty investment, and, perhaps more appropriately, a deficit: Mashah gains clothing only on credit. Thirdly, the concluding pages of the chapter introduce a theme that is important not only in this text, but in much of Yezierska's oeuvre: the idea that investment in the New World does not demand liquidation of assets brought from the Old. Sara's political and spiritual economy is one that honors a traditional matrilineal past embodied in the old woman, Muhmenkeh. But her practice of capitalism requires investment of labor and of self not only in the past, but also in the future. And, finally, her social economy relies on the tradition of *tsedakah* — social justice based on charitable distribution of wealth.[9]

The rest of the novel includes three basic examples of investment — traditional male religious garb as investment in tradition, speculative investments in clothing and assimilated identity, and the investment of the American future with a feminine Old-World past. Sara's discovery of capitalism can be contrasted to at least two other investments in *Bread Givers*: the father's speculative purchase of a grocery store in Elizabeth, New Jersey, and Max Goldstein's venture into the garment industry. The father wants to make a quintessentially capitalist gesture: to get something for nothing.[10] But he also wants to sustain a traditional patriarchy. His investment is divided between what he sees as absolute values (of Old World patriarchy) and what are fluctuating values, values that rise and fall with investment or debt, desire or deficit.[11] Two confidence men convince Reb Smolinsky that a store, basically a grocery space with empty boxes of product on the shelves, is a thriving business. Inept in matters of business because of his devotion to the Torah and to the life of a "schnorer," Smolinsky is taken in by the get-rich-quick scheme. He realizes too late that one of the men who cheated him has left town with the money, also cheating his own partner. This sequence of events marks a turning point in the novel, after which Sara decides to leave New Jersey and go back to their old neighborhood. The business scheme and its fallout represent the "struggle" of the novel's subtitle — a struggle between a father of the Old World and a daughter of the New, a struggle in which the daughter must learn the ways of the New World precisely because the father remains willfully ignorant of them, a struggle between absolute and negotiable values. Later in the novel, after years of separation, Sara stumbles upon her father peddling flowers in the street. The father, unlike Sara or even Muhmenkeh, remains stuck in the past, unable to transform that past into cultural capital to be invested in his own future. Sara has already discovered (at age ten), what her father never comes to understand — the joy of making a profit through wise investment. However, she does so by investing in her own neighborhood and relying on her own community — on Muhmenkeh, the embodiment of Old World roots and connectedness rather than the patriarchal Old-World orthodoxy of the father. The father borrows from outsiders and sets up shop away from the neighborhood. Sara, in her small way, works within the ethnic economy of Hester Street.

However, the joy that Sara gains from this particular kind of profit — selling fish she has bought from Muhmenkeh to her own neighbors — is as far as she will go in becoming a capitalist. She will not go as far as Max Goldstein, a young man who courts Sara briefly, but whom she dismisses because he is more concerned with money than with ideas, and because he embraces a new-world version of her father's Old World patriarchy. During their courtship, Max tells Sara all about his rise out of rags and into riches. He begins to gain American capital when he becomes the assistant to a pushcart peddler who instructs him to walk the streets declaiming: "Pay cash clothes," but because of his poor English manages only to sing: "Pay cats coals" (189). But despite his inexpertness with the language, Max manages to become a secondhand clothes merchant on Hester Street by the end of his first week in America. His inability to pronounce the words of the pushcart peddler do not keep him down, nor does this inability with colloquial English keep him from learning the language of business, very much in the mold of David Levinsky. He tells Sara that he doesn't want to talk much, that "I talk enough all day, buying and selling" (192). Max condemns school and claims that money is the most important part of advancing one's self in the world, "Only dumbheads fool themselves that education and colleges and all that sort of nonsense will push them on in the world. It's money that makes the wheels go round. With money I can have college graduates working for me, for my agents, my bookkeepers, my lawyers" (199). For Sara, "The man seemed to turn into a talking roll of dollar bills..." (199). This is the ultimate logic of capital in which commodities are turned into money, and people are alienated from the use value of these items, as well as from real human relations with each other — he is a "talking roll of dollar bills," and "He could buy everything." Max, in Sara's eyes, is the kind of entrepreneur who mistakenly imagines that financial investment leads to emotional pay off: that he can "buy" a wife and children. For him, the family becomes the only commodity with use value, and is not just another part of the circulation of commodities in the system of exchange. On the other hand, Sara invests in education and college. She invests her books with the kind of positive magical fetishism that gives them life and substance: "Nothing was so beautiful as to learn, to know, to master by the sheer force of my will even the dead squares and triangles of geometry. I seized my books and hugged them to my breast as though they were living things" (201). While Max sees everything as being reducible to exchange value, Sara sees lifeless objects transformed into living things with a positive fetishism. These things, like the books, hold promise, or, like a featherbed, convey memory.[12]

In contrast to Max, Sara does not see money as buying family, but, rather, family — with all its struggles as well as its harmony — as an intellectual treasure. He values family by the measure of cash; she sees the lessons of emotional struggle as more valuable than money: "The fight with Father to break away from home, the fight in the cafeteria for a piece of meat — when I went through those experiences I thought them privations and losses; now I saw them treasure chests of insight. What countless riches lay buried under the ground of those early years that I had thought so black, so barren, so thwarted with want!" (223). Her profit is ambiguous. Certainly she draws on her ghetto privations, ironically, to gain a wealth of intellectual insight. But do these profits come at the expense of her groundedness in the ghetto community, or do they draw her back closer to Muhmenkeh? The fact that, by this point in the novel, Muhmenkeh has completely disappeared, suggests that her grounding presence was fleeting, that Sara has now become assimilated into an Anglo-American intellectual frame of mind, if not into the American dream of middle-class comfort.

But Yezierska seems to suggest that clothing has the potential to change everything. Sara's struggles with her father, with Max, and with the Anglo-American system of education and assimilation have reinforced her connection to the past — to Muhmenkeh. Her love of clothing, however, threatens to cut her off from the spiritually rich past. Once out of college, Sara declares, "The dark night of poverty was over. I had fought my way up into the sunshine of plenty" (238). Basking in that sunshine, she seems to adopt all the accoutrements of assimilated identity. She finds a neat and humble flat in which she realizes the ideals advocated by settlement houses and homes for women, an almost complete absence of what was considered vulgar ornamentation, and the achievement of "that marvelous thing, 'a place for everything and everything in its place'" (241). More importantly for our interest in clothing, Sara imitates the simple elegance she so admired in the garb of her fellow students at college: "Finally, I decided on a dark blue." Her first experience in a department store leads Sara not to ornamentation but to plainness: "Plain serge only! Yes. But more style in its plainness than the richest velvet. I tried it on in a beautiful fitting room lined with mirrors. From all angles I could see myself" (239). This newly minted "person of reason," now places herself at the center of her own vision. Both subject and object of her own gaze, Sara transforms herself from immigrant to *teacherin*. She has already learned that "it wasn't character or brains that counted. Only youth and beauty and clothes — things I never had and never could have" (220). But now she seems to have gained them, at least the clothes, which may not qualify her to do the work, but opens doors to that work. It is this investment in vestment (expenditure on clothes) that gains her a position at a local school, but threatens to separate her all the more from her origins. Her loss of the ethnic past can be seen most vividly in Sara's mother's death and funeral. It is during the funeral that Sara refuses to have, according to the Jewish traditional rite, a hole cut into her plain suit of blue serge. Yezierska leaves some ambiguity as to Sara's identity. Has she lost the intrinsic value of her initial investments — of self, of the past, of labor? Has she been so transformed that the wealth she gains is only an empty profit? What distinguishes Sara's profit from her father's loss and even from Max Goldstein's gains is that hers is grounded not in Old-World patriarchy, nor in an American capitalist traffic in commodities that transforms all objects into the negative fetishes of exchange value. Rather, hers is a profit made on the cultural capital of her particular past invested in the cultural and intellectual capital of the present and the future.

However, the conclusion of *Bread Givers* does not return to Muhmenkeh as the embodiment of the past. Rather, Sara finds a sense of place with Hugo Seelig, principal of the school where Sara teaches, a man who represents the combination of ethnic *shtetl* identity, and European Enlightenment values and their manifestation in American progressivism. At first, their relationship is based on his fine-tuning of her abilities in English pronunciation, suggesting both her continued grounding in East Side culture, and his escape from it. Once their professional relationship gives way to personal interaction, Hugo asks Sara, "What do you remember of Poland?" to which she replies, "Nothing — nothing at all. Back of me, it's like black night" (278). But Hugo narrates for her a past with a "mud hut ... cows, the chickens ... the dark rainy morning ..." and the journey to America (278). Sara recognizes the shared identity: "We talked one language. We had sprung from one soil." He tells her "You and I, we are of one blood." (278). But this shared identity cuts off the past, like a vestigial limn, rather than re-investing the present with elements of that past: "As I talked my whole dark past dropped away from me" (278). While Seelig orchestrates a rapprochement between Sara and her father, we are left with a sense that the kind of joy that Sara found in her investment of Muhmenkeh's money, stock, and advice is completely lost. Muhmenkeh herself has disappeared from the novel, and will not reappear in Yezierska's work until she writes a later novel, *Arrogant Beggar*, in which Muhmenkeh returns to ensure that the American future is invested with the rich Jewish cultural past.

Examining the historiography of immigrant self-fashioning in the United States, historian Virginia Yans-McLaughlin suggests: "*Shtetl* culture allowed expressions of female autonomy that easily translated into both labor activism and an ideology of a worker community in the United States."[13] By negotiating past, present, and future, Sara exhibits what McLaughlin has observed in Jewish immigrant oral narratives: that "Jewish descriptions of the self in history correspond with the actual history of the Jews, who, in order to survive as a people and make their way in the New World, cultivated a sense of responsibility to themselves and to others as well as an appreciation of power relationships and skills for dealing with them" (273). The relationship between Muhmenkeh and Sara suggests this kind of imagining of the "self in history." But the task of imagining the "self in history" led Yezierska — who *imagined* characters in stories, as well as a self in history — through various possibilities before hitting upon her most complete answer to the problem.

Refashioning Immigrant Women: Shenah Pessah and Sonya Vrunsky

While Sara makes an early profit, her later investments seem less profitable; they give her some financial and some emotional payback, but generally, her loss is greater than her gain. She loses her mother and a sense of continuity with her maternal past. She gains Hugo Seelig as a husband, and she reconnects somewhat with her father. But the kind of reward she gained in her association with Muhmenkeh seems lost forever, and is never mentioned after that first chapter. Her loss echoes other losses in Yezierska's work, other bad investments such as the giving away of family heirlooms and the loss of rich memories and the history they symbolize, and the selling of a character's sense of self for the gain of the dry and spiritually impoverished stock of Anglo-American intellectual life personified in recurring images of young and handsome scholars. Such loss and empty gain characterize Shenah Pessah and Sonya Vrunsky's narratives in "Wings" and *Salome of the Tenements*, respectively.

The 1920s, when these stories were published, witnessed "a remarkable shift in the way the average consumer allocated money: savings shrank and debt blossomed."[14] In this decade, the nineteenth century ideal of frugality and saving was replaced by the normalization of debt and credit. This normalization of debt influenced and was, perhaps, influenced by literary representation. In F. Scott Fitzgerald's *The Great Gatsby*, for example, the loan sharking of Meyer Wolfsheim, a Jewish gangster, is contrasted from Nick Carraway's trafficking in legitimate bonds. Ultimately, that novel, according to Michael Tratner, reflects a social milieu in which "private loans and lenders were still suspect, but ... were rapidly becoming a normal part of life" (74). As disorienting as it may have been, this shift had some clear boundaries, one in especial being the image of the Shylock.[15] Meyer Wolfsheim, in *Gatsby*, represents an ethnic stereotype that marked the limit of the normalization of debt. Debt was no longer dangerous, unless one was indebted to a Jew. Jewish writers themselves — including Yezierska — were unable to avoid this image in their own work, either subconsciously pandering to their readers, occasionally as a corrective to racist representations, or as a way of distancing their own Americanized identities from racial stereotypes.

As the wider American attitude towards money shifted from an ideology of parsimony to one of expenditure and debt, for Jewish immigrants, part of the process of assimilation involved "adapting to abundance."[16] For protagonists like Sonya in *Salome of the Tenements* (1923) and Shenah Pessah in "Wings"(1919) notions of borrowing and saving have a great deal to do with the ethnic past. What aspects of the ethnic past are to be saved? What aspects of a new ethnic identity must be borrowed? What, as in both Shenah's and Sonya's cases, must be pawned? In "Wings," Shenah pawns her past in order to borrow her future, to "pay" for it, as it were, in installments, and in *Salome of the Tenements*, Sonya borrows much more from Americanizing values than she saves from her ethnic past. Both literal and metaphoric debt and credit are at work in these stories. In both cases, it is, ironically, the Jewish pawnbroker — an image of the Shylock — who establishes the terms of ethnic and identitarian debt.

In "Wings," Yezierska brilliantly portrays the way in which objects vested with personal meaning become invested with monetary value as the immigrant owners of these *things* pawn them, thereby exchanging their Old-World memories for American upward mobility. As Shenah Pessah, the protagonist of this story from the collection *Hungry Hearts*, enters Zaretsky's pawn shop, she becomes keenly aware of how lifeless the objects on his shelves have become: "The weird tickings that came from the cheap clocks on the shelves behind Zaretsky, seemed to her like the smothered heart-beats of people who like herself had been driven to barter their last precious belongings for a few dollars."[17] These clocks can be contrasted to one on Shenah's mantle as she awaits the arrival of John Barnes — the Anglo-American sociologist with whom she is infatuated: its "ticking ... seemed to throb with the unutterable hopes compressed in her heart" (19). The lifeless items in Zaretsky's pawn shop represent the loss of the past, its transformation into a quantifiable amount of value, and its ultimate sale. As monetary value is created, emotional, aesthetic, familial, and ethnic values are lost. By contrast, the new American household objects — the ticking clock — express an as yet unattained future in Shenah's "unutterable hopes." In Zaretsky's "morgue of dead belongings" Shenah witnesses the transformation of the household object from a positive fetish to a negative fetish. As a positive fetish, the clock or coat or mattress draws on the cultural meanings of pre-capitalist societies in which household items speak history and memory. The status of household objects as gifts or as items of everyday use — in either sacred or mundane activities — saturates these items with familial, cultural, and ethnic memory.[18]

Karl Marx's coat went in and out of pawn to support his work as a writer, but Shenah's featherbed goes into pawn and stays there so that she can purchase a dress and hat with which to impress the Anglo-American object of her desire. The featherbed was a gift from her mother, her "last memory from Russia" (*Hungry Hearts* 15), the "only thing left from [her] dead mother" (14). The memory it contains and conveys is, more specifically, that of her mother's labor — her picking of feathers to make it over the course of many winters. When she pawns it to Zaretsky, she tells him that her mother "began it when I was yet a little baby in the cradle — and —," at which point Shenah covers "her face with her shawl" (16) and cannot continue telling the tale. The feathers ironically signal the "wings" of the title of this story, but this molting of the feathers of the past will allow her to gain her new wings of ready-to-wear garments, and the ability to fly into the heights of Anglo-American intellectual life — Barnes will teach her English and take her to the public library. The featherbed would traditionally have been an important part of a bride's trousseau in Russia, and the shawl with which she covers herself is transformed from a garment of modesty to a sartorial sign of shame. Thus, once she has pawned the featherbed her past becomes abject, and she becomes alienated from the objects that would connect her with that past and she prepares to "fly" up into the heights of an American future. She is a female ethnic Icarus whose upward mobility destroys the "wings" she inherited from her mother.

The "wings" that she hopes to gain are materially the hat and dress that she hopes will lift her out of the darkness of her basement flat as tenement janitress and carry her into the world of her "miraculous stranger," John Barnes.[19] The straw hat that Shenah purchases is adorned with cherries, and, because they remind her of "the green fields of her native Russia," she buys a dress of the "greenest, crispest organdie" (17). And yet, this choice not only derails Shenah's pursuit of class mobility but also further distances her from her past. First, the dress and hat comprise a pale substitute for the featherbed she has pawned. The hat and dress distance her from the very past of which the cherries seem to remind her because she has had to pawn the last real memory of Russia to gain them. Secondly, the gaudy colors and tacky adornment of her new outfit amplify her greenhorn ethnic identity rather than concealing it from John Barnes who values austerity and simplicity in women's dress in general and especially as a means of assimilation.

Shenah becomes painfully aware of her miscalculation, and of Barnes's disapproval, on their trip to the public library, the site of her discursive assimilation into American middle-class aspirations. Shenah notes "the librarians' simple attire" just when Barnes states that he "like[s] to see a woman's face above her clothes" (21). In the library, she feels not only his eyes, and the librarians' eyes upon her, but feels that "the electric lights are like so many eyes looking you over" (22). All of these eyes discipline Shenah into middle-class white American assimilation — through their gaze, she sees herself from an Americanizing viewpoint, and from this moment on she can let go of those memories vested in her mother's featherbed. A social worker (Barnes), and a librarian are agents of Americanization who usher Shenah into her new identity as she signs her name for a library card, a symbolic act of surrender to assimilation.

Much like Shenah, Sonya Vrunsky in *Salome of the Tenements* longs for the love of a young and handsome Anglo-American intellectual: John Manning, a philanthropist interested in the uplift and assimilation of Jewish immigrants. Also like Shenah, her attempt to win his love leads her to the door of a pawnbroker, Honest Abe Levy. Moreover, Sonya too comes to realize that her investments of labor and emotion in her dream of upward mobility and interethnic romance have amounted to a momentary loss of personal integrity. *Salome* centers on Sonya's realization that John Manning's charitable giving and his interest in the Jewish working class is a thin veneer beneath which hides not only a confused and dangerous sexuality, but also a sense of racial superiority that Manning is unable to shake, despite his ostensible disavowal of his family's classism and racism. Sonya, whose dream is to become a fashion designer of the people, learns that Jacques Hollins/Jaky Solomon, a celebrated Jewish designer, is more appropriate. However, the creation of a utopia of fashion — a "high" aesthetic for the "lower" classes — makes for a treacherous negotiation of race.[20]

However, *Salome of the Tenements* ultimately fails to recover Sonya's Jewish identity in at least two ways. First, it does not establish her Jewish identity in terms of cultural memory to begin with. Rather, it establishes Jewishness through the racialized portrayal of Honest Abe Levy the pawnbroker and Mr. Rosenblat, Sonya's landlord. And while the novel offers Jacques Hollins — a Jewish designer passing for an exotic Frenchman serving a Fifth-Avenue clientele — as Sonya's acceptable husband, he is acceptable only because he has successfully suppressed or shed his "primitive oriental" racial characteristics of the Eastside Jew, though he lapses into this characteristic in defending her from John Manning at the end of the novel.[21] Secondly, the narrative hinges on Sonya's mismanagement of her financial affairs specifically in her dealings with Honest Abe.[22] Sonya fails because she is unable to invest her future with a sense of her past, a sense of cultural memory, and this misplacement of identity is plotted out in the novel in terms of financial failure. Furthermore, Sonya's bad investment of self is mediated by three Jewish men whose identities reduce Jewishness to fairly broad racial stereotypes. Like Shenah, Sonya finds herself pleading with a pawnbroker to finance her romantic dream of marrying an American Adam. But by the time she meets Honest Abe, Sonya has already gained two important material requirements for her courtship with John Manning: a simple elegant dress designed by Jacques Hollins and a clean and newly painted apartment reluctantly supplied by the sexually threatening Jewish landlord, Mr. Rosenblat.

To gain the dress, Sonya has convinced Jacques/Jaky that designing a dress for her will make him worthy of his art. Jacques, formerly Jaky Solomon, is an Eastside Jewish designer trained in France. His work, while celebrated, is limited to meeting the demands and fulfilling the whims of wealthy American clients. She appeals to him not only in terms of how well he can design a dress, but also in terms of how he can refashion her identity. She tells him that she has come to him because only he can create "a dress that will express me — myself" (23). He is among those "clothes artists that could make me look like myself" (16). His status as an Eastside Jew passing as a French designer along with Sonya's own desire to emulate the standards of beauty set by Anglo-intellectual John Manning's doctrines of assimilation suggest that this refashioning of the self involves an estrangement of Jewishness. When Jacques sees her in his "Challais model," he sees her transformed, freed from her recognizably ethnic identity. What shared ethnicity they have is expressed not in a shared cultural memory, but in an identical racial essence, "a sharp personal thrill that came straight from the racial oneness of the two of them." At the end of the novel, once she has left John Manning and joined Jaky in a business and a romantic partnership, Manning comes to repent and reclaim Sonya only to confront Hollins who devolves into "the primitive oriental guarding his woman" (180). Thus, while Hollins/Solomon promises to produce a becoming vestment, and a vestment of becoming, he does nothing to transform an ethnic identity based not on becoming, but on being. Essence is all.

But before she goes through these ups and downs of assimilation, Sonya must gain not only a dress, but also a home. In a dress Hollins has custom-designed for her, Sonya approaches her landlord, Mr. Rosenblat, who has already rejected her request that he clean and paint her room — dismissing her because of her shabby clothes. She approaches him now refashioned, and he is "Fooled by a skirt and a pair of silk stockings" (54). He agrees to her demands: "I want first of all this ugly paper torn down. [...] My walls are to be painted a light soft gray to match this dress I'm wearing. I want white woodwork and a new hardwood floor. Not only do I want to have my own room done. But the entrance hall and the stairway to be plastered, painted and cleaned" (55).[23]

Both of these encounters — with Jaky/Jacques and Rosenblat — are financial ventures with two different versions of Jewish male stereotype. First, Jacques is the effeminate dandy passing as cosmopolitan intellectual. Rosenblat, on the other hand, is hyper-heterosexualized, and echoes the kind of sexual pathology associated with the first iteration of David Levinsky in Cahan's 1913 version of that narrative, embedded in editorial decisions at *McClure's* that rendered the figure threatening to women.[24] In this case, Rosenblat plays out one stereotype when Sonya approaches him in her "rags" and another when she is dressed as a refined assimilated Jewish woman. Ultimately, these stereotypes — Jacques as effeminate dandy, Rosenblat as usurer and sexual predator — focus on Sonya's failed costuming of self, not on her failed investments in a future identity. The dress Jacques makes for her does not, in fact, make her more her self, but, rather, leads her into a humiliating relationship with her Anglo-American object of desire. Moreover, Rosenblat's decoration of her domestic space makes her seem, to Manning, a frugal and efficient immigrant rather than the vamp who tricks her landlord into spending money on her apartment. Ironically, what she thinks will reveal her true self simply fabricates a more elaborate disguise.

By the time, then, that she meets Honest Abe, Sonya has convinced two Jewish men to assist her, either willingly or unwillingly, to achieve her goal of marrying an Anglo-American man. Honest Abe, even more than Jacques and Rosenblat, introduces the narrative knot to be unraveled later because it is the deal she strikes with him that later destroys her marriage with Manning. Having achieved a new identity through habit and habitation, Sonya need only furnish her room. Sonya goes to Honest Abe to borrow money for the simple elegant furniture she wishes to buy, but has nothing to leave as collateral. When Abe asks her "on what" he should loan her the hundred dollars, she says, "On my hopes for the future" (59). Interestingly, this appeals to Abe because, as we find out from his own lips, he too was, in his youth, in need of money that was not forthcoming. In the old country, he had been a singer in his synagogue, and then, "life had purpose and meaning. Then was he the soul and spirit of his people" (60). However, his swollen tonsils threatened to put an end to his calling in life. His only hope was to appeal to his neighbors for a loan. However, none of these gave or loaned him the thousand rubles necessary for surgery, and he did, eventually, lose his voice, and through it his "purpose and meaning," "the soul and spirit" that he would have given for his people. Honest Abe recognizes what it is to trade on one's hopes for the future. Thus, at first, Abe seems to appeal precisely to the kind of cultural memory that Sonya herself so lacks. But it becomes clear that he is simply out for financial profit.

Abe even writes up a contract of her deal with him: "For value received, I promise to pay Five Hundred Dollars, to Abraham Levy, within one month of my marriage to John Manning. In case the marriage is delayed beyond two months from date this note must be renewed" (64). Sonya does, in fact, marry Manning but only after a delay that increases her debt to Abe by another five hundred dollars. Once married, she cannot find a way of obtaining the money without Manning finding out. In order to avoid further debt, and to forestall Abe's "honesty"—he threatens to tell Manning everything—she leaves her engagement ring in pawn with him (141), pawning, as it were, the very future she hoped to achieve. Though he does not, like Rumplestiltskin, come for her child (she has none), Abe is like that folktale figure in that he allows her, symbolically, to spin gold out of straw, and he does come to claim his price, a price that threatens her dream come true. But, unlike the miller's daughter, Sonya has not achieved domestic bliss, and her marriage with Manning is already under strain when she herself confesses to her dealings with Abe.

Here, it is Abe who has made an investment. Clearly, he wishes to make a profit. Despite his story about his own youth, he wishes for financial, not emotional return, though, perhaps, there is some avenging spirit to his investment in Sonya. And, although Sonya is in debt, and not making an investment here, she is, so to speak, trading on futures. Her failed investment brings Sonya back to her first emotional/financial speculation: she returns to Jacques Hollins. After working in a restaurant and then as a "sample hand" for the garment house of Ziskind, Sonya joins Hollins both as romantic and business partner. It would seem that this reunion between two whose "racial oneness" had brought them together might promise a return to ethnic identity, a reclaiming of her Jewishness through union with a Jew. However, the bottom line is a net loss of Jewish cultural memory and a gain only of Jewishness as racialized identity.

First, unlike Shenah in "Wings," Sonya's Jewish past seems confused. Two stereotypes of immigrant identity collide to make her cultural memory hazy at best. Yezierska gives us two conflicting versions of her birth and childhood. Either Sonya embellishes her story of her childhood, or Yezierska leaves an inconsistency in her novel. Early in the novel, Sonya tells John Manning:

> Even as a little girl, holding on to my aunt's skirts, on the ship to America, the sea, the sky called to me 'Fly, fly, free, like the sea-gulls!' But I was roped off, herded, like cattle, in the steerage, choked with bundles and rags and sea-sick humanity. Then later, in the factory, tied to a machine, windows barred and iron doors — and yet my heart was still on wings [34].

Here, Sonya's past reflects the statistics, but is also a romantic rags-to-riches tale. From her "aunt's skirts" and the "bundles and rags" of steerage, she goes to the "machine" of the factory. She rises to the level of stenographer in a beautiful office, and finally the journalist she is now.

However, later in the novel, the narrator tells us that Sonya was "Born in the blackest poverty of a Delancey Street basement," but that this birth did not stop her from demanding that mother obtain "a red silk hair ribbon" for the first day of school "like the American children" (83). In one version of Sonya's past, she crosses the Atlantic, and leaves behind her past. In this version of her history, she is born into an American ghetto where the past is already lost. In this second version, Jewishness is much more a construct than in the first; identity is imagined from scratch, not remembered from another time and place. But rather than negotiating identity, a play on costuming as passing and passing on, this second construction of identity is tenuous and ephemeral. Sonya's own Jewishness seems less essencializing, but more easily shed than Abe's, Rosenblat's, or, even, Hollins's. Most importantly, her identity is not essential, but, rather, completely artificial.

The pawnbrokers Honest Abe Levy (in *Salome*) and Zaretsky (in "Wings") present a grotesque caricature of the Shylock who demands a pound of flesh, the last memory of the old world, or the ultimate dream of the new, leaving their customers in debt. In Yezierska's work, then, there is the investment of patriarchal order exemplified in Reb Smolinsky and Max Goldstein (*Bread Givers*), there is the pawning of cultural memory ("Wings"), the unconvincing costume of a seemingly new self (*Salome*), and the threatening sexuality of the oriental Jew (Hollins and Rosenblat in *Salome*), all of which impedes the female protagonists' claim upon personal integrity in the face of assimilation. But it is not only Jewish immigrant characters that make bad investments in their own identities. Indeed, the Anglo-American characters to which they often appeal are, also, frequently caught in the bonds and stocks of a dying social order that promises no returns.

Muhmenkeh's Shoes

In *Arrogant Beggar,* Muhmenkeh is an old Russian Jew who works as a dishwasher to save money for her granddaughter's passage to America; she is the embodiment of what remains of Adele Lindner's past in America and what hope she has for herself in the future in Yezierska's 1927 novel. Muhmenkeh's saving of each penny implies the past's investment in the future, the grandmother's investment in her granddaughter. Most importantly, the development of Muhmenkeh's relationship with Adele is played out symbolically through the material and metaphor of clothing, as well as the reformulation of financial investment into investment of self and labor.

The novel follows Adele Lindner from her East Side tenement to a Working Girls settlement house run by Mrs. Hellman, a wealthy philanthropist. Adele first sees her entry into the Hellman Home as her first step toward entering the American middle class. Furthermore, she meets and falls in love with Mrs. Hellman's son, Arthur, who is, himself, a patron of the arts. Gradually, however, she becomes disillusioned with both the Hellman Home, and with Arthur. Both come to represent, for her, the failure of American institutions of charity to acknowledge the dignity of those they presume to serve. She leaves the Home, and works to become independent. But it is ultimately her dependence on Muhmenkeh that drives her, after Muhmenkeh's death, to open a restaurant in the old woman's own tenement room and name it Muhmenkeh's Coffee Shop. She marries Hellman's musical protégé, Jean Rachmansky, and saves enough to send for Muhmenkeh's granddaughter, Shenah Gittel, from the Old World. The novel is a narrative of rags to riches, but one that attempts to re-imagine the American dream as something that allows for the living memory of the Old World to continue in the New. The anticipated arrival of Shenah, the matrilineal heir of Muhmenkeh, suggests Adele and Jean's anticipated arrival of a future invested with the past.

As with many of Yezierska's heroines, Adele is introduced to us with careful attention to her clothing. She is dressed in a tam and a coat, and she is as aware of this outfit as we are, as she sizes up her own appearance. Furthermore, clothing is an important part of her heritage, her father having been a tailor in Poland, and, much like Honest Abe in *Salome of the Tenements,* having been a singer whose hopes of success had been dashed. Adele, as narrator, notes that he would rob himself of lunch money in order to take her to the opera. In this link between his vocation of tailoring and his avocation of music we find one of Yezierska's recurring thematic treatments of dress — clothing is an art, and even the simplest tailor can be an artist. Adele's own art, we will learn by the end of the novel, is in the realm of cuisine. But throughout the novel, we also see a motif of clothing presented as either art or commodity, and therefore as an ambiguous marker of identity.

Once Adele enters the Hellmen Home, she becomes aware of how the gaudiness of her peers marks them as East Siders. She tries, as much as possible, to distinguish herself from them. On the evening that Mrs. Hellman and her son are to attend a celebration at the Home, Adele "decided on [her] plain black dress" which would differentiate her from the flamboyance of the "cheap fancy styles of the girls."[25] Adele's clothes are also contrasted from the "stooped shoulders, the baggy, shapeless coat" of Shlomoh Hershbein, her grad-student neighbor who falls in love with her (14). Cloth and clothing come to represent the difference between the East Side and the Working Girls Home. The tenement's stuffy old featherbeds hanging to dry, "dank with the smell of dead generations," are contrasted with the "smooth mattress between two fresh, clean sheets" that she finds in her room at the Home (26). Most importantly, for a young woman who will later become a restaurateur, Adele notes more than once the emblem of East Side domesticity: the oilcloth in the kitchen as ubiquitous adornment and practical covering.

Within the Hellman Home, Adele not only becomes more aware of how clothes can help her in the process of assimilation, she also begins to understand the unspoken dress codes that her patrons establish, and how they police such codes. The Hellman Home's system of surveillance and discipline is clearly established in order later to contrast this kind of "charity" with Muhmenkeh's way of giving. When Adele is given certain privileges and responsibilities that allow her to serve the patrons at their board meetings, she overhears the board members of the Hellman Home commenting on the clothes of the girls at the home. Most of the members are up in arms about what they see as the pretensions of the girls they are helping — their silks and furs transgressing unwritten sumptuary limits on how "shop girls" should dress. In fact, Adele is overhearing a debate that echoes the real debate that Yezierska must have heard in political and civil discourse over benevolent societies and settlement houses. Ellen Richardson, who founded the domestic science movement, was taken aback by the showiness of the clothing of poor immigrant girls: "Did you ever go down to one of the city settlements full of the desire to help and lift up the poor shop girl? There must be some mistake you thought. They looked better dressed than you did. Plumes on their heads, a rustle of silk petticoats, everything about them in the latest style." Yezierska's fictional Mrs. Stone — a member of the board of the Hellman Home — echoes these exact sentiments when she says, "The way they dress these days. Shop girls wearing silk stockings, fur coats. Where's it all leading to?" (*Arrogant Beggar* 63). In response to the real life attitudes of Richardson, Jane Addams advocated on behalf of immigrant women to dress as they would. In "The Subtle Problems of Charity," Addams wrote, "The poor naturally try to bridge the difference by reproducing the street clothes which they have seen; they therefore imitate, sometimes in more showy and often in more trying colors, in cheap and flimsy materials, in poor shoes and flippant hats, the extreme fashion of the well-to-do." While there is still a tone of condescension in Addams's critique of showy and trying colors, and of cheap and flimsy materials, her words are also a critique of the culture of consumption that implicates wealthy Americans as well in a ridiculous and "extreme fashion."[26]

The attitude that ultimately prevails in Yezierska's fictional reproduction of this debate, however, is the word of a certain "preacher of efficiency," one Mrs. Gessenheim, the only character whose name suggests the German Jewish background of the women who would have been running the Clara de Hirsch Home for working girls when Hattie Mayer—Yezierska's Americanized name—lived there around 1899.[27] She advocates a kind of economic efficiency and moral economy that begins to stifle Adele, and that echoes in the moral/economic code that Mrs. Hellman repeats to her later: a penny saved is a penny earned. Adele comes to realize that this economy produces what she calls the mortgaging of her own soul. She has been searching for a sartorial aesthetic that avoids the same showiness that her benefactors deplore, but in achieving such an aesthetic, she begins to suspect that her taste for clothes might have been policed and shaped by a system that denies her and other Jewish women not only their ethnic identity, but also their human dignity.

When Adele begins to be disillusioned with the charity of the home, a charity that belittles its recipients, her frustration is expressed more and more through the image of clothing and through the language of investment and debt. When she gets in trouble one night for returning home too late, it is because she has lingered too long on Essex Street back in the East Side looking for bargains on stockings and a spool of cotton (26–27). This incident underlines the importance of the discourse of efficiency and frugality in the settlement movement as Yezierska experienced it. Settlement houses for working women encouraged them to live frugally and to be home before a certain hour. Yezierska attempts, here, to show the impracticality of these ideas in settlements that are situated in middle-class neighborhoods. Adele walks to the East Side and in looking for pushcart stockings for 29c rather than stockings to be found near the home for 49c, she is delayed and gets in trouble. This is only the first in a series of hypocrisies in the novel.

When Mrs. Hellman decides to award Adele with a scholarship in Domestic Science at a Training School for women, she also gives Adele some second hand clothing. Adele might have profited from Thoreau's injunction to avoid any profession that requires new clothes. The school will help Adele "fit [her]self to serve in a large way" (44), and an apron becomes her badge of servitude (39). Adele is excited about the clothes, and takes stock of them: "An afternoon dress, a party dress, silk stockings with little holes, linen collars slightly frayed, a sweater a little worn at the sleeves. But one thing was almost new — a brown suit with a hat to match, just the thing that I would have chosen for myself if I ever had the money" (47). The clothes suggest a new self, one given to her by a white American philanthropist. It is a moment filled with possibilities — both liberating and confining.

Ultimately, this gift of clothing "turned into lead in my hands" when Adele observes in a mirror Mrs. Hellman wiping away Adele's kiss of gratitude. Mirrors are important symbolically in this novel, as they are in *Bread Givers*, "Wings," and "The Miracle." According to art historian Anne Hollander, while mirrors are sometimes used to verify objective evidence about the body — for plucking eyebrows or shaving — they are most often used to produce a flattering and self-deceptive image of the subject. Looking into a mirror "is at best an exercise in art, at worst one in self-deception — or at the very worst, perhaps a path to death and damnation."[28] The mirror in this scene reveals Hellman's betrayal of an honest expression of friendship and thanks. It is as if mirrors tell comforting lies when looked at directly — recall Shenah Pessah's reflected self in her broken bit of mirror in "Wings" — but reveal uncomfortable truths when viewed from an angle, revealing the other. The scene also leads immediately to another mirror image, this time Adele's own reflection in a store window, a moment similar to David Levinsky's reflected image in a store window when he first comes to America in Cahan's *The Rise of David Levinsky*. For Adele, as well, the self reflected in the window of a consumerist space underscores her feeling of alienation: "I caught a glimpse of myself in the mirror of a passing shop window. A worried stare lurked in my eyes. Thought I had on a more becoming hat and suit than I had ever worn in my life, yet I could not hold my head as high as before" (48). The shop window is a particularly charged surface on which to reflect the self. A portal into commodity fetishism, the window gives back a ghostly reflection of Adele's ideal, assimilated self. Having achieved, at least outwardly, the identity she has always desired — a costume of simple elegance — Adele realizes the fraudulent ego she has constructed out of the borrowed clothes of the rich, the imposed ideologies of a dominant class and ethnicity. She has, like so many of Yezierska's characters, been forced to see herself as others see her. She begins to see that she cannot rely on wealthy charitable Americans to construct an identity for her. But her disillusionment is not yet complete. There is one more step.

Mrs. Hellman has asked her to make a list of other items she will need once she begins her training in Domestic Science. The list she comes up with is composed primarily of clothing:

> Coat for winter $25.00
> Shoes 10.00
> Warm gloves 1.50
> Four pairs silk stockings .... 5.00 [50].

Hellman, however, proceeds to economize the list further, offering Adele one of her daughters "two new [coats] that she really doesn't need" (51). With this, Hellman imparts one of the economic lessons that will come to haunt Adele later in the novel: "a penny saved is a penny earned" (51). In terms of investment, this notion seems to impart a kind of moral economy. The list also brings Adele's hopes about her future down to the level of cold cash, which her benefactor gives only under certain circumstances. Adele begins to realize that she is giving her self away in exchange for $47.50 in U.S. currency.

Lost as to her own true loyalties after Hellman's rebuff, Adele sends for Shlomoh Hershbein, her old neighbor who has earned a Ph.D. in sociology, and it is to this Jewish sociologist, a young man nurtured on his deceased father's religious belief and his mother's care, that Adele confesses that her soul has been mortgaged. He comes to her with hopes of marriage, and his own attire becomes symbolic of his greenness. He wears a tie that is "too stiff and narrow," overcompensating for another tie that Adele had told him was "too broad and shapeless." By the end of their date, Shlomoh is left drenched and dripping—caught in the rain because he spent his car fare on flowers he had brought for Adele. But Shlomoh's greenhorn aesthetic is, in relation to Adele's borrowed clothes and borrowed sense of self, a sign of his authenticity, his unmediated sense of self, a subjectivity not constructed around white middle-class liberalism, but grounded in a transplanted *yiddishkeit*.[29]

Adele becomes increasingly aware that American society plays an all-or-nothing game. It urges the immigrant to speculate on the future, without investing the past into that future. This is a risky game to play: "But it isn't just the hash," she complains to Shlomoh, "It's this *mortgage on my soul* I've given them for letting me live here, for sending me to Training School" (58 emphasis added). What she had thought of as self help or uplift ends up being something very different, something best expressed through financial metaphors: a mortgaging of her past, a submission of who she was and is in exchange for very little in return. At the peak of her frustration, Adele expresses that frustration publicly when she has to deliver a speech thanking her patrons at the Hellman House. However, this moment becomes an occasion for expressing her repressed anger, and she concludes her speech with this accusation: "A pound of flesh you want for every ounce of help — worse than Shylocks! Shylock only wanted the man's flesh. You want his soul. You robbed me of my soul, my spirit. You robbed me of myself" (86). What she had earlier called the mortgaging of her soul for a decent place to live now becomes outright robbery. Furthermore, she turns the epithet of Shakespeare's stereotypical Jew back against her white patrons.

This, in fact, is the turning point in Adele's investment of self in America. Finding that she has bought the spiritual equivalent of junk stocks, she cuts her losses and returns to the East Side and there begins to invest not only in her future, but to reinvest in her past. Adele's relationship with an old woman of the Old World allows her to build a future sponsored and informed by her ethnic past. Muhmenkeh and her shoes play an important role in allowing Adele to invest her future with a bit of her past. Muhmenkeh, an old dish washer saving for her granddaughter's passage to America, enters Adele's life with the simple act of washing Adele's shirtwaist, as if to mark Adele's first step in a return journey to her East-Side self. Having left the Hellman Home in confusion and poverty, Adele is drawn to restaurant work out of sheer hunger. There she washes dishes alongside Muhmenkeh, whom she first sees merely as another old woman, a painful reminder of Old-World poverty and tenement life. Seeing things still through the worldview of assimilation, Adele is repulsed by the woman's age and shabbiness: "From under [her] lids" Adele sees in her mind's eye, "Mrs. Hellman's dining room." When she opens them she sees Muhmenkeh, a "shriveled old woman bent over the pile of greasy plates," and this woman "gave [her] the creeps" (92). Muhmenkeh is a "humped bunch of rags" (92). She wears a "rusty old coat," and Adele can't "bear to have her touch" her. The woman is "old enough for the grave" (93). Her age, her work, and, especially her clothing — rags and a rusty old coat — link her to the world that Adele has been running from for so long.

When Adele passes out from fatigue, Muhmenkeh takes her home and lets Adele sleep in her own featherbed, and when she awakes, it is as if Adele's vision has been changed and she now sees Muhmenkeh differently. She is the archetype of the poor huddled masses, the icon of the Old World, of maternal nurturing, and of home. This idea of Muhmenkeh is conveyed through the *music* of washing clothes: "There was something so familiar and reassuring in the steady rub, rub, rub of the washboard. The song without words of the poor" (94). At this moment, Adele experiences a rebirth: "Her leaning forward and pulling back at the tub was as soothing as rocking a child to sleep in the dusk. A long forgotten picture of my mother flashed up in me" (94). This rebirth connects Adele to her past and to a matrilineal inheritance. She is given a new lease on life, as it were, after having "mortgaged her soul" to the Hellman House.

Muhmenkeh's first gesture for the new Adele is to wash her shirtwaist. Scrubbing the waist as she does in the gray suds of the washtub saturates the garment in the "song without words of the poor." The clinical sanitized influence of the Home is replaced by an authentic and organic connection to something like home: Muhmenkeh represents "the real world I knew," and being with her is a "homecoming" (97). When Adele falls ill with flu, Muhmenkeh and her neighbor take care of her, with some clumsy help from Arthur Hellman who has begun to fall in love with his mother's ward after Adele's outburst at the Home. When he shows up with a nurse, however, Adele is put off by the nurse's "spick-and-span uniform" and prefers the ministering of her ragged Muhmenkeh (106). Most importantly, Adele wishes to avoid being personally or financially indebted to Hellman. Adele is now careful about how she invests — how she invests her labor, her money, and her self.

When Muhmenkeh dies, Adele sees Muhmenkeh's clothes as material metaphors keeping her memory alive. Clothes have a crucial function in memory and mourning. In *Bread Givers*, the clothing of the mourners at a Jewish funeral serve an especially symbolic purpose when they are cut in metonymical sympathy with the dead. In *Arrogant Beggar*, Muhmenkeh's clothes become highly symbolic objects, containing and conveying the essence of Muhmenkeh's identity into Adele's reconstructed self: "The day of Muhmenkeh's funeral, I made a bundle of her clothes to give to Mrs. Mirskey. I went about quietly, gathering up her gray flannel petticoat, her black stockings, stiff with darns, her faded woolen dress, rubbed thin at the side where she carried her basket" (123). This is a crucial passage that demonstrates a great deal about the social and psychological function of clothing for poor immigrants in New York in the 1920s. First, gathered as a gift rather than an estate, the clothes act to weave a community together: Adele, Mrs. Mirskey, and Muhmenkeh are linked in an intergenerational web that binds past, present, and future — a temporal and spatial community held together literally and symbolically by garments. Secondly, Yezierska brings the reader as much as possible into the materiality of the clothes. The darned stiffness of the stockings makes the description almost palpable, and brings the clothing out of their strictly figurative function and, as it were, into the reader's hands. Most importantly, the material of the clothes bears the imprint of the human body and the mark of human labor, as the dress is "rubbed thin at the side where she carried her basket." The clothing embodies Muhmenkeh not only in a metaphorical but also and especially in a material way. Especially in contrast to the clothes that Adele is forced to borrow from Hellman's daughter, Muhmenkeh's clothes wrap Adele in her past, honor that past, and convey the dignity the middle-class garments had stolen from her.

Adele gives the clothes to Mrs. Mirsky, but she is unable to give up one item in the old woman's wardrobe: Muhmenkeh's shoes: "Her coat, her shawl, everything went. But when I picked up the cracked old shoes from under the bed, they seemed too much a part of Muhmenkeh for me to give up" (123). For Yezierska, Muhmenkeh's shoes are an authentic emblem of memory, labor, and a reclaimed and affirmed ethnicity. Adele reflects: "I put my hand into the torn lining, stained with sweat and mud. The crooked heels, worn almost to the sole. The toes split from patient trudging through endless streets, pushing up countless stairs. They were Muhmenkeh herself" (123). Muhmenkeh's clothing and especially her shoes become integrated completely into the material and spiritual life of a community. They convey the past.

However, Yezierska does not stop at re-imagining the social function of clothes out of exchange value and back into the life of the ethnic community. She also attempts to re-imagine the social function of investment. Figuratively, we cannot ignore the obvious suggestion that Adele must fill Muhmenkeh's shoes, and she does this in two ways, both involving financial, personal, and labor investment. She transforms Muhmenkeh's room into Muhmenkeh's Coffee Shop — which becomes a space of gustatory and intellectual nourishment for the Lower East Side — and, secondly, Adele takes on Muhmenkeh's project of saving for her granddaughter's passage to America. In these two related ways, Yezierska shows how investment need not be speculation on a future divorced from the past, but, rather, the reinvestment of the values of the past into the future. The novel ends with Adele and her new husband — the Polish composer, Jean Rachmansky — waiting for Shenah Gittel (Muhmenkeh's granddaughter) to disembark presumably at Ellis Island. When they see her walking toward them, "out of the many faces, we saw Muhmenkeh's face — Muhmenkeh's grandchild coming toward us" (152).

Conclusion

Behind this highly sentimental ending is the most serious of comments on a humanizing ratio of debt and investment. The last third of the novel is filled with references to indebtedness. Adele, in the Home, was mortgaging her soul to the idea of Americanization. Now, however, she takes up Muhmenkeh's "penny-to-a-penny" savings (111). When Arthur Hellman offers to pay Shenah Gittel's passage, Adele refuses. "Call it a loan," he says," but, arrogant beggar that she is, she declines. She sees that this, too, would be the same mistake she has already made with Arthur's mother. She responds in the same way when he proposes marriage. And, again, at the end of the novel, once she has saved enough to bring Shenah to America, Jean calls her a "funny little philanthropist [...] walking nobly in the footsteps of Mrs. Hellman" (151). However, Jean adds that the relation of benefactor and ward are much different, especially in his own relationship with her: "I ought to feel guilty for taking so much from you. But I don't. I love to be indebted to you" (152). One of the most important comments the novel makes is not only that commodities should be re-imagined away from their role in capitalist consumer culture and into their material function in an ethnic community, but also that other capitalist relations between "debtors" and "investors," between philanthropists and the poor should and can be re-imagined in ways that honor human dignity.

7. The Clothing of the American Frontier; or How the West Was Worn in Willa Cather

FOR HERMIONE LEE, THE POPULAR side of Willa Cather—her "memorializing of the pioneers and immigrants of the Western states and her disenchantment with the America of the 'closed frontier'"—is "very much of its time, and is strongly in sympathy with [Frederick Jackson] Turner's thesis."[1] Reworking Turner's three-stage development of the frontier, Cather, in "Nebraska: The End of the First Cycle," divides the settlement of the West into three successive generations, the third one of which "want to buy everything ready-made: clothing, food, education, music, pleasure."[2] Cather opens her list with clothes, and it is precisely in the recurring sartorial motif that she performs a literary historiography of the West similar to, though in important ways critical of the Turner hypothesis, especially Turner's personification of the frontier in the person and attire of the "frontiersman."[3]

Both Turner and Theodore Roosevelt refer to the garments of the frontiersman in their histories of the American West.[4] Roosevelt even saw the appropriation of Indian dress as crucial to what he called *The Winning of the West*. In the first stage of Turner's thesis, the "colonist" is still mastered by nature, the wilderness "finds him *a European in dress, industries, tools, modes of travel, and thought.*" The first settlers' European garb must be stripped away and replaced with more appropriate attire: The frontier "strips off *the garments of civilization* and arrays him in the hunting shirt and the moccasin."[5] Roosevelt provides an even more direct reference to the attire of the pioneer, describing a whole outfit characterizing the figure and achievements of the barely civilized pioneer:

> The backwoodsman's dress was in great part borrowed from his Indian foes. He wore a fur cap or felt hat, moccasins, and either loose, thin trousers, or else simply leggings of buckskin or elk-hide, and the Indian breech-clout. He

was always clad in the fringed hunting-shirt, of homespun or buckskin, the most picturesque and *distinctively national dress ever worn in America*. It was a loose smock or tunic, reaching nearly to the knees, and held in at the waist by a broad belt, from which hung the tomahawk and scalping-knife.[6]

Roosevelt's words here aim not only at writing history, but also at creating myth — creating an iconic image of national identity. Simple attire made from domestic materials (that is, materials not imported from England), had long symbolized republican ideals, political independence, and democracy in the United States.[7] Roosevelt seems to find a different kind of virtue in the simple dress of Americans. For him, the backwoodsman represents Europeans' inevitable conquest of America and its native people. The simple attire of the backwoodsman embodies the strenuous life of imperial ambition and national responsibility.

However, Roosevelt's celebration of Western expansion did not go unchallenged. In contrast to Turner and Roosevelt, Stephen Crane uses sartorial satire to represent and deconstruct the myth of the frontier in "The Bride Comes to Yellow Sky." When Scratchy Wilson, the town gunslinger, first appears, his outlaw identity is undercut by ironic reference to his clothes:

> A man in a maroon-colored flannel shirt, which had been purchased for purposes of decoration and made, principally, by some Jewish women on the east side of New York, rounded a corner and walked into the middle of the main street of Yellow Sky.... And his boots had red tops with gilded imprints, of the kind beloved in winter by little sledding boys on the hillsides of New England.[8]

On the one hand, Crane's story reinforces the Turner thesis: for Scratchy and those like him, the frontier is closed, and they are left out. At the same time, Crane critiques any nostalgia for the rugged past of the West because the holdouts from that era are not pathetic but laughable. It is those like Jack Potter and his wife, the sons of Boston Brahmins sledding down New England hills, and Jewish women in New York factories — or, rather, the bosses of Jewish women in New York factories — who really win the West.

Crane's critique also points out the increasingly important practice of conspicuous consumption, even among the supposedly hardy, independent, and practical pioneers of the American West. His portrait of the newlyweds underscores this point:

> A newly married pair had boarded this coach at San Antonio. The man's face was reddened from many days in the wind and sun, and a direct result of his new black clothes was that his brick-colored hands were constantly performing in a most conscious fashion. From time to time he looked down respectfully at his attire. ... The bride was not pretty, nor was she very young. She wore a dress of blue cashmere, with small reservations of velvet here and there and

with steel buttons abounding. She continually twisted her head to regard her puff sleeves, very stiff, straight, and high. They embarrassed her [347].

Jack Potter and his new wife are clearly conscious of their own clothing. Neither seems particularly comfortable, but Jack, at least, regards his own clothes (not necessarily his own self) with respect while she regards hers with embarrassment. In either case, they belie any notion of the settlers of the frontier as hardworking pioneers whose simple attire speaks eloquently of their hardy lives.

Somewhere between Roosevelt's archetypal backwoodsman and Crane's laughable cowboy Willa Cather produced a veritable compendium of the clothing of the American frontier. Cather deals with American self-fashioning, and, ultimately, she relates the craft of the dressmaker to her own craft as novelist and to the task of the "historian" of the American West in three ways. First, many of Cather's characters are ill-suited for the West, like Turner's colonist attired and limited by his European clothes. These characters cling to a European identity, consume conspicuously, and/or masquerade in inauthentic costumes. A second set of characters represent the pioneer ideal both in their actions and in their garments. Cather's portraits of Scandinavian immigrant women in particular — Alexandra Bergson (*O Pioneers!*) and Thea Kronborg (*The Song of the Lark*) — emphasize their deft ability to refashion identity. Thirdly, the craft of the dressmaker appears as a parallel to the art of the novelist and the scholarship of the historian. Lena Lingard in *My Ántonia* and Augusta in *The Professor's House* work in tandem with characters who narrate: Jim Burden as classicist and narrator, and Professor St. Peter as historian and narrator of the nation. Most importantly, the thematic and narrative links that Cather makes between clothes and the writing of history in *The Professor's House* suggest a conception of American national identity fashioned upon distinctly imperial designs: St. Peter's writing of conquest (the title of his book is *Spanish Adventurers in North America*) is made possible and inspired by, in large part, Augusta's work on the family's clothes.

Dudes and Dandies

A number of dandies, conspicuous consumers, masqueraders, and degenerate cowboys people Cather's novels of the American West. In her narratives of how the West was won, Cather includes portraits of those unable to gain the West for themselves. This pattern within her work produces critiques not only of those who cling too tightly to a narrow European past, but also those who perpetuate old rivalries, and even those who exemplify the degeneration of Turner's or Roosevelt's frontiersman ideal.

Old-World dandyism cannot survive in the American West. Frank Shabata — Marie's jealous husband in *O Pioneers!* — is a case in point. His inability to shed his "Bohemianism" displays his deeper inability to assimilate into the American frontier. Frank "had a way of drawing out his cambric handkerchief slowly by one corner, from his breast-pocket, that was melancholy and romantic in the extreme." Marie's father "characterized Frank Shabata by a Bohemian expression which is the equivalent of stuffed shirt." In recalling his first appearance on the Great Divide, the narrator reflects that "He was easily the buck of the beer-gardens, and on Sunday he was a sight to see, with his silk hat and tucked shirt and blue frock coat, wearing gloves and carrying a little wisp of a yellow cane."[9] These visible and sartorial images of his dandyism and his abiding European past indicate his inability to become a farmer and frontiersman. He may *do* some of the things required of the pioneer, but he is unable to become one. Alexandra Bergson reflects that he "had flung himself at the soil with savage energy" (209), but by the end of the novel he declares — in prison and stripped of his Old-World attire — "I guess dat place all go to hell what I work so hard on ... I not care a damn" (282).

Marie says that "Frank would be all right in the right place," but his dandyism is a social handicap in the brave new world of the American frontier, and Frank's "little wisp of a yellow cane" is an especially important marker of his inability to transform his identity. One winter evening, while she and Marie are poking around Marie and Frank's attic in search of crochet patterns for an old neighbor, Alexandra discovers Frank's old clothes, including "a slender elastic yellow stick" which he had "brought from the old country." Marie calls it "foolish" and Alexandra says, "He must have looked funny!" But Marie points out that his style depended on context: "No, he didn't, really. It didn't seem out of place. He used to be awfully gay like that when he was a young man" (233). Like the "foreign stamps" (234) that Marie also finds in her attic, this cane is Frank's index of foreignness. Cather returns to Frank's foreignness at the end of the novel, after he has shot and killed Marie and Emil, and is now in prison for his crime of passion. When she first sees Frank in his prison uniform, Alexandra "tried not to see his hideous clothes" (281). For Alexandra, "Frank seemed to have undergone a change of personality" (292), and to restore her former image of him, Alexandra, again, recalls the yellow cane, a mnemonic wand she uses to change this frog back into the prince he might have been in an urban European context.

> Alexandra remembered the little yellow cane she had found in Frank's clothes-closet. She thought of how he had come to this country a gay young fellow, so attractive that the prettiest Bohemian girl in Omaha had run away with him. It seemed unreasonable that life should have landed him in such a place as this. She blamed Marie bitterly [282].

The cane points to the past and the Old Country where Frank belongs. It points out his dandiacal body, to borrow a phrase from Thomas Carlyle, who described the Dandy as "a Clothes-wearing Man, a Man whose trade, office and existence consists in the wearing of Clothes." Carlyle states that "as others dress to live, [the Dandy] lives to dress," and Frank seems to follow this model. Frank is unable to shed his clothes as Thoreau would have the American citizen do in moments of personal crisis and transformation.[10] This inability to shed his sartorial skin prevents Frank from becoming a new man and taking those steps necessary in the mutual transformation of land and body, of landscape and self, that Turner imagined as producing the American nation and character.

Similarly, in *My Ántonia*, Mr. Shimerda's fastidiousness about his own wardrobe and his inability to keep his family well-clothed mark him as an inassimilable immigrant and a failed pioneer. Despite being "a weaver by trade," Shimerda is better suited to making "tapestries and upholstery materials" than to fashioning the rugged clothes of the West; his work is distinctly domestic and decorative rather than rustic and practical.[11] In the Nebraska winter, the inadequacy of the father's and the entire family's wardrobe becomes clear when Otto Fuchs tells the Burden family that the Shimerdas "ain't got but one overcoat among 'em over there, and they take turns wearing it." In fact, their "crazy boy," Marek, "never wears the coat" (47). Shimerda takes to making rabbit-skin caps, but these, too, are woefully inadequate for frontier winters, and present a marked contrast to Anton Jelinek's "long wolfskin coat" (68). Jelinek, who comes to help the Shimerdas after the father's suicide, seems well-suited for the frontier.

Mr. Shimerda's suicide is, itself, marked by his attention to dress, a fastidiousness completely out of keeping with the rugged, free, and open style of Jelinek and others. Again, Otto, whose own chaps, boots, and spurs mark him as a cowboy, takes note of Shimerda's attention to sartorial details in planning and executing his own death:

"He shaved after dinner, and washed hisself all over after the girls had done the dishes. Ántonia heated the water for him. Then *he put on a clean shirt and clean socks*, and after he was dressed he kissed her and the little one and took his gun and said he was going out to hunt rabbits. He must have gone right down to the barn and done it then. He layed down on that bunk-bed, close to the ox stalls, where he always slept. When we found him, everything was decent except"—Fuchs wrinkled his brow and hesitated—"except what he couldn't nowise foresee. *His coat was hung on a peg*, and his *boots was under the bed*. He'd took off that silk neckcloth he always wore, and folded it smooth and stuck his pin through it. He *turned his shirt at the neck and rolled up his sleeves*" [63, emphasis added].

Even after his death, the inadequacy of his *production* of clothing marks him as an inassimilable immigrant. At his funeral, Ántonia is wearing "the rabbit-skin hat her father had made for her" while her father is "draped in a black shawl" and his head "bandaged in white muslin, like a mummy's" (75).

Like Old-World dandies, American conspicuous consumers are also important figures in Cather's characterization of those ill suited for the frontier. Clothing as a sign of pecuniary waste figures prominently in *The Professor's House* when Tom Outland goes to Washington, D.C. to get help in protecting the artifacts he and Roddy Blake have unearthed at the Blue Mesa. He finds only bureaucrats concerned with their own advancement, more interested in their own suits than in the Mexican blankets or cloth-wrapped remains of Pueblo mummies. The official Tom works with is Mr. Bixby, who is "in office" in the War Department. Tom takes note of his and his wife's "slavery" to pecuniary culture, which is represented in the satin dress Mrs. Bixby requires for a reception given by the Secretary of War:[12]

> Then for a week they talked about nothing but what Mrs. Bixby was going to wear. They decided that for such an occasion she must have a new dress. Bixby borrowed twenty-five dollars from me, and took his lunch hour to go shopping with his wife and choose the satin. That seemed to me very strange. In New Mexico the Indian boys sometimes went to a trader's with their wives and bought shawls or calico, and we thought it rather contemptible. On the night of the reception the Bixbys set off gaily in a cab; the dress they considered a great success. But they had bad luck. Somebody spilt a claret-cup on Mrs. Bixby's skirt before the evening was half over, and when they got home that night I heard her weeping and reproaching him for having been so upset about it, and looking at nothing but her ruined dress all evening [210].

Because of this and other signs of their submission to invidious comparison, the civil servants Tom encounters strike him as "people in slavery, who ought to be free" (211).

Louie Marsellus, in *The Professor's House*, is both conspicuous consumer and dandy. Like his brother who is "engaged in the silk trade" in China (26), has an eye for clothing and cloth. When he first sees the Mexican blanket that becomes a key metaphor of family, community, nation, and empire in *The Professor's House* (see my discussion below), he wants to acquire it not as an heirloom but as a commodity. Louie wants it only as an item of luxury, seeing neither its importance as a marker of identity (Roddy's "skin") nor its symbolic signification of friendship and trust between Roddy and Tom. Dressed in his "golf stockings, and a purple jacket with a fur collar," as he enters St. Peter's study Louie "pounce[s] upon the purple blanket, thr[ows] it across his chest, and, moving aside the wire lady, studie[s] himself in Augusta's glass. 'And a very proper dressing-gown it would make for Louie, wouldn't it?' Louie says in a self-congratulatory way" (144). Louie is interested in the blanket as an adornment for his dandiacal body.

Double Cross-Dressing: The Ambiguous Gender and Ethnicity of the Pioneer

Cather scholars have long been concerned with what Susan Gubar originally called authorial disguise. Since Gubar, Eve Kosofsky Sedgwick, Judith Butler, and others have addressed Cather's destabilization of gender and sexuality through cross-dressing and masquerade.[13] Cather's own authorial cross-dressing — beginning with her ghost writing of S.S. McClure's autobiography — usually involves both the crossing of gender *and* of ethnicity. In the McClure autobiography, we see Cather write in the voice of an Irish-American man, telling the story of immigration and rise to prominence. With the autobiographical amalgam that Gubar associates with *My Ántonia*—Jim Burden the Anglo-American man and Ántonia the Czech immigrant woman — Cather dons a costume of national origin and of gender. We could add to these figures Cather's various protagonists, many of which are at least partly autobiographical: Thea Kronborg is, perhaps, the clearest case, especially as discussed by Susan Rosowski.

Cather's costuming of her characters, like her authorial and autobiographical masquerades, is a complex element of her work. Costuming points both to the successful appropriation of exotic identities — just as the frontiersman adopts the dress of the American Indian — and to a failed performance of identity. In some instances, costume expresses the essential self of the wearer, at other times costume fails to convey that essence. Most importantly, costume occasionally points to the persistence of the past — in the cases of Marie in *O Pioneers!* and in the cases of Louie Marsellus and Scott McGregor in *The Professor's House*.

In *O Pioneers!*, the costuming of Emil and Marie points to Emil's successful but ill-advised appropriation of a Mexican aesthetic and to Marie's inability to transcend her European past. When Emil Bergson, Alexandra's younger brother, returns from a one-year journey through Mexico, Alexandra takes him to a costume party. Cather describes Emil as:

> a strikingly exotic figure in a tall Mexican hat, a silk sash, and a black velvet jacket sewn with silver buttons. Emil had returned only the night before, and his sister was so proud of him that she decided at once to take him up to the church supper, and *to make him wear* the Mexican costume he had brought home in his trunk. "All the girls who have stands are going to wear fancy costumes," she argued, "and some of the boys. Marie is going to tell fortunes, and

she sent to Omaha for a Bohemian dress her father brought back from a visit to the old country" [*O Pioneers!* 240, emphasis added].

Marie's costume is also exotic, and points to her inability to become American: "Marie wore a short red skirt of stoutly woven cloth, a white bodice and kirtle, a yellow silk turban wound low over her brown curls, and long coral pendants in her ears" (243). But unlike Emil's costume—which is an exotic masquerade, the adoption of the clothes of another, more picturesque national identity—Marie's costume links her to her own origin; it expresses a racial essence while Emil's enacts a cultural performance. Marie's costumed mystique has more in common with her husband, Frank's dandyism than it does with her lover, Emil's exoticism. Marie is, in fact, drawn to Emil's exoticism; she asks him: "Do the men wear clothes like that every day, in the street?" Grabbing Emil "by his sleeve," Marie says: "Oh, I wish I lived where people wore things like that! Are the buttons real silver? Put on the hat, please. What a heavy thing! How do you ever wear it?" (243). Marie's excitement registers a longing to be somewhere other than the American frontier, and, at the same time, conveys a desire for Emil as other. Ultimately, it is Emil and Marie's mutual desire for each other's costumed identities that leads to their affair and ultimately to their deaths.

Cather's exoticization of Emil in Mexican garb is similar to David Spurr's characterization of Stephen Crane's depictions of Mexico. Spurr writes that Crane's "aesthetic functions as a form of colonization in itself, relegating Mexico to the status of an object to be appreciated for its beauty, pathos, and passion. Simultaneously, however, this cultivation of an aesthetic ideal opens up a space for domination in the realm of concrete practice." For Spurr, Crane can "escape the obligations of power by cultivating a purely aesthetic view" through the language of the painter. In Crane's aesthetic of Mexico, "the peasant remains a figure of sheer passivity." Similarly, Cather aestheticizes Mexican identity, but through costume and song, rather than through the aesthetics of painting, as does Crane. However, the result is similar to Crane's rhetoric of colonization that "sees the essence of Mexico in song and romance."[14] While Cather's depiction of Mexico is mediated through her narrator and through Marie's desire, it is clear from this image (and from the image of a Mexican blanket to be discussed later in this chapter), that Cather performs what we might call an aesthetic Mexicanismo in which Mexican identity—like the American Indian dress from which the frontiersman borrows—comes to be appropriated as a surrogate for an American, albeit, a failed American identity.

Another instance of costuming in Cather's work suggests that some Americans hold on too tightly to their European past, and as such play out national conflicts best left behind in Europe — or the "Old World" more generally, including the "Orient." When, in *The Professor's House,* Professor Godfrey St. Peter dresses up his sons-in-law for a tableau vivant to "commemorate the deeds of the early French explorer among the Great Lakes," he relishes the comic element of costuming Scott McGregor as the Plantegent and Louie Marsellus as Salah ud-Din.

> He posed his two sons-in-law in a tapestry-hung tent, for a conference between Richard Plantegent and the Saladin, before the walls of Jerusalem. Marsellus, in a green dressing-gown and turban, was seated at a table with a chart, his hands extended in reasonable, patient argument. The Plantegent was standing, his plumed helmet in his hand, his square yellow head haughtily erect, his unthoughtful brows fiercely frowning, his lips curled and his fresh face full of arrogance. The tableau had received no special notice, and Mrs. St. Peter had said dryly that she was afraid nobody saw his little joke. But the Professor liked his picture, and he thought it quite fair to both the young men [59–60].

Not only are Scott and Louie dressed in European and Oriental costume, respectively, they are also posed in roles of ancient Old-World rivalry and racial and religious antagonism. St. Peter, as a character, is not necessarily focused on these connotations. What he sees is the comic irony of costumes revealing the real Scott and Louie — the real Scotsman and the real Semite — rather than covering those true identities. But for Cather, perhaps, and for her readers, the broader questions of race, civilization, and culture come to the fore in this image of Saxon stubbornness and Oriental inscrutability. Costuming indicates the persistent tyranny of the Old World.

Clearly, then, some images of dress in Cather reinforce Turner's notion of the closing of the American frontier. In Cather's fiction, those stuck in European (or urban, or exotic) costumes are not true frontiersmen, nor can they contribute substantively to the winning of the West. However, what is interesting about Cather's sartorial motif is that she does not spare the frontiersman himself from her social satire. Cather seems to suggest, in *A Lost Lady* (1925), for example, that the frontiersman could, at least in succeeding generations on the frontier, degenerate into a perversion of the iconic figure to be found in Turner or Roosevelt's histories. Like Stephen Crane's Scratchy Wilson, Cather's Ivy Peters is a parody of the frontiersman, but while Crane's image is that of comic irony, Cather's Ivy represents a darker caricature, one in which the frontiersman comes across as hideous and savage. Also like Crane's Scratchy, Ivy is contrasted to conspicuous consumers who are no less the objects of a social satire, though again one that is more tragic or pathetic than comic.

Early in *A Lost Lady*, Ivy is "dressed in a shabby corduroy hunting suit, with a gun and a game bag;" he "never wore a straw hat, even in the hottest weather," but wore instead "a heavy black felt hat."[15] Ivy is an example of the ugly side of the rugged outdoorsman or of Roosevelt's notion of the individual living the strenuous life for the glory of his nation's imperial destiny. "He was an ugly fellow, Ivy Peters, and he liked being ugly" (15). When Neil Herbert, the novel's protagonist and the focus of the novel's pathos, returns from college, Ivy notices him on the train, taking special note of Neil's attire. The stark contrast between the two characters favors Neil's tastefully understated gray and blue, and dramatizes Ivy's childish costuming of self: "As he strolled through the Pullman he noticed among the passengers a young man in a grey flannel suit, with a silk shirt of one shade of blue and a necktie of another. After regarding this urban figure from the rear for a few seconds, *Ivy glanced down at his own clothes with gloating satisfaction*. It was a hot day in June, but he wore the black felt hat and ready-made coat of winter weight he had always affected as a boy" (87 emphasis added). His affectation of this style of dress reinforces his inappropriate use of the land — his usurping of the frontier — because what the Forresters had kept as marsh land, a kind of wildlife preserve, he transforms into wheat crop grown not for sustaining a population but for making a profit. Mrs. Forrester — and her ailing husband — are now under his control just as surely as the woodpecker was under his black felt hat at the opening of the novel.

At a party given by Mrs. Forrester, the young people in attendance express a concern for clothes, a concern that exposes both those ill suited for life in the West through their inappropriate and ugly attire (Ivy), and those concerned only with the new and expensive: "They were talking about clothes; Joe Simpson, who had just inherited his father's clothing business, was eager to tell them what the summer styles would be" (136). Here, Cather is certainly critiquing a younger generation's concern with things, with "buying whatever is expensive and ugly,"[16] but the real target of the satire in this scene is, again, Ivy who takes his peers to task for their interest in fashion: "You fellows are like a bunch of girls" he says, "always talking about what you are going to wear and how you can spend your money. Simpson wouldn't get rich very fast if you all wore your clothes as long as I do. When did I get this suit, Joe?" (136–37). In having this ugly and savage character accuse his friends of talking "like a bunch of girls," Cather addresses the problem of gender in the construction of the frontiersman archetype. Earlier in the novel, when he is about to blind the woodpecker in the Forresters' marsh-land, he accuses Neil of being a "Miss Female" for not wanting to injure the bird. Ivy's hyper-masculinity seems to represent the perversion of the image of the frontiersman made famous by Turner, and is part of a wider gendered critique of the discourse of the frontier that leads to Cather's own equally iconic figures, like Alexandra Bergson whose own cross-dressing (she wears a man's coat) only reinforces her as an image of the frontiers*woman*.

While Cather *does* depict a degenerate version of the frontiersman in Ivy Peters, she includes portraits of men who are, in fact, model woodsmen. In *My Ántonia*, much is made of the inadequacy of Mr. Shimerda's rabbit-skin caps. The Shimerdas are, generally, a family bereft of clothing appropriate to the frontier, and the father's handcrafted hats are sorry excuses for the woodsman's outfit. By contrast, Anton Jelinek appears shortly after Shimerda's death not only to help his countrymen in need, but also to provide an example of how to dress for the West: "I remember exactly how he strode into our kitchen in his felt boots and long wolfskin coat, his eyes and cheeks bright with the cold. At sight of grandmother, he snatched off his fur cap, greeting her in a deep, rolling voice which seemed older than he" (67). In boots, cap, and coat, Jelinek epitomizes the frontiersman but a frontiersman fashioned both from his encounter with the frontier *and* by Old-World tailoring: "Jelinek put on his long wolfskin coat, and when we admired it, he told us that he had shot and skinned the coyotes, and the young man who 'batched' with him, Jan Bouska, who had been a fur-worker in Vienna, made the coat" (70). Jelinek is all that Ivy fails to be.

If Cather critiques the perversion of the frontiersman in the figure of Ivy Peters, she also, as is well known, rethinks the image of the pioneer as woman. As noted above, Cather's gendered cross-dressing has been an important part of Cather criticism for almost twenty-five years, beginning with Susan Gubar's "Blessings in Disguise" (1981).[17] However, very few of these critics, with the exception of Katrina Irving, have noted the link between Cather's gendered cross-dressing and what we might call her ethnic cross-dressing.[18] On one level, this chapter is a consideration of Cather's use of ethnic cross-dressing. Specifically, in examining a character like Alexandra Bergson, for example, we must read her donning of masculine dress in relation to Cather's use of a Scandinavian woman as protagonist — indeed, heroine — of a Romance of the American Midwest.

Imperial Designs

Cultural historian Patricia Williams has observed that specifically ethnic traditions informed dress adaptation among immigrant women in the Midwest. While Norwegian immigrant women gradually gave up their traditional national dress in order to adopt American ready-to-wear, they held on to their ethnic identity in subtle ways, especially in the early generations: "Wearing part of the national dress kept her in touch with the homeland and was a source of ethnic pride."[19] Later, in the period when Cather is writing, Hulda Garborg, a Norwegian sartorial traditionalist, "introduced the term *bunad*, meaning clothes, to indicate the conscious effort to reconstruct a traditional style or to create new apparel designs based on old traditions" (106). Cather would have been aware, from her childhood and her adult interest in fashion, that these kinds of national/ethnic adaptations were part of the material process of becoming American for Norwegian, and more generally, Scandinavian immigrants in the Midwest.

It is in this context that we must read the following characterization of Alexandra Bergson, in which a complex crossing of gender overlaps with a "redressing" of Turner's frontiersman as frontierswoman thereby complicating Turnerian historiography: "His [young Emil's] sister [Alexandra], was a tall, strong girl, and she walked rapidly and resolutely, as if she knew exactly where she was going and what she was going to do next. *She wore a man's long ulster* (not as if it were an affliction, but as if it were very comfortable and *belonged to her*; carried it like a young soldier), and a round plush cap, tied down with a thick veil" (*Early Novels and Stories* 140). Like the Norwegian women of Williams's study, Alexandra reshapes her cultural identity sartorially, and Cather's heroes and heroines, in general, indicate their fitness for the West through various forms of dress and undress. But rather than depicting this appropriation of Western dress as a Rooseveltian conquest, Cather represents the process of dressing for the West as a Whitmanesque weaving of identities.

Various states of undress — though usually not complete nudity or nakedness — mark two of Cather's protagonists (Godfrey St. Peter and Thea Kronborg) and one of her most important supporting characters (Lena Lingard in *My Ántonia*) as figures well-suited for the American frontier. Godfrey St. Peter's nakedness, for example, is an echo not of his Anglo-American and French Canadian forefathers, but of his spiritual ancestors — the Spaniards about whom he writes. First, St. Peter's nakedness simply reveals his physical beauty and athleticism. The narrator tells as that "for looks, the fewer clothes [St. Peter] had on, the better," and that this undressing revealed a body "built upon extremely good bones, with the slender hips and springy shoulders of a tireless swimmer." This observation of attractiveness and physicality also reveals a literal ethnic identity and another, perhaps spiritual, identity: Though St. Peter comes from "mixed stock (Canadian French on one side, and American farmers on the other)," he is "commonly said to look like a Spaniard" (4). As a physical and intellectual ideal, St. Peter can be read as an archetype that challenges Roosevelt's racialist history of the American West; for Roosevelt the ideal American is an unadulterated Anglo, while for Cather the ideal American is of mixed racial heritage and ambiguous physical appearance.

St. Peter is the author of a frontier history, *The Spanish Adventurers in*

North America, and even his mixed-stock physique (the racially blended "new man" of Crèvecoeur's answer to the question "what is an American?")[20] symbolically resembles the body of one of the first Europeans to land on the American mainland—Alvar Núñez Cabeza de Vaca. In his *Journal*, Cabeza de Vaca describes how he was washed ashore naked, and that his nakedness became for him a sign of his rebirth as a man of the New World.[21] As the first Europeans to explore the interior of the North American continent, Spaniards present an important European type for St. Peter, and for Cather. The history of the Spaniards is the first history of the American frontier. As one of the few nudes in Cather's work, St. Peter is symbolic not of modern man, per se, but of the American as a newborn race. He is, furthermore, a refutation of Roosevelt's Anglo-Saxon model of American racial and national identity.

In *My Ántonia*, Lena Lingard appears as an undressed avatar of the plains; herding her father's cattle, she appeared "bareheaded and barefooted, scantily dressed in tattered clothing...." For Jim she is "something wild, that always lived on the prairie." The body exposed to the elements becomes emblematic of adaptation to an American landscape: "her legs and arms, curiously enough, in spite of constant exposure to the sun, kept a miraculous whiteness which somehow made her seem more undressed than other girls who went scantily clad." Lena — seeming more undressed than other girls — is "not embarrassed by her ragged clothes" (106). Lena's scantily-clad body drives one man to distraction and raises the ire of a scandalized community, but Jim recounts this in terms of that community's conventional and slavish adherence to tradition, which Lena transcends. The land itself is her *habitus*. When, the "Norwegian preacher's wife ... begged Lena to come to church on Sundays," "Lena said she hadn't a dress in the world any less ragged than the one on her back." Lena agrees, eventually, and appears at church in "shoes and stockings, and the new dress, which she had made over for herself very becomingly." However, this is not enough to hide the "swelling lines of her figure [which] had been hidden under the shapeless rags she wore in the fields" (108). Clothes cannot contain her body.

In a similar vein, Thea Kronborg, in *The Song of the Lark*, experiences a deep connection with the Pueblo inhabitants of Panther Canyon and a sense of belonging to the landscape of the West when she takes a hiatus from her career as opera singer—just as Cather took a hiatus from her writing career between the publication of *Alexander's Bridge* and *O' Pioneers*. During this six-month retreat, Cather "did no writing down there, but [she] recovered from the conventional editorial point of view."[22] Cather reproduces her own experience in relating Thea's life—the life of the artist as a young woman. Thea's seclusion from society brings her back to her own body, a process aided by her physical connection to the American landscape, to the ghosts of the native inhabitants of the South West:

> It seemed to Thea that a certain understanding of those old people came up to her out of the rock shelf on which she lay; that certain feelings were transmitted to her, suggestions that were simple, insistent, and monotonous, like the beating of Indian drums. They were not expressible in words, but seemed rather to translate themselves into attitudes of body, into degrees of muscular tension and relaxation; the naked strength of youth, sharp as the sun-shafts; the crouching timorousness of age, the sullenness of women who waited for their captors.[23]

Her only covering on some of these days in the high cliffs in Panther Canyon seems to be "a roll of Navajo blankets" (547). She returns from her morning swims to long days of inactivity during which she "stretched her body on [the] warm surfaces" of the "wooly red-and-gray blankets" (548). Just as St. Peter's nakedness suggests the nakedness of a Spanish explorer — perhaps, even, reflecting the stripping away of the European self experienced by Cabeza de Vaca — so does Thea's bodily connection with Navajo blankets and Pueblo cliff-dwellings link her to the "Ancient people" of America and strip her of her European identity. However, Thea's stripping away of European garb occurs within a thematic tension that also privileges Europe — imagined broadly as including Spanish as well as English or French elements, Catholic and Jewish elements as well as Protestantism. As Thea's aunt Tillie puts it: "In older countries ... *dress and opinions and manners are not so thoroughly standardized as in our own West*" (351 emphasis added).

Thea's Panther Canyon episode, is just one step in a longer journey that promises to give her what she and her friend Ray Kennedy refer to as a feeling of empire over the landscape of the West. However, Cather's feeling of empire owes more, as Guy Reynolds has argued, to Michelet's pluralistic model of history than it does to Frederick Jackson Turner's or Teddy Roosevelt's Anglo-Saxon or Teutonic models of historical development.[24]

One important way that Cather weaves identities into history is through ethnic cross dressing. In preparing for her "musical evening" at Mrs. Nathanmeyer's in Chicago, for example, Thea protests that she hasn't "got the right clothes for that sort of thing." But Fred Ottenburg tells her not to worry, "Mrs. Nathanmeyer has a troop of daughters, a perfect seraglio, all ages and sizes. She'll be glad to fit you out, if you aren't sensitive about wearing kosher clothes" (528). These "kosher clothes" allow Thea, ironically, to transcend her Scandinavian parents' conventionalities. The "kosher clothes" point to a process of Americanization that a German Jewish family in Chicago will probably have mastered more quickly than Scandinavian farmers in Colorado. The figure of Mrs. Nathanmeyer points out that the American frontier was not transformed into "America" by solitary Teutonic men who appropriated American Indian dress and forged a new national identity. Rather, the "clothing" of the American frontier was accomplished through a plurality of influence and action. Ironically, then, the "kosher clothes" Americanize Thea.

Cather's well-known, though ultimately ambiguous anti–Semitism notwithstanding, her portrayal of American ethnic identity acknowledges the cultural influence of Jews in America. Though essentialist in his assessment, Thea's friend Fred Ottenburg expresses something Cather, herself, probably acknowledged: that Mrs. Nathanmeyer's "perceptions — or her grandmother's, which is the same thing — were keen when all this was an Indian village. ... She will like you because the Jews always sense talent, and ... they admire certain qualities of feeling that are found only in the white-skinned races" (530). Though Ottenburg expresses an essentialist assessment of racial qualities, he also expresses a pluralism not inconsistent with Cather's imperial designs. However, as some readings of Cather suggest, she deploys pluralism often at the expense of the earliest known inhabitants of the Americas: the American Indians. Guy Reynolds has thoroughly examined how Cather's Progressivism informed her imperialism, and Walter Benn Michaels has observed how Cather's "multiculturalism" is an expression rather than a denial of essentializing and, even, racist conceptions of identity. Cather is no less invested in imagining American history as a history of empire than was Teddy Roosevelt. As Reynolds puts it, Cather accomplished a historiographic version of what Alan Trachtenberg calls the "incorporation of America." This is a process of "financial, administrative, and social integration of America as a modern industrial society," and that Reynolds interpolates as "a transformation in historiographical discourse." Reynolds argues that in *The Professor's House*, especially, history becomes "the history of mankind" (Reynolds 127–7). This history is distinctly social Darwinist, presenting a version of recapitulation in which primitive races represent the childhood of human development: "Savages and barbarians are simply races that have remained in phases of culture which more civilized races have outgrown" (Reynolds 131). Cather's depiction of Jewish identity places them in some intermediate stage of development, characterized by a love of adornment and finery as is clear from the description of "kosher clothes" in *The Song of the Lark*. Her cross-dressing of characters like Thea expresses a desire to weave various ethnicities into a grand narrative of racial evolution and nation-making. Thea's ethnic masquerade and St. Peter's mixed-blood and Spanish physiognomy suggest a weaving of pluralism into nativism, as Micheals has suggested.[25]

It is clear, then, that Cather refashions American identity — or more accurately, American whiteness — along imperial lines. A key example of her imperial designs is the relationship between Ray Kennedy and Thea in *The*

Song of the Lark. Ray conveys his "feeling of empire" to Thea when he gives her the gift of a turquoise stone he has looted from an Indian burial ground. In describing the perfectly preserved remains of an Indian woman — who is, perhaps, a precursor to Mother Eve, the mummy that Tom Outland finds on the Blue Mesa in *The Professor's House*— Ray carefully describes her clothes: "She was preserved as perfect as any mummy that ever came out of the pyramids. She had a big string of turquoises around her neck, and she was wrapped in a fox-fur cloak, lined with little yellow feathers that must have come off wild canaries." The elegantly dressed figure provides a model for Thea as she gradually becomes an artist and an American. At the same time, the stone re-enforces some aspect of European identity as the colors connote Thea's Swedish heritage: "I got this from her necklace," Ray tells Thea, "See the hole where the string went through? ... You like it, don't you? They're just right for you. Blue and yellow are the Swedish colors." Again, Cather weaves a broadly imagined European past into an imperial American design premised on the looting of native artifacts: "As she drew in that glorious air [in Panther Canyon] Thea's mind went back to Ray Kennedy. *He, too, had that feeling of empire; as if all the Southwest really belonged to him because he had knocked about over it so much, and knew it, as he said, 'like the blisters on his own hands'*" (485 emphasis added).

Even more dramatically than Thea's Navajo blankets, a Mexican blanket comes to symbolize the national fabric in *The Professor's House*. Tom Outland gives St. Peter the blanket, an artifact originally given to Tom by his comrade, Roddy Blake (144). This blanket — as cloth and clothing — functions at ever-increasing circles of identity, beginning with Roddy himself as individual, moving outward to Roddy and Tom's friendship, extending further to the family's sense of community once it is in the St. Peters' possession, and finally including even the broader circles of nation and empire.

First, it functions as clothes generally do to construct a sense of individual identity in the form of a supplement.[26] "It was like his skin," Kathleen tells her father when she first learns that he has kept Roddy's blanket in his office. When Tom first meets Roddy, Roddy is lining his clothes with money he has won from gambling in Mexican Town: "The bills he folded and put inside the band of his hat. He filled his overalls pockets with the gold, and swept the rest of it into his big red neckerchief" (161). But Roddy's acquisition of this blanket seems to transform him from a man whose clothes only function to carry his money to a man whose clothes truly define his personhood. Like a supplement which is both essential to identity and an appendage of it, the blanket constructs and reflects Roddy's identity. When it makes its way into the St. Peter household it brings Kathleen and her father together, and links them to Roddy and Tom. The blanket reminds Kathleen of the legend of "*Amis* and *Amile*," the French knights whose friendship and devotion to each other serve as a prototype for the friendship between Roddy and Tom. This European legend not only links these two friends, but points to the transplanting of European civilization into the United States. It is through a Mexican fetish object ("Kathleen stroked it thoughtfully," 111) that Kathleen recalls a European legend linked with the Crusades and coming out of Oriental sources. As a fetish object, the blanket also conjures up memories for Kathleen that she associates with Roddy and her sense that the American West is truly hers: "Now that Rosamond has Outland, I consider Tom's mesa entirely my own" (112).

Like Ray Kennedy's looted Indian woman in *The Song of the Lark*, Mother Eve — the mummified remains of a Pueblo woman on the Blue Mesa in *The Professor's House* — provides a key figure for understanding Cather's explorations of gender, and also her fabrication of national identity.[27] In contrast to the conspicuously consuming Bixby household, the ancient people of the Blue Mesa strike Tom Outland as having perfected the fine arts of domestic life.[28] Tom and Roddy's most important find are the remains of what appears to be an entire pueblo family: Mother Eve (a mummified "pueblo" woman), two other women, and one man. This household echoes the St. Peter family (St. Peter, his wife, and their two daughters), and the figures in St. Peter's office (St. Peter, Augusta, and the two female forms). As a kind of Ur-family in America, their presence is important as archetype for St. Peter's epic history of the early frontier, and again, clothes come to signify familial and national identity simultaneously: "They hadn't moved away, for they had taken none of their belongings, not even their clothes. Oh, yes, we found clothes; yucca moccasins, and what seemed like cotton cloth, woven in black and white. Never any wool, but sheepskin tanned with the fleece on them" (191). Thus, in Cather, the truly American fabric is never black crape or blue serge as in James or Yezierska. Nor is it the "kosher clothes" of assimilated Jews. Rather, it is the ancient artifacts of worn Indian blankets, but artifacts acquired by an incorporating or imperial modernity.[29]

Fashion and Narration: History, the Novel, and the American Fabric

But these artifacts alone cannot make the American nation, cannot form the American fabric into a becoming national garment, a task accomplished in Cather's novels by historians and dressmakers. Cather's dressmakers — Lena Lingard in *My Ántonia* and Augusta in *The Professor's House* — practice arts that are linked to history and to nation. Lena's material fashioning of a nation, "her untiring interest in dressing the human figure" (179), is linked to Jim's discovery of Virgil as a poet of empire and nation, and Augusta's work as dressmaker for the St. Peter family is linked to St. Peter's work as historian of the earliest European-American frontier. Augusta's role as dressmaker is introduced immediately in *The Professor's House*, and the same room that houses Augusta's dressmaking tools also contains Godfrey St. Peter's manuscripts and notebooks on the history of the West.

Guy Reynolds has observed that Randolph Bourne and Willa Cather shared an interest in American folk art, and, in particular, in American fabric crafts. Bourne uses the image of weaving and fabric to describe his transnational America: "America is coming to be, not a nationality but a trans-nationality, a weaving back and forth, with the other lands, of many threads of all sizes and colors. Any movement which attempts to thwart this weaving, or to dye the fabric any one color, or disentangle the threads of the strands, is false to this cosmopolitan vision" (Bourne in Reynolds 93). Most who link Cather to Turner note Turner's Anglo-Saxonism — his notion that it was partly the racialized qualities of Anglo-Americans that formed the spirit of the frontier (Reynolds 66).[30] Cather was interested, as we have seen, in a broadening of whiteness to include Catholics, "Bohemians," French, and others in American identity. Lena's interest in dressing the human figure and Augusta's role as dressmaker of the St. Peter family represent Cather's own narration of the nation. Just as Lena's work with cloth is linked to Jim Burden's education in the classics, just as Augusta's dress patterns are interwoven with St. Peter's epic history of the American West, so is Cather's writing of the West a novelist's response to Turner and Roosevelt's Anglo-Saxonist histories. In realizing her goal to become a dressmaker Lena Lingard represents the literal and figurative fashioning of a nation. Her own nakedness (or half-nakedness) makes her part of the landscape — as if rising out of it rather than coming to it from across the Atlantic — so that once she begins to *produce* garments, these garments come as if from the land itself.

You will recall from the preceding section that Jim Burden (or Cather) goes to great lengths in describing Lena as a "scantily clad" nymph of the prairie — a kind of naked avatar of the frontier itself. In the same breath, Cather/Burden introduces her, ironically, as a dressmaker. In the same sentence that describes Lena as always appearing "bareheaded and barefooted," Jim Burden recalls that Lena was "always knitting as she watched her herd" (106). She "was always knitting stockings for little brothers and sisters, and even the Norwegian women, who disapproved of her, admitted that she was a good daughter to her mother" (107).

In her seminal study of Cather's authorial cross-dressing, "Blessings in Disguise," Susan Gubar claimed that Jim Burden and Ántonia Shimerda together comprise an autobiographical coupling — complementing each other in Cather's autobiographical amalgam. However, we might look at Lena as an even more apt complement to Jim. Lena's ambition to become a dressmaker parallels Jim's desire to become a scholar: as Jim learns the classics of Western civilization — especially Virgil as a poet of empire and nation formation — Lena learns to sew and eventually opens her shop in Lincoln, where Jim is at college. While Lena runs her dressmaking shop in Lincoln, Gaston Cleric, Jim's Latin teacher, introduces him to Virgil's *Georgics*, pastoral poems in which Virgil describes the establishment of a community in the countryside, a model for settling and, eventually, "closing" the American frontier.

While Jim begins to see the Midwest of his youth as the "Mincio" of Virgil's Italy, Lena is plying her trade as a dressmaker, a profession that she has chosen — to Jim's view — as a direct response to her childhood as an undressed avatar of the American frontier. Jim reflects:

> Evidently she had great *natural* aptitude for her work. She knew, as she said, "what people looked well in." She never tired of poring over fashion-books. Sometimes in the evening I would find her alone in her work-room, draping folds of satin on a wire figure, with a quite blissful expression of countenance. I couldn't help thinking that *the years when Lena literally hadn't enough clothes to cover herself might have something to do with her untiring interest in dressing the human figure* [179, emphasis added].

Lena's *natural* aptitude comes directly out of her experience of scarcity and survival on the American frontier.

After traveling to the Klondike where she makes a fortune, Tiny Soderball, another of the "Hired [Scandinavian] Girls" in Book II of *My Ántonia*, settles with Lena in San Francisco where the two not only form a domestic partnership but also a complementary pairing of vestments and investments. Central to Frederick Jackson Turner's claims about the modernization (or closing) of the American frontier is the idea of economic development. In Cather's novels this development is most often embodied in women: Alexandra Bergson and, here, Tiny Soderball. Cather complements this feminized economic expansion of the American West with the image of a feminized fashioning of the nation. Settling in the great Western metropolis of their time — and yet a city that had already acquired a reputation for bohemianism if not a gay subculture — Lena and Tiny embody Cather's conception of the West: a West that is broader in its conceptions of gender, sexuality, and ethnicity than Turner's or Roosevelt's historical model.

In the case of *My Ántonia,* Cather presents Lena and Tiny as ideals of pragmatic national and cultural development. As women, as Scandinavian immigrants, and as a homosocial if not lesbian pairing, Lena and Tiny offer an image of the new nation. By the end of the novel, Lena has moved to the Bay Area and Lena's fashion and Tiny's wealth work dialectically:

> Tiny lives in a house of her own, and Lena's shop is in an apartment house just around the corner. It interests me, after so many years, to see the two women together. Tiny audits Lena's accounts occasionally, and invests her money for her; and Lena, apparently, takes care that Tiny doesn't grow too miserly. 'If there's anything I can't stand,' she said to me in Tiny's presence, 'it's a shabby rich woman.' Tiny smiled grimly and assured me that Lena would never be either shabby or rich. 'And I don't want to be,' the other agreed complacently [212].

Tiny reflects that her own status as a wealthy woman is incomplete without Lena's contribution as a dressmaker: "[Lena] keeps an eye on me and won't let me be shabby. When she thinks I need a new dress, she makes it and sends it home — with a bill that's long enough, I can tell you!" (194).

Conclusion: Writing and Sewing

Nothing establishes the important connection between clothing and national identity in Willa Cather's fiction more forcefully than Godfrey St. Peter's office space in *The Professor's House*. In the "house" in question — Professor St. Peter's first home, his scholarly retreat from his family's material concerns in their new and more expensive residence — the Professor shares his study with Augusta, his daughters' German Catholic dressmaker. In a "box-couch," St. Peter's manuscripts for his book on *Spanish Adventurers in North America* are mingled with Augusta's dress-patterns for St. Peter's daughters:

> At one end of the upholstered box were piles of note-books and bundles of manuscript tied up in square packages with mason's cord. At the other end were many little rolls of patterns, cut out of newspapers and tied with bits of ribbon, gingham, silk, georgette; notched charts which followed the changing stature and figures of the Misses St. Peter from early childhood to womanhood. In the middle of the box, *patterns and manuscripts interpenetrated* [13, emphasis added].

In this interpenetration, this very weaving of sewing and writing, and of fashion and history, Cather establishes at the outset of this novel the link between the story of a family and the narrative of a nation. Seeing his manuscripts mixed in with Augusta's patterns does not, as it might any other scholar, fill St. Peter with anxiety. "Fairly considered, the sewing-room was the most inconvenient study a man could possibly have, but it was the one place in the house where he could get isolation, insulation from the engaging drama of domestic life" (16). The room provides "insulation," but the seeming clutter also provides its own pattern, and St. Peter says to Augusta:

"I see we shall have some difficulty in separating our life work, Augusta. We've kept our papers together a long while now" (14).

In addition to the "patterns," there are the "forms," and these also play an important role in the novel's interweaving of family history and national history. The forms remind St. Peter of his daughters and of their growth and development. When St. Peter's daughter Rosamond asks him how he can work with these dressmaker's dummies in his office, he replies: "They remind me of the times when you were little girls, and your first party frocks used to hang on them at night when I worked" (48). St. Peter remembers these frocks — embodied not through the daughters themselves but by the "forms" on which they are draped — at pivotal moments in the novel, reminding him of his work, and reminding Cather's readers of the link between Augusta's work as "sewing-woman" and St. Peter's work as historian of the American West:

> How much she reminded him of, to be sure! She had been the most at the house in the days when his daughters were little girls and needed so many clean frocks. It was in those very years that he was beginning his great work....
> During the fifteen years he had been working on his *Spanish Adventurers in North America*, this room had been his center of operations. There had been delightful excursions.... But the notes and the records and the ideas always came back to this room. It was here they were digested and sorted, and *woven* into their proper place in his history [16].

The closing words in this passage — "his history" — point simultaneously to his individual life, and to the life of the nation he writes. Augusta's role seems to be even more important than St. Peter's own role as historian because she provides, in fact, the conceptual framework upon which he hangs or drapes his own historical narrative.

Whenever St. Peter reflects upon the role of Augusta and the place of the "figures" in his study and his life, he pieces together the different parts of his life and work into what the narrator calls a "tapestry":

> He had grown to like the reminders of herself that she [Augusta] left in his work-room — especially the toilettes upon the figures. Sometimes she made those terrible women entirely plausible.
> ...When he was writing his best, he was conscious of pretty little girls in fresh dresses.... His mind played delightedly with all those incidents. Just as Queen Mathilde was doing the long tapestry now shown at Bayeux, — working her chronicle of the deeds of knights and heroes, — alongside the big pattern of dramatic action she and her women carried the little playful pattern of birds and beasts that are a story in themselves; so, to him, the most important chapters of his history were interwoven with personal memories [84–85].

Not only, then, does this passage link St. Peter's work to that of Augusta, but it links history to fabric. The tapestry (actually embroidery) of Bayeux depicts the Norman Conquest, and like St. Peter's choreography of his sons-in-law in a *tableaux vivant* depicting the Crusades, this image links St. Peter's history back to European history, an aspect of Cather's historiography that diverged from Turner's notions of American empire and exceptionalism.

In order to understand Cather's own sense of narrating the nation, we must fully appreciate the place of Augusta in the life and work of St. Peter, for, like Lena and Jim, Augusta and St. Peter form an amalgam: the dressmaker and the historian fabricating and documenting national history. Cather returns to this again in the closing pages of the novel: "Augusta, he reflected, had always been a corrective, a remedial influence. ... Very often she gave him some wise observation or discreet comment to begin the day with" (255–56). During their breakfast conversations, she would provide information on illnesses and funerals, and speak "about death as she spoke of a hard winter or a rainy March, or any of the sadnesses of nature." She is the perfect historian, beyond how her sewing tells the story of the family. She speaks without romance and without drama of the lives and deaths of a people: "Solid and sound and on the solid earth she surely was, and, for all her matter-of-factness and hardhandedness, kind and loyal" (256). Together, Lena and Augusta point to an important metaphor in Cather's work — the link between textile and text and between clothing and history. For Cather herself, this link was no less than a metaphor for the writer's work as historian and narrator of the nation. While Cather's sartorial historiography of the American West challenges Turner's and Roosevelt's Anglo-Saxonism, broadening the racial fabric of the American nation, her novels share with these histories a conception of America as empire.

Postscript: A Scarf, a Shawl, *un Rebozo*

THIS STUDY BEGAN WITH THE IMAGE of Cabeza de Vaca stripped of his clothing on the North American continent. It concluded with a discussion of Cather's imperial sartorial designs, including the image of a naked Professor St. Peter, the author of a history of Spanish exploration of North America. St. Peter is even described as being built along Spanish lines of physique, and of having the body of a "tireless swimmer," which Cabeza de Vaca would have to have been. While Cather explored the aesthetics of dressmaking in juxtaposition with the importance of historical narrative, she seems also to have responded to an older ideological position: that the adornment and covering of modern existence is best stripped away to reveal the naked truth. However, for the purpose of masculine modesty it might be best to cover these naked figures of Cabeza de Vaca and St. Peter with a simple cloth — a shawl, a blanket, a *rebozo*. Three contemporary writers — Carol Shields, Cynthia Ozick, and Sandra Cisneros — use the image of a versatile piece of fabric (a scarf or shawl) as a way of imagining and negotiating social and cultural identities. In the globalized fashion industry of the twenty-first century, the problems of the ready-made industry of the early twentieth century have shifted. And in the postmodern and postcolonial aesthetic context, the materiality of dress has become more fragmentary: reduced to remnants of fabric. Nevertheless, the important relation between the sartorial and the literary persists, and the material meanings of cloth for identity continue to inform contemporary fiction.

One of the themes that has emerged from this study is the notion that text and textile are not unrelated. As an editor of a daily periodical — a manufacturer of mass-produced and widely distributed text — Cahan told the story of a designer of fashionable garments: a manufacturer of mass-produced and widely consumed textile. Furthermore, Willa Cather equates the narration of national history with the work of a seamstress who fashions a family's clothes. Both writers were responding to the centrality of cloth in a consumer society. Cahan explored the ways in which clothing gave meaning to identity, and how the production of that clothing involved a transformation of individuals producing and consuming it, and a transformation of the society embodied in dress. Cather seems to be attacking conspicuous consumption, either valorizing St. Peter's naked body, stripped of any cloth, or privileging the art of hand crafted clothes — whether by the hands of idealized noble savages of the American South West or those of an immigrant dressmaker employed by a historian of the same region. This connection between text and textile continues to inform postmodern meta-fictional writing, as in Carol Shields's story, "A Scarf." The protagonist and narrator of Shields's story is, like herself, a writer of fiction. This writer is dismissed — also in some ways like Shields — as the author of light literature, what has come to be called chick lit, today. In that story, the narrator embarks on a book tour, during which she searches for a gift for her daughter, finding for her what she thinks is the perfect item: a silk scarf. Also on this journey she becomes reacquainted with an old writing colleague, Gwen. Gwen, it turns out, had lifted one of the narrator's images and inserted it in one of her own novels. Similarly, when Gwen meets the narrator unexpectedly, she sees the beautiful silk scarf and mistakenly thinks it is a gift for her. She says to the narrator: "It's just that it's so beautiful.... Finding it, it's almost like you made it. You invented it, created it out of your imagination."[1] The metafictional connotation here is unmistakable: Gwen's plagiarizing of the narrator's language is embodied here in her unconscious (or conscious?) theft of the scarf: "A scarf, half an ounce of silk, maybe less, floating free in the world" (23). In the postmodern context, this free-floating sartorial signifier embodies the ways in which we are *disconnected* from materiality. Shields attempts to reconnect us to that materiality, ironically, through the immaterial method of story-telling, of fabrication.

Haunting Shields's story is a secondary character, Danielle Westerman, a mentor and author who "wrote ... amid the shadows of the Holocaust" (11). This figure offers a kind of ballast, some measure of gravity in a story in which a silk scarf floats in and out of signification. She may, in fact, be Shields's homage to another writer — Cynthia Ozick — whose story "The Shawl" also uses cloth as a sartorial signifier, but this time not of the slipperiness of language and meaning, but of the dialectics of loss and survival, memory and forgetting. Readings of Ozick's famous story have tended to psychologize the shawl as a "transitional" psychological object or as a symbol of life's dichotomies — both swaddling cloth and shroud.[2] However, read within the context of Jewish American literary history, Ozick's use of cloth places her in the company of Cahan, Yezierska, and, also, Mary Antin, who described her own experience of immigration through the metaphor and materiality of cloth and clothing. For Mary Antin, writing in 1912, a "long past vividly remembered is like a heavy garment that clings to your limbs when you would run."[3] And yet, much of Antin's autobiography, *The Promised Land*, involves the weaving of Old-World Jewish material culture into New-World literacy, as she often juxtaposes her sister Frieda's work with textiles alongside her own reading and writing.[4] And writing almost eighty years later, another immigrant writer, Jamaica Kincaid, uses precisely the same trope to describe her own past: "Oh, I had imagined that with my one swift act — leaving home and coming to this new place — I could leave behind me, *as if it were an old garment never to be worn again*, my sad thoughts, my sad feelings, and my discontent with life in general as it presented itself."[5] But, of course Lucy, in Kincaid's novel of migration, cannot so easily leave behind a past, suggesting that Antin's wish was idealistic at best, and perhaps self-deceptive. But both instances of this trope point to how fabric functions in this metaphor: the impermanent materiality of cloth — a tissue that embodies the past but that is gradually and eventually worn away to nothing — allows for the dialectic of memory and forgetting. In "Rosa," the sequel to "The Shawl," in which the mother of the murdered child is living in Florida and has the shawl in which she hid her child restored to her, a fellow survivor, Persky, tells Rosa: "Sometimes a little forgetting is necessary."[6] As noted earlier through the work of Peter Stallybrass, cloth and clothing are especially important material embodiments of memory. People's clothes retain their smells, their posture, their ghostly remainders. When Stella — Rosa's niece and the person Rosa holds responsible for her baby daughter's death, despite Magda's own pain and loss as an adolescent survivor of the Holocaust — restores the shawl to Rosa, Rosa finds in the shawl the "memory of Magda's smell, the holy fragrance of the lost babe" (31). Ironically, it is Stella who has developed a complete, though perhaps clinical, understanding of the material and symbolic significance of the cloth, associating it with "trauma" and calling it a "fetish," words she has learned from taking psychology courses (31). Throughout eastern Europe and the Middle East, dating back to the Byzantine period, the simple cloth — the head scarf or shawl — has been an important part of women's attire and a tissue of socialization, one by no means limited to Muslim societies but rather entering Islam through these earlier Christian and Jewish manifestations. In Ozick's story, the shawl functions in another postmodern capacity, not, like Carol Shields's scarf, as a floating sartorial signifier, but, rather, as a figure of an ambivalent memory. Consciousness is spared if, simply, the body remembers.

And this same bodily memory is at work in Sandra Cisneros's speculations on the significance of an unfinished yet intricately designed *rebozo*, or shawl, that weaves its way through her novel *Caramelo*. In recounting a multi-generational narrative of migration from rural Mexico to Mexico City and from Mexico City to Chicago, Cisneros embodies storytelling itself in the figure of an unfinished *rebozo*, one crafted and designed on exquisite and intricate patterns, one so complex that no other *rebocero* (shawl maker) can complete it, but that Cisneros herself completes by writing her own intricate novel. As if in response to Cather's association of a white historian of Spanish-America with a German immigrant seamstress, Cisneros reclaims storytelling and history for her own Chicana voice. Indeed, the intricacies of the *rebozo* and the intricacies of Cisneros's novel can be thought of in terms of the Chicana aesthetic of *rasquachismo*. This is a distinctly postmodern "sensibility," characterized by the mixing of high art and low culture. "The rasquache inclination," according to Tomas Ybarra-Frausto, "piles pattern on pattern, filling all available space with bold display. Ornamentation and elaboration prevail, joined to a delight of texture and sensuous surface."[7] Clearly, Cisneros continues to work in this tradition not only in describing the *rebozo*'s intricacy, but in embodying it in her own fiction. Cisneros, in a footnote characteristic of this postmodern novel, writes that the *rebozo*, as a form of material culture, is a product of Mexican culture itself, evolving from the simple cloth used by Mexican Indian women to swaddle their infants, but influenced by Chinese silk, Spanish art, and even Arab influences.[8] Sewing, weaving, embroidery, and even the art of wearing the *rebozo*, all come to be associated in Cisneros's novel with storytelling itself. Furthermore, the fact that the *rebozo* is unfinished and that it travels from rural Mexico to the quintessential Spanish-American city, and to Chicago — the same city where Carrie Meeber fetishizes shoes and dresses — can be read in relation to the real global networks of labor, fashion marketing, and capital that make up today's garment industry. While some aspects of today's global fashion market are very different from the garment industry as it existed in 1899 when a young woman like Carrie Meeber might have worked in a shoe factory or in 1917 when Cahan published *The Rise of David Levinsky*, some labor historians trace today's sweatshops back to those beginnings, and see the place of women's clothing and women laborers as central to more recent developments such as the notion that styles and identities are negotiated.[9] Cisneros, whose work is always concerned with materiality, attempts this kind of negotiation by reclaiming agency through cloth, and retelling history through fabric. Thus, cloth and clothing continue to inform contemporary fiction as they did the American realists. Understanding the relations between text and textile, between garment industry and the mass production of popular fiction at that time can help us understand some of these same questions in the context of postmodern fiction.

Chapter Notes

Preface

1. Claudia Kidwell and Margaret Christman established this scholarly line of inquiry in their comprehensive and visually rich book, *Suiting Everyone: The Democratization of Dress in America* (Washington, D.C.: Smithsonian Institution Press, 1974) which argued that the technical and material transformation of American dress between the 1830s and the early 1900s effected an ideological shift in that anyone could, now, afford to dress well. By the early 1990s, American studies scholars Patricia A. Cunningham and Susan Voso Lab, their edited volume, *Dress in American Culture* (Bowling Green, OH: Bowling Green State UP, 1993) were complicating Kidwell's work by examining more closely a range of ideological implications of dress, from Cunningham's own examination of simple dress and its symbolic and material meanings in the wardrobes of American presidents and diplomats to Patricia Williams's examination of Norwegian immigrant dress in the nineteenth century. The essays Cunningham and Voso Lab collected in *Dress in American Culture* complicate the "democratization" thesis by examining specific contexts of power and resistance in American dress history. More recently, Michael Zakim, in *Ready-Made Democracy: A History of Men's Dress in the American Republic, 1760–1860* (Chicago: U of Chicago P, 2003) argues, against Kidwell's thesis, that while ready-made clothing produced a rhetoric of democratization, it established an economic hierarchy and division of labor that had powerful political implications in terms of class, gender, and race. The work of Cunningham, et al., as well as that of Zakim suggests that dress is important as part of the material history studied by political scientists as well. For example, in "Why Thomas Jefferson and African Americans Wore Their Politics on Their Sleeves: Dress and Mobilization between American Revolutions" (*Beyond the Founders: New Approaches to the Political History of the Early American Republic*, ed. Jeffrey L. Pasley, Andrew W. Robertson, and David Waldstreicher [Chapel Hill: U of North Carolina P, 2004], David Waldstreicher builds on Cunningham's work to explore how both written and unwritten sumptuary laws attempted to define identity and power, but also how these laws were resisted and challenged.

2. See, for example, Shane White's *Stylin': African American Expressive Culture from Its Beginnings to the Zoot Suit* (Ithaca: Cornell UP, 1998). Also, as we shall see, Russian Jewish immigrants played an important role in resisting and challenging hierarchies of labor as well as discourses of ethnic exclusion and assimilation as they entered and eventually controlled much of the burgeoning garment industry in New York City. See, for example, John Higham's *Send These to Me* (Baltimore: Johns Hopkins, 1987); Ronald Sanders's *The Lower Eastside Jews* (Dover, 1999); and Hadassa Kosak's *Cultures of Opposition: Jewish Immigrant Workers, New York City, 1881–1905* (Albany: SUNY, 2000).

3. See, especially, Susan A. Glenn's *Daughters of the Shtetl: Life and Labor in the Immigrant Generation* (Ithaca: Cornell UP, 1990); Elizabeth Ewen, *Immigrant Women in the Land of Dollars: Life and Culture on the Lower East Side, 1890–1925* (New York: Monthly Review Press, 1985); and Barbara Schreier's, *Becoming Americana Women: Clothing and the Jewish Immigrant Experience, 1880–1920* (Chicago: Chicago Historical Society, 1994). See also Andrew

Heinze, *Adapting to Abundance: Jewish Immigrants, Mass Consumption, and the Search for American Identity* (New York: Columbia UP, 1990), particularly Chapters 3 and 5.

4. Michaels, *The Gold Standard and the Logic of Naturalism* (Berkeley: UC Press, 1987) 5.

5. Kaplan, *The Social Construction of American Realism* (Chicago: U of Chicago P, 1988) 8–9, emphasis added.

6. Seguin, *Around Quitting Time: Work and Middle-Class Fantasy in American Fiction* (Durham: Duke UP, 2001) 40–41.

7. Trachtenberg, *The Incorporation of America: Culture and Society in the Gilded Age* (1982; New York: Hill and Wang, 2007) 5, emphasis added.

8. Wilson, *Adorned in Dreams: Fashion and Modernity* (Berkley: UC Press, 1985) 12.

9. Crane, *Fashion and Its Social Agendas: Class, Gender, and Identity in Clothing* (Chicago: U of Chicago P, 2000) 1.

10. See Stallybrass, "Worn Worlds: Clothes, Mourning, and the Life of Things," *The Yale Review* 18.2 (April 1993): 35–75; and "Marx's Coat," *Border Fetishisms: Material Objects in Unstable Spaces*, ed. Patricia Syper (New York: Routledge, 1998): 183–207.

11. There are, of course, studies of individual texts, but no comprehensive book-length study of dress and American realism. See, for example, Blanche H. Gelfant, "What More Can Carrie Want? Naturalistic Ways of Consuming Women," *Prospects: An Annual of American Cultural Studies* 19 (1994): 389–417; and Linda Morris, "Behind the Veil: Clothing, Race, and Gender in Mark Twain's *Pudd'nhead Wilson*," *Studies in American Fiction* 27.1 (1999): 37–52.

12. See, especially, endnotes to Chapter 6, below for a thorough discussion of literary critical responses to Anzia Yezierska. See, also, Babak Elahi, "The Heavy Garments of the Past: Mary and Frieda Antin in *The Promised Land*," *College Literature* 32.4 (2005) 29–49.

13. See Anne Hollander, *Seeing through Clothes* (New York: Viking, 1978). More recently, see Clair Hughes, *Dressed in Fiction* (Oxford: Berg, 2005). For important single-author studies see Hughes, *Henry James and the Art of Dress* (London: Palgrave, 2001). Hughes work on James remains relatively formalist in approach, though she does consider James's both symbolic and material use of dress. Perhaps the most important work on dress and literary representation is Mark Anderson's *Kafka's Clothes: Ornament and Aestheticism in the Habsburg* Fin de Siècle (Oxford: Oxford UP, 1992).

14. To these two figures we must add the important presence of Mary Antin. Antin's *The Promised Land* (1912; New York: Penguin, 1997) explored questions of assimilation and resistance by using dress in both symbolic and material ways. Antin will not be covered in this book. For a thorough discussion of Antin's exploration of sartorial assimilation and resistance, see Elahi, "The Heavy Garments of the Past."

Chapter 1

1. Alvar Núñez de Cabeza de Baca, *Interlinear to Cabeza de Vaca: His Relation of the Journey, Florida to the Pacific, 1528–1536*, trans. Haniel Long (Buffalo, NY: Frontier Press, 1969), excerpted in *Aztlan: An Anthology of Mexican American Literature*, eds. Luis Valdez and Stan Steiner (New York: Vintage, 1972) 41.

2. Gayle Veronica Fischer, "'The Daughters of Sion Are Naughty': Clothing and Sexual Oppression in Puritan New England," *Journal of Unconventional History* 3.1 (1991): 27–50; Linzy A. Brekke, "The 'Scourge of Fashion': Political Economy and the Politics of Consumption in the Early Republic," *Early American Studies* 3.1 (2005): 111–139; and Gary North, "The Puritan Experiment with Sumptuary Legislation," *Freeman* 24.6 (1974): 341–355.

3. For discussions of simplicity in dress and the use of homespun as material and metaphoric embodiments of American democratic ideals see David Waldstreicher, "Why Thomas Jefferson and African Americans Wore Their Politics on Their Sleeves: Dress and Mobilization Between American Revolutions," *Beyond the Founders: New Approaches to the Political History of the Early American Republic*, ed. Jeffrey L. Pasley, Andrew W. Robertson, and David Waldstreicher (Chapel Hill: U of North Carolina P, 2004): 79–103; Michael Zakim, *Ready-Made Democracy: A History of Men's Dress in the American Republic, 1760–1860* (Chicago: U of Chicago P, 2003); and Patricia A. Cunningham, "Simplicity in Dress: A Symbol of American Ideals," *Dress in American Culture*, ed. Patricia A. Cunningham and Susan Voso Lab (Bowling Green, OH: Bowling Green State UP, 1993): 181–99.

4. See Claudia B. Kidwell and Margaret Christman, *Suiting Everyone: The Democratization of Dress in America* (Washington, D.C.: Smithsonian Institute Press, 1974).

5. See Kidwell 27–37. See also Walter Light, *Industrializing America: The Nineteenth Century* (Baltimore: Johns Hopkins UP, 1995) 22–25 and 35–43.

6. Carol Nackenoff, *The Fictional Republic: Horatio Alger and American Political Discourse* (New York: Oxford UP, 1994). Nackenoff explains how Alger popularized the Protestant ethic and a Franklinian capitalist spirit. Within this context, clothing was an emblem of character. Educator Horace Mann stated, for example, that "Nudity and rags are only human idleness or ignorance *out on exhibition*" (quoted in Nackenoff 135).

7. See Zakim, and Kidwell.

8. Joanne B. Eicher and Barbara Sumberg, "World Fashion, Ethnic, and National Dress." *Dress and Ethnicity: Change Across Space and Time*, ed. Joanne B. Eicher (Oxford: Berg, 1995). In discussing "world fashion" in relation to ethnic and national identity, anthropologists Eicher and Sumberg define "dress as an assemblage of modifications of the body and/or supplements to the body" (298). See also Cavallaro and Warwick, *Fashioning the Frame Boundaries, Dress and Body* (Oxford: Berg, 1998) v.

9. Referencing Jean Jacques Rousseau, Henry Adams argued that the educated "Ego" is "a manikin on which the toilet of education is to be draped in order to show the fit or misfit of the clothes. The object of study is the garment, not the figure." John Carlos Rowe quotes Adams in *Henry Adams and Henry James: The Emergence of a Modern Consciousness* (Ithaca: Cornell UP, 1976), 24.

10. The Brooks Brothers history is quoted in Harry A. Corbin, *The Men's Clothing Industry: Colonial through Modern Times* (New York: Fairchild, 1970) 24.

11. For a discussion of the ideology of mass market magazines see Christopher Wilson, "The Rhetoric of Consumption: Mass Market Magazines and the Demise of the Gentle Reader, 1880–1920," ed. Richard Wightman Fox and T.J. Jackson Lears, *The Culture of Consumption: Critical Essays in American History, 1880–1980* (New York: Pantheon, 1983). Also, according to Elizabeth Wilson, "Journalism, advertising and photography have acted as mass-communication hinges joining fashion to the popular consciousness." See Wilson's *Adorned in Dreams* (Berkeley: UCP, 1985) 157. And Christopher Breward writes, "The rise of the department store and the expansion of women's fashion magazines, both designed to serve all classes, undoubtedly transformed and 'modernized' the culture and consumption of dress in the second half of the [nineteenth] century." Breward, *The Culture of Fashion* (Manchester: Manchester UP, 1995) 166.

12. Alan Trachtenberg, *The Incorporation of America: Culture and Society in the Gilded Age* (New York: Hill and Wang, 2007). Responses to Trachtenberg attempt to complicate the notion of "incorporation" by describing it as "social construction," as "modernity," or as a reconstruction of ethnicity and race. However, Trachtenberg's narrative of incorporation remains compelling in its discussion of how literary realist literature was both a challenge and yet remained a part of this broad economic, political, *and* cultural incorporation of the nation. Amy Kaplan, *The Social Construction of American Realism* (Chicago: U of Chicago P, 1988); Robert Seguin, *Around Quitting Time: Work and Middle-Class Fantasy in American Fiction* (Durham: Duke UP, 2001). For a discussion of the failure of realism to address questions of race, see Kenneth Warren's *Black and White Strangers: Race and American Literary Realism* (Chicago: U of Chicago P, 1993). For a discussion of *intra*-class conflicts debated within literary realist discourse, see Phillip Barrish, *American Literary Realism, Critical Theory, and Intellectual Prestige, 1880–1995* (Cambridge, UK: Cambridge UP, 2001). Also, though not concerned specifically with literary realism as institution, Katrina Irving's *Immigrant Mothers: Narratives of Race and Maternity, 1890–1925* (Urbana: U of Illinois P, 2000) deals with the failure of a group of texts by and about immigrant women to transcend Fordist mechanisms of production-consumption. Trachtenberg's model, while already aware of race and ethnicity, can still be revised through the critical prisms offered by these later studies. This revised Trachtenberg vision is useful in considering how, in the context of the current study, mass produced ready-made clothing also contributed to the material, cultural, and ideological incorporation (or investment) of America.

13. For a discussion of the transformation of authorship along with the commodification of literature during the realist period, Kaplan. For a discussion of individual vs. collective agency within realist representations of labor

and middle-class fantasy, see Seguin. For specific discussions of clothing and the self in society in American realism see, for example, Ruth Bernard Yeazell, "The Conspicuous Wasting of Lily Bart," *ELH* 59 (1992) 713–734; Blanche H. Gelfant, "What More Can Carrie Want? Naturalistic Ways of Consuming Women," *Prospects: An Annual of American Cultural Studies* 19 (1994): 389–417, reprinted in the Norton Critical Edition of *Sister Carrie* (Norton: New York, 2006), Donald Pizer, ed., 554–573. See also the work of Clair Hughes: *Dressed in Fiction* (Oxford: Berg, 2005), and *Henry James and the Art of Dress* (Hampshire, UK: Palgrave, 2001).

Chapter 2

1. Historians of clothing agree that the distinction between modern and pre-modern clothing can be made in terms of the fitted and the draped — modern clothes being sewn or buttoned or otherwise fitted to the body, medieval and primitive clothes hanging loose around it. See Breward, *The Culture of Fashion* (Manchester: Manchester UP, 1995); Laver, *Costume and Fashion: A Concise History* (New York: Thames and Hudson, 1995); and Wilson, *Adorned in Dream Dreams: Fashion and Modernity* (Berkley: UCP, 1985).

2. Edward J. Lowell, "Clothes: Historically Considered." *Scribner's Magazine* 14.3 (September 1893): 288–305. *The Making of America*. Cornell U Library. 16 November 2006. <http://cdl.library.cornell.edu/moa. 288>.

3. Others who wrote on this question of biology and clothing included George Van Ness Dearborn in his "The Psychology of Clothing," *Psychological Monographs* 26 (1918) and G. Stanley Hall in "Some Aspects of the Early Sense of Self," *American Journal of Psychology* (1898), excerpts of which are published in *Fashion Foundations: Early Writings on Fashion and Dress*, ed. Kim K.P. Johnson, Susan J. Torntore and Joanne B. Eicher (Oxford: Berg, 2003)

4. See "Dress as an Expression of the Pecuniary Culture," Chapter 7 of *The Theory of the Leisure Class* (1899) (New York: Penguin, 1994) 167–187. However, Veblen was less inclined towards social Darwinism than was Webb.

5. Susan Glenn, *Daughters of the Shtetl: Life and Labor in the Immigrant Generation* (Ithaca: Cornell UP, 1990): 5

6. Addams outlines this view in "Charitable Effort, *Democracy and Social Ethics* (1902), reprinted in John Stuhr, ed., *Pragmatism and Classical American Philosophy* (New York: Oxford U. Press, 2000) 631–644.

7. See John J. Appel and Selma Appel, "The Huddled Masses and the Little Red Schoolhouse," *American Education and the European Immigrant: 1840–1940*, ed. Bernard J. Weiss (Urbana: U Illinois P, 1982): 17–29.

8. Ruth Bernard Yeazell, "The Conspicuous Wasting of Lily Bart," *ELH* 59 (1992): 723.

9. See James Laver, *Costume and Fashion: A Concise History*, (1982; New York: Thames and Hudson, 1995): 180–183.

10. Robert Lauer and Jeanette Lauer, *Fashion Power: The Meaning of Fashion in American Society* (Englewood Cliffs, New Jersey: Prentice-Hall, 1981): 251 and 255. See especially the authors' footnotes.

11. Laver 200. But even the triumph of the Rational Dress movement attests to the desire for Americans to attain independence in dress as they had in politics.

12. Ronald Takaki, *A Different Mirror: A History of Multicultural America* (Boston: Back Bay Books, 1993) 288. See also Odassa Kosak, "Chapter Three: Jewish Immigrants and the New York Clothing Industry," *Cultures of Opposition: Jewish Immigrant Workers, New York City, 1881–1905* (Albany: SUNY, 2000) 61–80.

13. Both John Higham and Takaki quote from *The Rise of David Levinsky* in presenting the history of nineteenth century immigration in the U.S. Higham, *Strangers in the Land; Patterns of American Nativism, 1860–1925* (New Brunswick, N.J.: Rutgers UP, 1955).

14. See Elizabeth Ewen, *Immigrant Women in the Land of Dollars: Life and Culture on the Lower East Side, 1890–1925* (New York: Monthly Review Press, 1985). The long *Tribune* quote and preceding statistics are from pages 24–27, and the discussion of "homework" can be found on pages 121–122. Ewen is an especially important source for this chapter. Her examination of her grandmothers' generation through their "closets" (13) lends itself to the present analysis of dress as metaphor and material for identity.

15. See Lauer and Lauer, *Fashion Power*, especially Chapter 5, "Fashion and National Identity." In this chapter, Lauer and Lauer focus on how in the 1910s commentators on fashion placed a great deal of importance for the need of creating "American fashions" for American women.

16. In "The Nation Form: History and Ideology," (trans. Chris Turner) Etienne Balibar argues that the nation-state constructs identity by naturalizing a particular racial-linguistic group as its "fictive ethnicity," an ethnic identity that it presents as its ideal self. This is not, as is often argued, a primordial identity, but a future-looking one, one that hopes to secure the racial identity of the nation's progeny rather than celebrating the racial purity of the ancestors. This fictive ethnicity is produced when a language community — insufficient in and of itself to construct ethnic identity — is given the *supplement* of race. Balibar calls this combination of a language community and the symbolisms of race a fictive ethnicity, a "fabrication" (Balibar 96). See Etienne Balibar and Immanual Wallerstein. *Race, Nation, Class: Ambiguous Identities* (London: Verso, 1991): 86–106.

17. In *Whiteness of a Different Color: European Immigration and the Alchemy of Race* (Cambridge, MA: Harvard UP, 1998), Matthew Jacobson describes race as a "fabrication," and, of course, the idea of ethnicity and race as "fabricated" lends itself intuitively to a metaphor of clothing, but the connection goes beyond this intuitive link. In discussing "world fashion" in relation to ethnic and national identity, anthropologists Joanne Eicher and Barbara Sumberg define "dress as an assemblage of modifications of the body and/or *supplements* to the body" (298). In historical moments of mass migration — like the beginning and end of the twentieth century — cosmopolitan or world fashions come into conflict, and also into productive combination with ethnic and national dress. Eicher and Sumberg argue that "individuals' wardrobes in many places contain both cosmopolitan and ethnic dress ensembles, allowing them to adapt with ease to communicate effectively with others and establish their desired image as any given situation demands" (305). See Eicher and Sumberg, "World Fashion, Ethnic, and National Dress," *Dress and Ethnicity: Change Across Space and Time*, ed. Joanne B. Eicher (Oxford: Berg, 1995).

18. See, for example, Troy Duster, "The 'Morphing' Properties of Whiteness" in *The Making and Unmaking of Whiteness* edited by Rasmussen et al. (Durham: Duke UP, 2001).

19. See Dani Cavallaro and Alexandra Warwick, *Fashioning the Frame Boundaries, Dress and Body*. Oxford: Berg, 1998). This discussion of clothing as a literal supplement to ethnic identity can be developed in a parallel direction. Cavallaro and Warwick discuss clothing as a figurative supplement *of* identity. Using the term supplement in its Derridean connotations, they argue that "the supplement operates simultaneously as an optional appendix and as a completing and hence necessary element" of identity. This notion of clothing as supplement resonates with Balibar's definition of race; both uses of the term point to the fabrication of identity through an ambiguous process. As Elizabeth Wilson puts it: if "the body with its open orifices is itself dangerously ambiguous, then dress, which is an extension of the body yet not quite part of it, not only links that body to the social world, but also more clearly separates the two. Dress is the frontier between the self and the not self." Wilson 2–3, also quoted in Cavallaro and Warwick, xv.

20. Linda Morris, "Behind the Veil: Clothing, Race, and Gender in Mark Twain's *Pudd'nhead Wilson*," *Studies in American Fiction* 27.1 (1999): 37–52, reprinted in *Pudd'nhead Wilson and Those Extraordinary Twins*, ed. Sidney E. Berger, Second Edition (New York: Norton, 2005): 381–395.

21. Orlando Patterson defines slavery in terms of the "natal alienation" of the slave: "the loss of ties of birth in both ascending and descending generations" (7). Patterson's full definition of slavery is "the permanent, violent domination of natally alienated and generally dishonored persons." The loss of an inheritance plus the loss of a child embodies natal alienation. Orlando Patterson, *Slavery and Social Death* (Cambridge, MA: Harvard UP, 1982).

22. Morris 387.

23. Werner Sollors, *Beyond Ethnicity: Consent and Descent in American Culture* (Oxford: Oxford UP, 1987): 162.

24. In reading Jake/Yekl's distancing of himself and his Jewish identity from its ethnic moorings, Sabine Haenni examines this same quote. She notes that, "Cahan does not comment on Jake's alleged ability to transform a vehicle of labor (the sewing machine) into a vehicle of leisure (a train), nor does he specify Jake's visions, but the scene makes clear that Jake is 'carried away,' determined by an urban-industrial machine, and that his visions and performances can be read as a replication of and — to the extent that they translate industrialism into nontechnological performance —

a defense against urban-industrial culture." Sabine Haenni, "Visual and Theatrical Culture, Tenement Fiction, and the Immigrant Subject in Abraham Cahan's *Yekl*," *American Literature* 71:3 (1999): 493–529. 515.

Chapter 3

1. Jean-Christophe Agnew, "The Consuming Vision of Henry James" in *The Culture of Consumption: Critical Essays in American History 1880–1980*, edited by Richard Wightman Fox and T.J. Jackson Lears (New York: Pantheon Books, 1983): 65–100. 75.

2. See Agnew, 82, and Richard Adams, "Heir of Propriety: Inheritance, 'The Impressions of a Cousin,' and the Proprietary Vision of Henry James," *American Literature* 71:3 (1999) 463–91.

3. Agnew borrows Karl Marx's evocative phrase. He argues that in the late nineteenth century in the United States, the commodity form "dissolved" the material "attributes as the identifiable properties of particular human artifacts," transforming them into abstract exchange values. Agnew concludes by quoting Marx: "All that is solid melts into air." Agnew 71.

4. See Ross Posnock, "Affirming the Alien: The Pragmatist Pluralism of *The American Scene*," *The Cambridge Companion to Henry James*, ed. Jonathan Freedman (Cambridge, UK: Cambridge UP, 1998) 224–246. Jonathan Freedman provides a more thorough analysis of James's representation of ethnicity and Jewish identity, in particular, within broader anti-Semitic and assimilationist discourses in *The Temple of Culture: Assimilation and Anti-Semitism in Literary Anglo-America* (London: Oxford UP, 1999). See, especially, Chapter Four, "Henry James and the Discourses of Anti-Semitism" (117–154).

5. Peter Stallybrass, "Worn Worlds: Clothes, Mourning, and the Life of Things," *The Yale Review* 81.2 (1993) pp. 35–75. p. 39.

6. Stallybrass borrows the observation about "counter memory" from Elaine Showalter. Stallybrass, "Worn Worlds," p. 43–44.

7. Henry James, "The Romance of Certain Old Clothes," (1868) *Complete Stories, 1564–1874* (New York: The Library of America, 1999) 243–44.

8. Mary Hallab, "The Romance of Old Clothes in a Fatal Chest," *Henry James Review*, 16:3 (1995): 315–320, 317–318.

9. James, *The Portrait of a Lady*, ed. Robert D. Bamberg, 2nd ed. (1881/1908; New York: Norton, 1995) 175. The Norton Edition reproduces the 1908 version, with James's changes, rather than the 1881 original publication. T. J. Jackson Lears quotes this passage in *No Place of Grace* (New York: Pantheon, 1981), arguing that as the United States became more urbanized, "increasing numbers of Isabel's countrymen were willing to side with Madame Merle" (36). John Carlos Rowe quotes the very same passage in *Henry Adams and Henry James: The Emergence of a Modern Consciousness* (Ithaca: Cornell UP, 1976), arguing that the debate between Madame Merle and Isabel reflects James's own struggle to find a language that can express modern consciousness. Rowe sees the dialectic between Merle's socially constructed self and Isabel's essential self as James's confrontation with the conflict at the center of modern consciousness as it emerged at the end of the nineteenth century — the disappearance of old certainties about object, subject, and self (37). Jean-Christophe Agnew brings this passage into his discussion of the "commodity form" in relation to James's narrative form (85). Ruth Bernard Yeazell examines the same passage in terms of James's revision for the New York edition of 1904, arguing, like Rowe, that James was searching for a new discourse with which to express new realities. See Yeazell's *Language and Knowledge in the Late Novels of Henry James* (Chicago: U of Chicago P, 1976)

5. Clair Hughes comments directly on the question of dress in this passage in her *Henry James and the Art of Dress*, 50.

10. Henry James, *The Reverberator*, 1888 (New York: Grove, n.d.) 14.

11. This chapter leaves out a study of a few key texts in James's oeuvre, but ones that fall outside the comparison of "A Romance of Certain Old Clothes" and "Crapy Cornelia." In addition to his significant references to dress in *The Portrait of a Lady*, James uses dress as a key motif in a number of novels and stories. For example, both Hyacinth Robinson's (the protagonist of the novel) mother and "foster" mother or guardian are dressmakers. Hyacinth's later adoption into high society and its material beauty is informed by this fact of his birth — we are made aware of the fabric of aesthetic beauty. In *The Turn of the Screw*, the clothing of the "ghost" Quint allows for a careful and subtle exploration of the narrator's anxieties about social class and what were, by the end of the nineteenth century, unwritten

sumptuary laws. What is most frightening about Quint, one might argue, is not that he is a monstrous ghost but that he boldly goes about the grounds hatless. Furthermore, it is clear that he had stolen some of the master's clothes, so that the theft of sartorial property is as frightening as any supernatural quality of the narrative. Moreover, at the climactic moment in *What Maisie Knew*, when Maisie faces Sir Claud, the narrator describes Mrs. Wix dressing Maisie for the occasion, dramatizing the idea that clothes — the sartorial component of what William James called the "material me" (see chapter 2, above) — form an important part of the social construction of self. Furthermore, during his master phase, James produced novels centrally concerned with materiality and with clothing. While these are all important moments in James's oeuvre and suggest a consistent interest in materiality and fashion, a full exploration of these issues would require a book-length study of dress in James, a task ably accomplished by Clair Hughes in *Henry James and the Art of Dress*.

12. As Leon Edel has suggested, James felt that he "could finance the trip in part by writing a book of 'impressions' — it would have to be 'for much money.'" Edel, *Henry James: The Master: 1901–1916*, (1972; New York: Avon-Discus, 1978) 225–226. By 1909, when "Crapy Cornelia" and "The Velvet Glove" were published, and a year after "The Jolly Corner" came out, James complained to his agent that "in no year had he so 'consummately managed to make so little money as this last'" (Edel 436). So during the time he was writing these stories about old property and new money, James was keenly aware of his own financial difficulties, at least relatively speaking, and realized that he, too, was implicated in America's new economy.

13. Henry James, "Crapy Cornelia," 1909, *Complete Stories 1898–1910* (New York: Library of America, 1996) 826.

14. In "The Velvet Glove," the commercial French writer, Amy Evans, uses her own glove to ask English writer John Berridge to write a preface to her new book titled *The Velvet Glove*. The story ends with Berridge's refusal, signified by a wave of his hat in the very last line of the story: "He too fell back, but could still wave his hat for her as she passed to disappearance..." (*Complete Stories 1898–1910*, 220). In "John Delavoy," the narrator describes stuffing into his hat the proofs of an article he has written about the deceased author, Delavoy. The significance of hats in *The Turn of the Screw* and *What Maisie Knew* is discussed briefly above in note 11.

15. Henry James, *The American Scene* (1904; New York: Penguin, 1994) 249.

16. Henry James, "The Question of Our Speech," *French Writers and American Women Essays*, ed. Peter Guitenhuis (1904; Branford, Connecticut: Compass, 1960) 29.

17. The transformation of a *thing* into a commodity and into currency is not a one-way and once-and-for-all event, as Gayatri Spivak suggests in "Scattered Speculations on the Question of Value," *In Other Words: Essays in Cultural Politics* (New York: Routledge, 1988) 154–78. She argues that the development of natural objects into use-values, commodities, money, and ultimately capital is *not* a one-way, continuous process, but rather a discontinuous process. The oilcloth analogy that James uses points both to the commodity form of language as well as to its use-value. Furthermore, the notion of "English acquisition," which is so much in common parlance in our own day, suggests an analogy of language with capital. If, as Richard Adams has shown, James's work is centrally concerned with questions of proprietary inheritance versus commodity acquisition, then this theme comes to full fruition in *The American Scene*.

18. Martha Banta provides a detailed discussion of how James viewed middle- and upper-class white women in America, as the only ones who took care of the language, at least in Washington D.C., the "City of Conversation." Banta, "Men, Women, and the American Way," *The Cambridge Companion to Henry James*, ed. Jonathan Freedman (Cambridge, UK: Cambridge UP, 1998) 21–39

Chapter 4

1. Henry James, *The Wings of the Dove* (1902; New York: Penguin, 1985) 72.

2. According to William Pietz, the notion of fetishism emerged in the sixteenth century out of Portuguese imperialist ventures in West Africa. The fetish involves "the subjection of the human body ... to the influence of certain significant material objects that, although cut off from the body, function as its controlling organs at certain moments." By associating fetishism with African societies and dissociating it from themselves, Portuguese colonialists in West Africa (and later European imperialists

across the globe) distanced their own supposedly enlightened and humanistic concern with values from the superstitious beliefs of the savage. This was a "disavowal of the object." However, later Karl Marx "ridiculed a society that thought it had surpassed the 'mere' worship of objects supposedly characteristic of 'primitive religions.'" By contrast, what Marx identified as commodity fetishism was not the elevation of the consumer *object* itself to a sacred, supernatural, or animate level, but rather the elevation of the object's "invisible," "immaterial," "supra-sensible" exchange value to the level of economic as well as social and political power. European merchants and capitalists were "interested in objects only to the extent that they could be transformed into commodities and exchanged for profit on the market." Thus, we have the fetishism of things — the individual and collective investment of objects with important and even sacred personal and communal meaning — and the fetishism of commodities: the abstraction of value from objects, and the elevation of that abstracted value to the level of economic. See Peter Stallybrass, "Marx's Coat," in Patricia Spyer, editor, *Border Fetishisms: Material Objects in Unstable Spaces* (London: Routledge, 1997) pp. 184–87.

3. Philip Fisher, *Hard Facts: Setting and Form in the American Novel* (New York: Oxford UP, 1987) 132–33, quoted in Amy Kaplan's *The Social Construction of American Realism* (Chicago: U of Chicago P, 1988) 150.

4. Walter Benn Michaels, *The Gold Standard and the Logic of Naturalism* (Berkeley: UCP, 1987) 33.

5. In the field of psychology, William James argued that clothes, among other material things, were an important part of constituting the social self. See William James's *Psychology: The Briefer Course* (New York: Harper, 1961). See Chapter 2 above for a discussion of William James's theory in the context of American Realism.

6. Theodore Dreiser, *Sister Carrie*, ed. Donald Pizer, 3rd ed. (1899; New York: Norton, 2006) 3.

7. Kaplan argues that "the critical opposition associating sentimentalism with consumption and desire, and realism with work and deprivation, is already generated by the narrative strategies of *Sister Carrie*, as a way of imagining and managing the contradiction of a burgeoning consumer society" (143). The similarity between Hurstwood's work situation and his home life is a key instance of this critical opposition already at work in *Sister Carrie*.

8. Fisher pays close attention to this passage and to the "plot of decline" that the second half of *Sister Carrie* follows: "the New York half" of the novel can be divided into "a balanced and closely modeled double story that compels us to see and comprehend the rise of Carrie by means of the fall of Hurstwood" (169–170). Fisher's reading informs later readings of *Sister Carrie*, including this one.

9. Writing the same year as Dreiser, Veblen argued that the "process of progressive exemption from the common run of industrial employment will commonly begin with the exemption of the wife" (54). The most obvious way to make this exemption from labor, or simply, this leisure, conspicuous — to put it on display — is through clothes: "the more elegant styles of feminine bonnets go even farther towards marking work impossible than does the man's high hat" (171). Veblen, *The Theory of the Leisure Class* (1899; New York: Penguin, 1994).

10. In his analysis of Hurstwood's fall from riches to rags, Fisher argues that "Behind the plot of decline is the Darwinian description of struggle, survival, and extinction" (171). This broad Darwinian view is optimistic about large groups but pessimistic about the individual. Thus, it might be argued along Marxian lines that Hurstwood's extinction ensures the survival of capitalist society.

11. Both Robert Seguin and Amy Kaplan identify the "he" in this passage as Hurstwood. Kaplan writes: "When Dreiser comments on a policeman's ambivalence toward the strike, he notes that "of its true social significance, [Hurstwood] never once dreamed" (Kaplan 154). Hurstwood's name in brackets is in Kaplan's text, but clearly, the "he" here is a continuation of Dreiser's discussion of the policeman's ambivalence. Seguin writes: "In his heart of hearts, [Hurstwood] sympathized with the strikers...." Seguin puts Hurstwood's name in brackets and goes on to quote the passage up to the sentence "Strip him of his uniform, and he would have soon picked his side" (Seguin 47). However, given the quote in context the subject is the policeman, not Hurstwood.

12. Michael Tratner, *Deficits and Desires: Economics and Sexuality in Twentieth Century Literature* (Stanford, CA: Stanford UP, 2001) 76.

13. Quoted in Christopher Breward, *The*

Culture of Consumption (Manchester, 1995) 169.

14. Abelson quoted in Breward, 167–9.

15. Abelson in Breward, 169.

16. For a further discussion of department stores at the turn of the twentieth century, see the editor's note on pages 15–16 of the Norton Critical Edition of *Sister Carrie* (3rd Edition, 2006), edited by Donald Pizer. See, also, Chapter 5 of Christopher Breward's *The Culture of Consumption* (Manchester, 1995). According to Breward, the "visual world of the department store, like the world of the new magazines with their lavish plates and consumerist descriptions of shop goods or society events, was one that did not necessarily rely on the rationality of the market system or predominant social and cultural ideas...." Rather, department stores had a "fantastic and otherworldly character" (167). See also Mary Antin's *The Promised Land* (1912; New York: Penguin, 1997) 149.

17. See, for example, Kevin R. McNamara, "The Ames of the Good Society: *Sister Carrie* and Social Engineering," *Criticism* 34 (1992) 217–35, reprinted in the Norton Critical Edition of *Sister Carrie* (3rd Edition, 2006) 537–54.

18. Philip Fisher's well-known reading of *Sister Carrie*, "The Life History of Objects: The Naturalist Novel and the City" (in *Hard Facts*, Oxford U. P., 1986) quotes this passage focusing on the image of windows, and more recently, Robert Seguin quotes the same passage, developing Fisher's reading to discuss thresholds both in time and space within the novel. See Fisher, *Hard Facts*, 158, and Seguin, *Around Quitting Time*, 30.

19. Both Walter Benn Michaels and Amy Kaplan discuss the question of sentimentalism and realism or naturalism in their reading of *Sister Carrie*. This passage, which discusses Carrie's sympathies and fanciful imagining of working-class life, is a key example. However, Michaels downplays or even dismisses Dreiser's critique of capitalism by focusing on Carrie's desire for material objects. Attending to the description of materiality and a counter-capitalist kind of fetishism as defined by Stallybrass suggests that Dreiser's characterization of Carrie is not a simple embodiment of a capitalist logic of insatiable consumption.

20. Again, Fisher, Kaplan, and Seguin read this passage in similar ways. Seguin, for example, reads the passage as describing a threshold in time and space — between the world of work and the world of leisure, or quitting time. Seguin, 22–23.

Chapter 5

1. Veblen, *The Theory of the Leisure Class* (1899; New York: Penguin, 1979) 167.

2. Simmel, "Fashion," *Georg Simmel on Individuality and Social Forms*, ed. Donald Levine (Chicago: U of Chicago Press, 1971) 305. For a discussion of Simmel's importance to contemporary fashion historians see Diana Crane, *Fashion and Its Social Agendas: Class, Gender, and Identity in Clothing* (Chicago: U of Chicago Press, 2000) 6–7. Crane describes Simmel's theory as "a process of imitation of social elites by their social inferiors" (Crane 6). However, she argues that "the dissemination of fashion was more complicated than the process described by Simmel" (7). Citing Pierre Bourdieu, Crane argues that "Within social classes, individuals compete for social distinction and *cultural capital* on the basis of their capacity to judge the suitability of cultural products according to class-based standards of taste and manners" (7). However, ethnicity further complicates the situation.

3. Andrew Heinze, *Adapting to Abundance: Jewish Immigrants, Mass Consumption, and the Search for American Identity* (New York: Columbia U Press, 1990) 103.

4. Dani Cavallaro and Alexandra Warwick, *Fashioning the Frame: Boundaries, Dress and Body* (Oxford: Berg, 1998) xvi–xvii. Cavallaro and Warwick refer, here, to what Jacques Lacan calls the human infant's "jubilant assumption of his specular image" in the "mirror stage," when the child begins to be socialized into human culture, and into the first elementary function of language — differentiating between self and other. According to Lacan's psychoanalytic theory, the happy self-image of the pre-socialized infant dates, developmentally, to a time before "the deflection of the specular *I* into the social *I*" which results in "paranoic alienation." According to this semiotic view of human psychology, the pre-linguistic imaginary sense of self is "jubilant," while a language-bound symbolic sense of self is "paranoic" and "alienated" as the individual is socialized. Lacan, "The Mirror Stage," *Écrits: A Selection*, trans. Alan Sheridan (New York: Norton, 1977) 2–5.

5. The term was coined by Gilles Deleuze and Felix Guattari in *Kafka: Toward a Minor*

Literature (Minneapolis: U of Minnesota Press, 1986). The term suggests not just geographic or spatial deracination, but, moreover, linguistic and cultural unmooring. While there is a level of cultural alienation and social dissonance in any experience of exile or, even, migration, these experiences also result in what Eva Hoffman calls the "contrapuntal concept of home." See Hoffman's "The New Nomads" in *Letters of Transit: Reflections on Exile, Identity, Language, and Loss*, edited by Andre Aciman (New York: New Press, 1999) 35–63.

6. Others have made a similar argument for a variety of immigrant and exilic groups in the United States. See, for example, Gustavo Perez-Firmat, *Life on the Hyphen: The Cuban-American Way* (Austin: U of Texas P, 1994); Rosaura Sanchez, *Chicano Discourse: A Socio-Historic Perspective* (Houston: Arte Publico Press, 1994); Hamid Naficy, *The Making of Exile Cultures: Iranian Television in Los Angeles* (Minneapolis: U of Minnesota, 1993), and Daniel Boyarin and Jonathan Boyarin, "Diaspora: Generation and the Ground of Jewish identity," *Critical Inquiry* 19.4 (1993): 693–725.

7. Abraham Cahan, *The Rise of David Levinsky* (1917; New York: Penguin, 1993) 5.

8. See Chapter 4 of Alger's *Ragged Dick* (1867; New York: Scribner, 1998) "Dick's New Suit."

9. In *Capital: Volume One*, Marx writes that "By means of the value-relation ... the natural form of a commodity B becomes the value-form of commodity A, in other words, the physical body of commodity B becomes *a mirror for the value of commodity A*" (emphasis added). In his footnote to this passage, Marx explains that this mirroring relation between commodities is also at work in relations between man and man: "In a certain sense, a man is in the same situation as a commodity. As he neither enters into the world in possession of a mirror, nor as a Fichtean philosopher who can say 'I am I,' a man first sees and recognizes himself in another man. Peter only relates to himself as a man through his relation to another man, Paul, in whom he recognizes his likeness. With this, however, Paul also becomes from head to toe, in his physical form as Paul, the form of appearance of the species man for Peter." What is important about this passage is that it emphasizes a mediated relationship between people in terms of the mediated relationship between commodities. Commodities do not have absolute value in and of themselves. They have relative value in relation to other commodities. So, too, then, with people. In pertinent passages from *Levinsky*, this "reflected" or relative identity of people presents them as being *like* commodities, echoing a Marxist view of society. Karl Marx, *Capital: Volume One*, trans. By Ben Fowkes (New York: Vintage, 1977), 144 and note 19 on the same page.

10. David Engel defines modernity in relation to Cahan's novel as the "depiction of [a] radical process whereby new experiences are compounded to alter the boundaries of life, challenging the fundamental feel of experience itself." Drawing on Paul de Man, and especially on de Man's use of Nietzsche's "The Use and Disadvantage of History for Life," Engel explains that the "modern comes after. It begins with an awareness of change and develops into a sense of discontinuity" (Engel 73). Like the desire to study the past as history rather than to live it in the present as myth, "Modernity exists in the form of a desire to wipe out whatever came earlier, in the hope of reaching at last a point of origin that marks a new departure" (73). Engel's essay is a kind of elegy for what Levinsky loses by obliterating his past. Engel, "The Discrepancies of the Modern: Reevaluating Abraham Cahan's *The Rise of David Levinsky*," *Studies in Jewish American Literature* 5:2 (Winter 1979): 68–91, 71.

11. See note 9 above.

12. The German-style *gymnasium* was the modern secular counterpart to the traditional Jewish *yeshivah*.

13. For a discussion of the homosocial and homoerotic connotations of this scene, see Magdalena J. Zaborowska's "Americanization of a 'Queer Fellow': Performing Jewishness and Sexuality in Abraham Cahan's *The Rise of David Levinsky*," *American Studies in Scandinavia* 29.1 (1997): 18–27.

14. Andrew Heinze writes that "The male 'coquettes' of the Jewish quarter were a subject of commentary for the [*Jewish Daily*] *Forward* [which Cahan edited], which ran feature stories such as the one detailing the fate of a yeshiva student from eastern Europe who had turned into a womanizing 'dude' in New York City" (94). Furthermore, the very term used here and in the *Forward*, that is, *dude*, was one that Georg Simmel made famous in his essay on "Fashion" published, in fact, in New York in 1904 in the *International Quarterly* (Volume 10, 1904), reprinted in *Georg Simmel on Individuality and Social Forms*. Simmel argued that fashion allowed for the paradoxical combina-

tion of social obedience and individual conspicuousness precisely because at its extreme it allowed for flamboyance and deviance: "It is characteristic of *the dude* that he carries the elements of a particular fashion to an extreme; when pointed shoes are in style, he wears shoes that resemble the prow of a ship; when high collars are all the rage, he wears collars that come up to his ears; when scientific lectures are fashionable, you cannot find him anywhere else, etc., etc." (Simmel 305). Jake Mindels is Cahan's caricature of the "dude," but as Zaborowska argues, there is the added scandal of his ambiguous sexuality.

15. Zaborowska, "Americanization of a 'Queer Fellow'" 27.

16. The question of subjective agency has been central to Cahan criticism from some of the earliest critical readings of Levinsky's alienation to Phillip Barrish's response and critique of these. Characteristic of the earlier criticism that sites a loss of agency because of a loss of traditional Jewish identity is David Green's "The Price of Success: Use of the Bildungsroman Plot in Abraham Cahan's *The Rise of David Levinsky*," *Studies in American Jewish Literature* 12.2 (1993) 19–24. See also Richard S. Pressman's "Abraham Cahan, Capitalist; David Levinsky, Socialist," *Studies in American Jewish Literature* 12.2 (1993) 2–18. However, Phillip Barrish argues that "rather than undercutting his American rise, as is often claimed by readers of Cahan's novel and related immigrant stories from the period, the specific forms of Levinsky's self-division work as primary mechanisms of the rise, in both its cultural and economic aspects." See Barrish, "'The Genuine Article': Ethnicity, Capital, and *The Rise of David Levinsky*," *American Literary History* 5:4 (Winter 1993) 643–662.

17. According to Dalia Kandiyoti, Cahan "wrote his pioneering work" at "the very juncture" "between culture and mobility and between the local and the mobile." See Kandiyoti, "Comparative Diasporas: The Local and the Mobile in Abraham Cahan and Alberto Gerchunoff," *Modern Fiction Studies* 44.1 (1998) 77–122. 85.

18. Anderson reads *Amerika* as a traveling narrative in which Karl Rossman is continually expelled from familiar and familial relations and enters the world of *Verkehr*: "the movement of people, goods, money, or information... ." *Verkehr* involves "traffic, trade, commerce, exchange, social and sexual intercourse" (Anderson 99).

19. John Durham Peters, "Exile, Nomadism, and Diaspora: The stakes of Mobility in the Western Canon," in *Home, Exile, Homeland: Film, Media, and the Politics of Place*, ed. Hamid Naficy (New York: Routledge, 1999): 17–41. 18.

20. Ronald Sanders discusses the Jewish Workers' Bund and Cahan's journalistic connection to and political sympathies for the group at length in *The Lower East Side Jews: An Immigrant Generation* (New York: Dover, 1999) 330–34.

21. Daniel Boyarin and Jonathan Boyarin, "Diaspora: Generation and the Ground of Jewish Identity," *Critical Inquiry* 19.4 (1993): 693–725, reprinted in Jana Evans Braziel and Anita Mannur (eds.) *Theorizing Diaspora: A Reader* (Malden, MA: Blackwell, 2003): 85–118. 114. See also Dalia Kandiyoti's "Comparative Diasporas" where she uses the Boyarins' claims to support her own reading of Cahan. She argues that the "permanent diasporic state of the Jews and Judaism, considered an affliction by some Jews and non–Jews, put them in a particular position vis-à-vis territorial discourse they encountered and engaged. The turn-of-the-century immigrant writer's 'rediasporization' ... had to contend with the various, reterritorializing discourse of nativism" (112). While Kandiyoti argues that this "rediasporization" is ambiguous in Cahan, she also claims that he "staged the complexity of immigrant and Jewish multidimentionality" and walked "a tightrope of conflicting literary discourses and political visions in order to assert [a] politics of location" (112).

22. The Boston common is the place where Miss Dillingham sooths Mary's feelings of isolation from her own family. See *The Promised Land*, 215–216. It is also where Mary indulges in new-found patriotic reveries about what she calls "my country" (177).

23. In his essay, "The Uncanny," Sigmund Freud turns to Otto Rank's discussion of the double (*doppelgänger*). What is important for in this context is that the evolution of the idea of the double suggests that what was once an assurance of immortality became, over time, a "ghastly harbinger of death." Though Levinsky's doublings, either in mirrors or in his reflections on his own identity, do not suggest death, they do suggest the disintegration of the ego, and the production of feelings of homelessness. Freud, "The Uncanny" (1919) *Studies in Parapsychology* (1919; New York: Collier, 1971) 19–62.

24. "The acceptance of stylishness as an element of prestige among Jewish newcomers was reflected most clearly in the ritual of courtship. In traditional Jewish culture, three qualities determined the desirability of a prospective mate: scholarship, wealth, and yikhes." Yikhes means, roughly, "civilized": "a nobility of spirit, a compassionate involvement with other people that the Jews associated with great scholars and benefactors." However, "in urban America, where familiarity with American ways had become a priority, stylishness was viewed as a social asset" (Heinze, 97–8).

25. See Sanders for a full discussion of this history: 18–23.

26. Irving Howe, *World of our Fathers*, abr. ed. (1976; New York: HBJ-Bantam, 1980) 15.

27. Daniel and Jonathan Boyarin define Diaspora as a way of basing identity on race without linking race to land. "Race is here on the side of the radicals; space, on the other hand, belongs to the despots" (106).

28. In particular, Susan K. Harris, and Sam Girgus have read Levinsky as Cahan's self-stereotyping as a Jew. Girgus, in particular, reads David Levinsky's sexual indiscretions as part of a social psychosis. However, even this individual reading seems to place Levinsky in the stock character of the degenerate Jew who lusts after white women. See Harris, "Problems of Representation in Turn-of-the-Century Immigrant Fiction" in *Realism and the Canon*, edited by Tom Quirk and Gary Scharnhorst (Newark: U of Delaware Press, 1994) 127–142. See also, Girgus's *The New Covenant: Jewish Writers and the American Idea* (Chapel Hill: U of North Carolina P, 1984).

29. Robert Thacker, Introduction, *The Autobiography of S. S. McClure*, (Lincoln: Bison Books, 1997).

30. Chametzky, Introduction (1993) *The Rise of David Levinsky* (New York: Penguin, 1997).

31. Burton J. Hendrick's captions to illustrations on pages 125 and 142 of "The Jewish Invasion of America," *McClure's Magazine* 40.5 (March 1913) 125–165.

32. Hendrick, "The Jewish Invasion," 165. See Jules Chametzky's Introduction, xiv–xviii.

33. Sanders 396–420. Sanders provides a detailed and dramatic account of these events that involved "the large manufacturers, organized into the New York Clothing Association" (404) and "25,000 workers — more than two-thirds of the workers in the men's clothing industry" (405). By early 1913 — just before the publication of Hendrick's "Jewish Invasion of New York," and two months before the first publication of "The Autobiography of an American Jew"—Cahan's "*Forward* became the principal actor in the drama that was developing" (405). The *Forward* not only covered the garment workers strike of 1912–13, but became a key agent. According to Sanders, the Executive Committee of the United Garment Workers told Cahan that "it could not make its next move without the *Forward*'s support." Cahan offered the support, but also advocated compromise, which led to a rift between the leadership of the press (that is, Cahan) and the leadership of the garment workers (406). Given Cahan's involvement in these events, these problems would have been uppermost in his mind when *McClure's* approached him for a series of sketches about Jewish industries in New York. Sanders writes that "Cahan decided to create a fictitious character who could serve as a composite for numerous success stories in the garment industry.... The fiction form was meant just as a device for conveying a mass of information dramatically" (418). These events resulted in changed perceptions and realities within the garment industry, with Cahan contributing to both.

34. Cahan in Chametzky, with Chametzky's emphasis, Introduction, xvii.

35. Sam Girgus reduces David Levinsky's sexual misadventures with women to a "hatred of women" that "signals a deep sexual neurosis." More importantly, this reading of sexuality is part of Girgus's broader reading of *The Rise of David Levinsky* as a new American Jeremiad, and thus within a bounded conception of national identity. Girgus claims that Jewish American writers endorse and even shape what he calls "the American idea," that is to say, "the set of values, beliefs, and traditions of freedom, democracy, equality, and republicanism that are known as the American Way and that give America a unique identity in history" (3).

36. Matthew Frye Jacobson, "Anglo-Saxons and Others," *Whiteness of a Different Color: European Immigration and the Alchemy of Race* (Cambridge, MA: Harvard UP, 1998) 65–68.

37. Bram Dijkstra, *Evil Sisters: The Threat of the Female and the Cult of Manhood* (New York: Knopf, 1996) 280.

38. Cahan, "The Autobiography of an American Jew," *McClure's Magazine* 41.3 (July 1913) 118. This same passage appears verbatim in the 1917 *The Rise of David Levinsky*. See the Penguin edition, 1993/97, 443.

Chapter 6

1. While critics have examined both Yezierska's utopian tendency and her attention to clothing, no readers of her work have examined these two issues in relation to Yezierska's use of the theme and metaphors of investment and debt. Mary Dearborn, Magdalena J. Zaborowska, and Thomas J. Ferraro, focus, respectively on Yezierska's generally platonic affair with John Dewey and its significance for both her art and his philosophy; Yezierska's place among other immigrant writers of her time in the process of reimagining gender; and a reevaluation of her work in the context of upward social mobility. See Dearborn, *Love in the Promised Land: The Story of Anzia Yezierska and John Dewey* (New York: Free Press, 1988); Zaborowska, *How We Found America: Reading Gender through Eastern European Immigrant Narratives* (Chapel Hill: U of North Carolina P, 1995): 113–164; and Ferraro, "Working Ourselves Up in Anzia Yezierska's *Bread Givers*," *South Atlantic Quarterly* 89:3 (1990): 547–582. Delia Caparoso Konzett turns to Yezierska's use of language in the context of assimilation and Anglo-conformity. See Caparoso Konzett's "Administered Identities and Linguistic Assimilation: The Politics of Immigrant English in Anzia Yezierska's *Hungry Hearts*," *American Literature* 69:3 (1997): 595–619. Katherine Stubbs, Christopher Okonkwo, and Meredith Goldsmith have separately examined the themes of fashion, the garment industry, and assimilation in *Salome of the Tenements*, a few short stories, and *Bread Givers*. See Goldsmith, "Dressing, Passing, and Americanizing: Anzia Yezierska's Sartorial Fictions," *Studies in American Jewish Literature* 16 (1997): 34–45; Okonkwo, "Of Repression, Assertion, and the Speakerly Dress: Anzia Yezierska's *Salome of the Tenements*," *MELUS* 25:1 (2000): 129–45; and Stubbs, "Reading Material: Contextualizing Clothing in the Work of Anzia Yezierksa," *MELUS* 23:2 (1998): 157–173. All three refer back to a cultural historian and an art historian, Elizabeth Ewen and Barbara Schreier, respectively, who rely on Yezierska's fiction as documentary evidence in discussing the assimilation of eastern European women into American society in the early years of the twentieth century. See Ewen, *Immigrant Women in the Land of Dollars: Life and Culture on the Lower East Side, 1890–1925* (New York: Monthly Review Press, 1985); and Schreier's, *Becoming Americana Women: Clothing and the Jewish Immigrant Experience, 1880–1920* (Chicago: Chicago Historical Society, 1994). Okonkwo, Stubbs, and Goldsmith also draw on Thorstein Veblen's theory of conspicuous consumption to contextualize Yezierska's use of sartorial signifiers in narrating assimilation and resistance. Whether it is Mashah Smolinsky's desire for clothes in *Bread Givers* or Sonya Vrunsky's utopian fashion in *Salome of the Tenements*, these readings of Yezierska's fiction place significant emphasis on clothing as material history and literary metaphor, especially in the context of middle-class Anglo-American movements of urban reform, domestic science, Americanization, and social work. However, while these critics examine fashion, consumption, and labor, none examines investment — Yezierska's attention to questions of capital, debt, credit, and, ultimately, her use of financial themes and metaphors to represent the immigrants' emotional investments in community, work, and identity. For Yezierska, vestments are closely related to *in*vestments.

2. Walter Benn Michaels distinguishes between investment and speculation in his reading of William Dean Howells's *The Rise of Silas Lapham*. Investment, Michaels suggests, has a material or human foundation in natural or human resources. Speculation, on the other hand, is completely abstract and based on exchange rather than absolute values. For the Lapham family, whose fortunes rise on a tide of the natural resource of paint, speculation is like "gambling," its rewards are monstrously "disproportionate to the amount of value invested." See Michaels's *The Gold Standard and the Logic of Naturalism* (Berkeley: UC Press, 1987): 38–41.

3. See chapter 1.

4. *Bread Givers* (1925; New York: Persea, 1975) 297.

5. Stubbs and Goldsmith both focus on the importance of the religious connotations of clothing in this novel, and especially on Sara's negotiation of tradition and assimilation through Sara's careful adoption of a new sartorial self. See note 1 above.

6. In the *shtetl*, or east European Jewish villages of the nineteenth century, "Women often became breadwinners so that their husbands could devote themselves to study...." See Irving Howe's *World of Our Fathers* (Toronto: Bantam, 1976): 6.

7. According to Susan Glenn, "Women's economic obligation reached its most extreme degree in the families of religious scholars,

where wives performed a religious *mitzvah* (good deed) by working so their husbands might pursue a higher purpose... . The hardworking scholar's wife acted as a legitimating symbol of the female breadwinner for the masses of east European Jews." Glenn, *Daughters of the Shtetl: Life and Labor in the Immigrant Generation* (Ithaca: Cornell UP, 1990) 12.

8. Andrew Heinze discuss the crucial distinction in European Jewish culture between the "holy and the mundane," and shows how "Under the pressure of life in the American city, where the distinction between the holy and the mundane appeared suddenly tenuous and unstable, the old symbolism of luxuries dissolved." See *Adapting to Abundance: Jewish Immigrants, Mass Consumption, and the Search for American Identity* (New York: Columbia UP, 1990) 56.

9. Irving Howe defines *tsedakah* (or *tsdokeh*) as "charity, in the larger sense of communal responsibility," arguing that this tradition "remained powerful" into the twentieth century and into the American urban context, "lashing the suburban (and urban) Jews to feats of self-taxation that could not be matched in any other American community" (614).

10. In the context of American realism and naturalism, Walter Benn Michaels defines "speculation" as "the quintessentially capitalist gesture," as a risk whose rewards are "vastly disproportionate to the amount of labor invested" (*The Gold Standard* 40).

11. Michael Tratner uses these terms in his study of economics and sexuality in *Deficits and Desires: Economics and Sexuality in Twentieth Century Literature* (Stanford, CA: Stanford U Press, 2001).

12. In "Marx's Coat," Stallybrass distinguishes between pre-capitalist fetishism of things and the capitalist fetishism of their invisible exchange value in Karl Marx's concept of the commodity and money. In capitalist society since the sixteenth century, things have lost their ability to embody the identity (an un-alienated sense of self and an embodied sense of memory) that a positive fetishism infuses into the products of human labor. When things — and, for Stallybrass, especially clothes — are not subsumed into the capitalist system of exchange value, they allow the individual "to hold onto oneself" and "to hold onto a memory system." For Stallybrass, "What little wealth [workers] had was stored not in *money* in *banks* but as *things* in the *house*" (202).

13. Virginia Yans-McLaughlin, "Metaphors of Self in History: Subjectivity, Oral Narrative, and Immigration Studies" in *Immigration Reconsidered: History, Sociology, and Politics*, ed. by Virginia Yans-McLaughlin (New York: Oxford U Press, 1990) 265.

14. Tratner 72.

15. Tratner focuses on sexuality and tends to gloss over notions of deficit and desire in reconstructions of ethnic identity. But what, if anything, of *value* do immigrants *save* from their homeland and original ethnic community? What *values* must they *borrow* from their host culture? Tratner's analysis of *Gatsby* suggests that that novel posited new ideologies of economics and sexuality simultaneously — in both sex and money, saving up was no longer seen as safe or healthful, but as dangerous, limiting, repressive.

16. See chapter 5 on Abraham Cahan. Andrew R. Heinze coined this evocative phrase to discuss the process by which Jews migrating from the eastern European village to the North American city, found that despite the low wages they may have received in various forms of labor, they still had more opportunity to spend money on commodities than they did in their homelands. What had been considered luxuries in the old country — including fashionable clothes — suddenly became mundane, everyday items. This shift in the meaning of commodities affected how Jewish immigrants saw the importance and sacredness of items they brought with them from the old world. See Heinze, *Adapting to Abundance: Jewish Immigrants, Mass Consumption, and the Search for American Identity* (New York: Columbia Press, 1990), especially Chapter 3 and Chapter 5.

17. Anzia Yezierska, *Hungry Hearts* (1919; New York: Signet, 1996) 15.

18. As a negative fetish, an object loses its *thingness*, becomes a commodity, and is bereft of its ability to contain and convey a past and a personal as well as communal meaning. As negative fetish, the object is reduced to signifying monetary value, and this results in the alienation of human experience from the objects around them. See Peter Stallybrass, "Marx's Coat" and "Worn Worlds." See, also, Martin Heidegger's discussion of *thingness* in relation not to the commodity, but to the work of art in "The Origin of the Work of Art," *Poetry, Language, Thought* (New York: Harper and Row, 1971), reprinted in Mark C. Taylor, ed., *Deconstruction in Context* (Chicago: U of Chicago P, 1986) 256–279.

19. Mary Dearborn has suggested that John Barnes is modeled after John Dewey and his student Albert Barnes. Barnes and Yezierska were both enrolled in Dewey's graduate seminar in the fall of 1917. The two were Dewey's favorite students, according to Mary Dearborn's account. However, Barnes had expressed anti-Semitic attitudes, and, as Yezierska recollects, "did not even regard me as a human being." This combination of Dewey as champion of the immigrant, and the racist Albert Barnes in the character of John Barnes helps explain the divided self we find in his attitude to Shenah Pessah. Dewey was, as his poetry suggests, just as divided as his fictionalized counterpart. Barnes's character displays this cultural and emotional confusion. See Dearborn 122.

20. Critics of *Salome of the Tenements* and Yezierksa's biographers have focused on this novel in terms of Yezierska's critique of the condescension, sexism, and subtle and not so subtle racism of the benevolent movements that John Manning represents. Gay Wilentz — following the lead of Mary Dearborn and, before her, Louise Levitas Henriksen — suggests that the marriage and break up between John Manning and Sonya Vrunsky is modeled after the relationship between millionaire philanthropist Graham Stokes and Yezierska's close Jewish socialist friend, Rose Pastor. Wilentz goes further to add that Manning is also modeled after John Dewey — as Dearborn also suggests about Manning and a series of other characters throughout Yezierska's fiction. As Wilentz puts it: Yezierska "layered her own undeveloped affair with Dewey into the plot" and "expanded the focus of [Sonya's] activism from solely class-based to include that part of herself denied in the move toward Americanization — her Jewish identity." Gay Wilentz, introduction, Anzia Yezierska, *Salome of the Tenements* (Urbana: U of Illinois P, 1995) xvii. Louise Levitas Henriksen, *Anzia Yezierska: A Writer's Life* (New Brunswick: Rutgers UP, 1988). See especially Dearborn's biographical criticism of Yezierska's work, *Love in the Promised Land*. Dearborn's is the most complex analysis of the ways in which Yezierska's relationship with Dewey informed her creation of John Manning. For further analysis of what Wilentz observes about Sonya's Jewish identity, see Goldsmith.

21. Yezierska, *Salome of the Tenements* 180.

22. According to Goldsmith: "Oscillating between the elite women she dresses and the immigrant working-girls whom she inculcates into American Standards of beauty, Sonya carves out an agonizingly tenuous position in the Americanized Jewish middle-class. Performative self-revision brings Yezierska's heroines to the threshold of agency, yet the ephemerality of these performances reminds us of just how difficult it was, and just how few were permitted, to cross the threshold into American culture" ("'Democracy of Beauty'" 183). Focusing on Sonya's refashioning of self through costume and performance, Goldsmith adds to our understanding of Yezierska's difficulties with what Wilentz sees as her "expansion" of her radical critical focus to include Jewish identity. These readings, however, don't offer closer attention to Sonya's failed financing of a fashion utopia and her bad investments (emotional and financial) in her own upward mobility.

23. Goldsmith notes that Sonya aesthetic is based almost exactly on the "model apartment" that Lillian Wald, founder of the Henry Street Settlement, displayed for the benefit of immigrant women" ("'Democracy of Beauty'" 172). For Goldsmith, Rosenblat displays some of the stock stereotypes of threatening Jewish male heterosexuality. In more overt ways than Sonya's dealings with Hollins, her association with Rosenblat distances her from an estranged racialized Jewish essence. He is the unmeltable ethnic: no amount of assimilation can change his racial core.

24. See chapter 5 above.

25. Yezierska, *Arrogant Beggar* (1927; Durham: Duke UP, 1996) 29.

26. Richardson and Addams quoted in Schreier, 107.

27. Levitas Henriksen 17.

28. Anne Hollander, *Seeing through Clothes* (New York: Viking, 1978) 393. Hollander traces the image of clothing in mythology, painting, and modern literature. She devotes several pages to the symbolism of the mirror.

29. See the discussion of *yiddishkeit*, along with notes on Irving Howe's definition in chapter 5, above, on Abraham Cahan.

Chapter 7

1. Hermione Lee, *Willa Cather: Double Lives* (New York: Pantheon1989) 8.

2. Willa Cather quoted in Lee 8.

3. See Guy Reynolds, *Willa Cather in Context: Progress, Race, Empire*; Marianne Davidson's *Willa Cather and F.J. Turner: A Contextu-*

alization; and Joseph Urgo, *Willa Cather and the Myth of American Migration*. For links between Cather and Turner that predate Hermione Lee's analysis, see Lionel Trilling, *Speaking of Literature and Society*, ed. Diana Trilling (New York: HBJ, 1980), and James E. Miller, Jr., "*My Ántonia*: A Frontier Drama of Time," *American Quarterly* 4:10 (1958).

4. Alan Trachtenberg and Richard Slotkin have independently observed that Roosevelt's image of the backwoodsman appropriating native attire goes back to James Fenimore Cooper's Leatherstocking tales and continues long after Roosevelt and Turner are writing their histories. See Trachtenberg, "Dreaming Indian," *Raritan* 22:1 (2000) 58–81; and Slotkin, *Gunfighter Nation: The Myth of the Frontier in Twentieth-Century America* (New York: Atheneum, 1992) 33.

5. Frederick Jackson Turner, *The Frontier in American History* (New York: Holt, 1921) 4.

6. Theodore Roosevelt, *The Winning of the West, Volume I* (New York: G.P. Putnam's Sons, 1889) 114–15, emphasis mine.

7. See Preface and Chapter 1.

8. Stephen Crane, "The Bride Comes to Yellow Sky" (1896) in *Portable American Realism Reader*, ed., James Nagel and Tom Quirk (New York: Penguin, 1997) 353.

9. Willa Cather, *Early Novels and Stories*, ed. Sharon O'Brien (New York: Library of America, 1987) 280.

10. Thomas Carlyle, *Sartor Resartus*, 207.

11. Willa Cather, *My Ántonia* (1918) (Boston: Houghton Mifflin, 1988) 16.

12. Willa Cather, *The Professor's House* (1925) (New York: Vintage, 1990) 211.

13. See Susan Gubar, "Blessings in Disguise: Cross-Dressing as Re-Dressing for Female Modernists," *Massachusetts Review* 22:4 (1981) 477–508; Eve Kosofsky Sedgwick "Across Gender, Across Sexuality: Willa Cather and Others." *South Atlantic Quarterly* 88:1 (1989) 53–72. See also the following biographies: Susan Rosowski, *Voyage Perilous: Willa Cather's Romanticism* (Lincoln: U of Nebraska P, 1986), Hermione Lee, *Willa Cather*, and Janis Stout, *Willa Cather: The Writer and Her World* (Charlottesville: UP of Virginia). See also Judith Butler's "Dangerous Crossings," *Bodies that Matter: On the Discursive Limits of "Sex"* (New York: Routledge, 1993). While all of these critical studies and biographies attend, in some way, to questions of *gendered* cross-dressing, none examines the question of ethnic masquerade in any significant or systematic way. Only Katrina Irving's study of ethnicity and sexuality points out the importance of ethnic cross-dressing in Cather. See Irving, "Displacing Homosexuality: The Use of Ethnicity in Willa Cather's *My Ántonia*," *Modern Fiction Studies* 36:1 (1990) 91–102

14. David Spurr, *The Rhetoric of Empire: Colonial Discourse in Journalism, Travel Writing, and Imperial Administration* (Durham: Duke UP, 1994) 57.

15. Cather, *A Lost Lady* (1923; New York: Vintage, 1951) 13, 16.

16. Cather quoted in Lee 8.

17. In "Blessings in Disguise," (1981) Susan Gubar places Cather in the company of other "female modernists" who "escaped" confining gender roles by dressing as men. For Cather, the "male narrator is at least metaphorically a kind of mask worn by the female writer to attain the trappings of authority" (Gubar 485). Eve Kosofsky Sedgwick pursues this same line of investigation in "Across Gender, Across Sexuality" (1989). Cather's biographers, from Susan Rosowski (1986) to Hermione Lee (1989) to Janis Stout (2000) also read her costuming almost exclusively in terms of gender. Judith Butler (1993) has argued that Cather's use of a male author-narrator in *My Ántonia* is part of her wider use of "masculine names" in a generalized literary "cross-dressing" in her work (Butler, 145). These are Cather's "dangerous crossings," a term that Butler takes from "Tom Outland's Story" in order to analyze Cather's radical play with gender and sexual identity. Challenging readings of Cather as "masculine-identified," Butler offers Cather's dangerous crossings of geographical and bodily boundaries as the novelist's subversion of normative sexuality and gender. Butler moves from *My Ántonia* to Cather's early stories — "Tommy the Unsentimental" and "Paul's Case" — to suggest that her crossing of gender boundaries challenges both gender and sexuality through a complex sacrifice and appropriation of identity. Both male and female characters give up their own (senses of) self in order to appropriate normative identities for a sexually marginalized identity. Janis P. Stout's recent autobiography cautions us against assuming too much about Cather's personal clothing or her literary guises. What others have called her men's clothes were, according to Stout, masculine styles popular among many women of the time, and her deconstructive performance of gender was matched by her discovery of her essential sexual identity (Stout, 6 and 58).

18. Irving *does* begin to point us in the direction of how ethnicity and homosexuality cross. Irving makes a convincing argument that in *My Ántonia* ethnicity effectively displaces homosexuality. However, the potentially rich field of costume and clothing remains unexamined as a potential motif through which the link between sexuality and ethnicity can be negotiated.

19. Patricia Williams, "From Folk to Fashion: Dress Adaptations of Norwegian Immigrant Women in the Midwest" in Patricia A. Cunningham and Susan Voso Lab, eds., *Dress in American Culture* (Bowling Green, OH: Bowling Green State UP, 1993) 95–108, 105.

20. See J. Hector St. John de Crèvecoeur, *Letters from an American Farmer*, Letter III.

21. See Chapter 1 of the present study.

22. Cather, "My First Novels (There Were Two)," *Willa Cather on Writing: Critical Studies on Writing as an Art* (New York: Knopf, 1949) 92.

23. Cather, *Early Novels and Stories*, 550.

24. Guy Reynolds has observed that Cather's writing about the American frontier owes more to the historical model of Michelet than it does to that of Frederick Jackson Turner, because she sees America's coming of age not as exceptional, but as one manifestation of a form of nation building that goes back to the founding of Rome narrated in *The Aeniad* and that can be traced through the "amalgamation of races" that Michelet depicts in his history of France. See Reynolds, *Willa Cather in Context: Progress, Race, Empire* (New York: St. Martin's, 1996): 65–67 and 47.

25. See Walter Benn Michaels, *Our America: Nativism, Modernism, and Pluralism* (Durham: Duke U P, 1995). Michaels uses the term "nativist modernism" to describe Cather's adoption of "vanished races" of the Midwest and Southwest as her white protagonists' ancestors. He argues that in Cather, "identity is a function of inheritance, but what gets inherited is not just a biology, it's a culture" (37). And, "it was only because they *were* dead that [American Indians] could assume the status of cultural standard" (38).

26. See Dani Cavallaro and Alexandra Warwick, *Fashioning the Frame*. Clothing is a supplement, and "the supplement operates simultaneously as an optional appendix and as a completing and hence necessary element" of identity" (v). See Chapter 2 above.

27. John N. Swift, "Unwrapping the Mummy: Cather's Mother Eve and the Business of Desire," *Willa Cather and the American Southwest*, ed. John N. Swift and Joseph R. Urgo (Lincoln: U of Nebraska, 2002) 13–21.

28. According to Reynolds, "When we turn to Thorstein Veblen we discover a remarkably similar jeremiad on 'conspicuous consumption'" as the one Cather aims at "the modern businessman" (135). Reynolds states that "Cather and Veblen were satirists who illustrated the materialist inadequacy of contemporary America by juxtaposing their society against idealized, earlier civilizations" (133). Thus, even Cather's critique of American avarice relies on the imperialist fashioning of noble savagery.

29. Reynolds reads *The Professor's House* in relation to the Carnegie Museum as textual and institutional incorporations of American history. The importance of ancient artifacts in both underscores Cather's imperial designs: "to understand modern man and his achievements it was necessary to juxtapose contemporary exhibits [or characters and settings, in Cather's case] against artifacts drawn from the ancient or even prehistoric world" (Reynolds 28).

30. See also Marianne Davidson's *Willa Cather and F. J. Turner: A Contextualization* (Heidelberg: Universitätsverlag C. Winter). While Davidson defends and attempts to mitigate Turner's racial/racist theories about the American frontier, even she acknowledges the influence of Anglo-Saxonism on Turner's personal and professional thought. See, for example, 44–45.

Postscript

1. Carol Schields, *Dressing up for the Carnival* (New York: Penguin, 2000) 23.
See Billie J. Jones, "The Fabrics of Her Life: Cloth as Symbol in Ozick's *The Shawl*," *Studies in American Jewish Literature* 21 (2002) 39–51; and Andrew Gordon, "Cynthia Ozick's 'The Shawl and the Transitional Object," *Literature and Psychology* 40.1–2 (1994) 1–9.

2. Mary Antin, *The Promised Land* (1912; New York: Penguin, 1997) 3.

3. See Babak Elahi, "The Heavy Garments of the Past: Mary and Frieda Antin in *The Promised Land*," *College Literature* 32.4 (2005) 29–49.

4. Jamaica Kincaid, *Lucy* (1990; New York: Plume, 1991) 7.

5. Cynthia Ozick, *The Shawl* (1980; New York: Vintage International, 1983) 59.

6. Tomas Ybarra-Frausto, "Rasquachismo: A Chicano Sensibility," *Chicano Art: Resistance and Affirmation, 1965–1985*, ed. Richard Griswald del Castillo, Teresa McKenna and Yvonne Yarbro-Bejarano (Los Angeles: Wight Art Gallery, UC P, 1991) 157.

7. Sandra Cisneros, *Caramelo* (2002; New York: Vintage Contemporary, 2003) 96.

8. See Alan Howard, "Labor, History, and Sweatshops in the New Global Economy," *No Sweat: Fashion, Free Trade, and the Rights of Garment Workers*, ed. Andrew Ross (New York: Verso: 1997) 151–172; and Susan B. Kaiser, "Identity, Postmodernity, and the Global Apparel Marketplace," *Meanings of Dress*, ed. Mary Lynn Damhorst, Kimberley A. Miller, Susan O. Michelman (New York: Fairchild, 1999) 106–114.

Bibliography

Adams, Henry. *The Education of Henry Adams.* New York: Modern Library, 1931.

Adams, Richard. "Heir of Propriety: Inheritance, 'The Impressions of a Cousin,' and the Proprietary Vision of Henry James." *American Literature* 71:3 (Sept 1999) 463–91.

Addams, Jane. *Twenty Years at Hull House.* 1910. New York: Signet, 1981.

Agnew, Jean-Christophe. "The Consuming Vision of Henry James." *The Culture of Consumption: Critical Essays in American History 1880–1980.* Ed. Richard Wightman Fox and T.J. Jackson Lears. New York: Pantheon Books, 1983. 65–100.

Alger, Horatio. *Ragged Dick.* 1867. *Ragged Dick and Mark, the Match Boy: Two Novels by Horatio Alger.* Ed. Richard Fink. New York: Scribner, 1998.

Anderson, Mark. *Kafka's Clothes: Ornament and Aestheticism in the Habsburg Fin de Siècle.* Oxford: Oxford UP, 1992.

Antin, Mary. *The Promised Land.* New York: Penguin, 1997 (1912).

Appel, John J., and Selma Appel. "The Huddled Masses and the Little Red Schoolhouse." Ed. Bernard J. Weiss. *American Education and the European Immigrant: 1840–1940.* Urbana: U of Illinois P, 1982. 17–29.

Balibar, Etienne and Immanual Wallerstein. *Race, Nation, Class: Ambiguous Identities.* London: Verso, 1991. 86–106.

Banta, Martha. "Men, Women, and the American Way." *The Cambridge Companion to Henry James.* Ed. Jonathan Freedman. Cambridge: Cambridge UP, 1998. 21–39.

Barrish, Phillip. *American Literary Realism, Critical Theory, and Intellectual Prestige, 1880–1995.* Cambridge, UK: Cambridge UP, 2001.

———. "'The Genuine Article': Ethnicity, Capital, and *The Rise of David Levinsky.*" *American Literary History* 5:4 (Winter 1993) 643–662.

Behdad, Ali. *Belated Travelers: Orientalism in the Age of Colonial Dissolution.* Durham: Duke, 1994.

Berman, Marshall. *All That Is Solid Melts into Air: The Experience of Modernity.* New York: Penguin, 1988.

Berthold, Michael. "Cross-Dressing and Forgetfulness of Self in William Wells Brown's *Clotel.*" *College Literature* 20:3 (October 93) 19–30.

Blair, Sara. *Henry James and the Writing of Race and Nation.* New York: Cambridge UP, 1996.

Boyarin, Daniel, and Jonathan Boyarin. "Diaspora: Generation and the Ground of Jewish identity," *Critical Inquiry* 19.4 (1993): 693–725.

Brekke, Linzy A. "The 'Scourge of Fashion': Political Economy and the Politics of Consumption in the Early Republic." *Early American Studies* 3.1 (2005): 111–139.

Breward, Christopher. *The Culture of Fashion.* Manchester: Manchester UP, 1995.

Brooks Picken, Mary. *The Secrets of Distinctive Dress: Harmonious, Becoming, and Beautiful Dress—Its Value and How to Achieve It.* Scranton, PA: 1918.

Butler, Judith. *Bodies That Matter: On the*

Discursive Limits of "Sex." New York: Routledge, 1993.

Cahan, Abraham. "The Autobiography of an American Jew." *McClure's Magazine* 41.3 (July 1913).

———. *The Rise of David Levinsky*. 1917. New York: Penguin, 1993.

———. *Yekl and the Imported Bridegroom, and Other Stories of the New York Ghetto*. New York: Dover, 1970.

Cather, Willa. *Early Novels and Stories*. Ed. Sharon O'Brien, New York: Library of America, 1990.

———. *Later Novels*. Ed. Sharon O'Brien. New York: Library of America, 1990.

———. *My Antonia*. 1918. Boston: Houghton Mifflin, 1988.

———. *O' Pioneers!* In *Willa Cather: Early Novels and Stories*. Sharon O'Brien, Ed. New York: Library of America, 1990.

———. *The Professor's House*. 1925. New York: Vintage, 1990.

———. *Willa Cather on Writing: Critical Studies on Writing as an Art*. New York: Knopf, 1949.

Cavallaro, Dani, and Alexandra Warwick. *Fashioning the Frame: Boundaries, Dress and Body*. Oxford: Berg, 1998.

Cavanaugh, Cheryl Lynn. "Fashion, Class, and Labor: Clothing in American Women's Fiction." Diss. U of Illinois at Urbana-Champaign, 1998.

Chametzky, Jules. Introduction (1993). *The Rise of David Levinsky*. New York: Penguin, 1997.

Chesnutt, Charles W. *The Marrow of Tradition*. 1901. *The African-American Novel in the Age of Reaction*. Ed. William L. Andrews. New York: Mentor, 1992.

———, and Diana Crane. *Fashion and Its Social Agendas: Class, Gender, and Identity in Clothing*. Chicago: U of Chicago P, 2000.

Cisneros, Sandra. *Caramelo*. 2002. New York: Vintage Contemporary, 2003.

Corbin, Harry A. *The Men's Clothing Industry: Colonial through Modern Times*. New York: Fairchild, 1970.

Crèvecoeur, Hector St. John. *Letters from an American Farmer and Sketches of 18th-Century America*, New York: Penguin Books, 1981.

Cunningham, Patricia. "Simplicity in Dress: A Symbol of American Ideals." Eds. Patricia A. Cunningham and Susan Voso Lab. *Dress in American Culture* (Bowling Green, OH: Bowling Green State U Popular P, 1993): 181–199.

Davidson, Marianne. *Willa Cather and F. J. Turner: A Contextualization*. Heidelberg: Universitätsverlag C. Winter, 1999.

Dearborn, James Van Ness. "The Psychology of Clothing" *Psychological Monographs* 26 (1918). Excerpted and reprinted in Kim K.P. Johnson, Susan J. Torntore and Joanne B. Eicher, eds. *Fashion Foundations: Early Writings on Fashion and Dress*, Oxford: Berg, 2003: 37–40.

Dearborn, Mary. *Love in the Promised Land: The Story of Anzia Yezierska and John Dewey*. New York: Free P, 1988.

———. *Pocahontas's Daughters: Gender and Ethnicity in American Culture*. New York: Oxford UP, 1986.

Deleuze, Gilles, and Felix Guattari. *Kafka: Toward a Minor Literature*. Minneapolis: U of Minnesota P, 1986.

Dijkstra, Bram. *Evil Sisters: The Threat of the Female and the Cult of Manhood*. New York: Alfred A. Knopf, 1996.

Dreiser, Theodore. *Sister Carrie*. 1899. Ed. Donald Pizer. 3rd ed. New York: Norton, 2006.

Duster, Troy. "The 'Morphing' Properties of Whiteness." *The Making and Unmaking of Whiteness*. Ed. Rasmussen et al. Durham: Duke UP, 2001.

Edel, Leon. *Henry James: The Master: 1901–1916*. 1972. New York: Avon-Discus, 1978.

Edwards, Justin. "Henry James's 'Alien' New York: Gender and Race in *The American Scene*." *American Studies International* 36:1 (February 98) 66–80.

Eicher, Joanne B., and Barbara Sumberg. "World Fashion, Ethnic, and National Dress." *Dress and Ethnicity: Change Across Space and Time*. Ed. Joanne B. Eicher. Oxford: Berg, 1995.

Elahi, Babak. "The Heavy Garments of the Past: Mary and Frieda Antin in *The Promised Land*." *College Literature* 32.4 (2005): 29–49.

Emerson, Ralph Waldo. "Nature." *Ralph Waldo Emerson: Selected Essays*. Ed. Larzer Ziff. New York: Penguin, 1982.

Engel, David. "The Discrepancies of the Modern: Reevaluating Abraham Cahan's

The Rise of David Levinsky," *Studies in Jewish American Literature* 5:2 (Winter 1979) 68–91.
Evans Braziel, Jana, and Anita Mannur, eds. *Theorizing Diaspora: A Reader.* Malden, MA: Blackwell, 2003.
Ewen, Elizabeth. *Immigrant Women in the Land of Dollars: Life and Culture on the Lower East Side, 1890–1925.* New York: Monthly Review Press, 1985.
Ferraro, Thomas J. *Ethnic Passages: Literary Immigrants in Twentieth Century America.* Chicago: U of Chicago P, 1993.
Fischer, Gayle Veronica. "'The Daughters of Sion Are Naughty': Clothing and Sexual Oppression in Puritan New England." *Journal of Unconventional History* 3.1 (1991): 27–50.
Fisher, Philip. *Hard Facts: Setting and Form in the American Novel.* New York: Oxford UP, 1987.
Flannigan, John H. "Thea Kronborg's Vocal Transvestism: Willa Cather and the 'Voz Contralto.'" *Modern Fiction Studies* 40:4 (Winter 1994) 737–763.
Franco, Felluga D. "The Critic's New Clothes: Sartor Resartus," *Criticism* 37:4 (Fall 1995) 583–601.
Freedman, Jonathan, ed. *The Cambridge Companion to Henry James.* Cambridge, UK: Cambridge UP, 1998.
———. *The Temple of Culture: Assimilation and Anti-Semitism in Literary Anglo-America.* London: Oxford UP, 1999.
Freud, Sigmund. "The Uncanny." 1919. *Studies in Parapsychology.* New York: Collier, 1971. 19–62.
Gelfant, Blanche H. "What More Can Carrie Want? Naturalistic Ways of Consuming Women." *Prospects: An Annual of American Cultural Studies* 19 (1994): 389–417. Reprinted in ed. Donald Pizer. *Sister Carrie.* Norton: New York, 2006 (554–573).
Gilman, Sander L. *Difference and Pathology: Stereotypes of Sexuality, Race, and Madness.* Ithaca: Cornell UP, 1985.
Girgus, Sam B. *The New Covenant: Jewish Writers and the American Idea.* Chapel Hill: U of North Carolina P, 1984.
Glenn, Susan. *Daughters of the Shtetl: Life and Labor in the Immigrant Generation.* Ithaca: Cornell UP, 1990.
Goldsmith, Meredith. "'The Democracy of Beauty': Fashioning Ethnicity and Gender in the Fiction of Anzia Yezierska." *Yiddish* 11:3–4 (1999) 166–87.
———. "Dressing, Passing, and Americanizing: Anzia Yezierska's Sartorial Fictions." *Studies in American Jewish Literature* 16 (1997) 34–45.
Gordon, Andrew. "Cynthia Ozick's 'The Shawl and the Transitional Object." *Literature and Psychology* 40.1–2 (1994): 1–9.
Green, David. "The Price of Success: Use of the Bildungsroman Plot in Abraham Cahan's *The Rise of David Levinsky.*" *Studies in American Jewish Literature* 12.2 (1993) 19–24.
Gubar, Susan. "Blessings in Disguise: Cross-Dressing as Re-Dressing for Female Modernists." *Massachusetts Review* 22:4 (Autumn 1981) 477–508.
Haenni, Sabine. "Visual and Theatrical Culture, Tenement Fiction, and the Immigrant Subject in Abraham Cahan's *Yekl.*" *American Literature* 71:3 (1999) 493–529.
Hall, Stanley. "Some Aspects of the Early Sense of Self." *American Journal of Psychology* (1898). *Fashion Foundations: Early Writings on Fashion and Dress*, Ed. Kim K.P. Johnson, Susan J. Torntore and Joanne B. Eicher. Oxford: Berg, 2003: 43–50.
Hallab, Mary. "The Romance of Old Clothes in a Fatal Chest." *Henry James Review*, 16:3 (1995) 315–320.
Harris, Susan K. "Problems of Representation in Turn-of-the-Century Immigrant Fiction." *American Realism and the Canon.* Ed. Tom Quirk and Gary Scharnhorst. Newark: U of Delaware P, 1994. 127–142.
Haviland, Beverley. *Henry James's Last Romance: Making Sense of the Past and the American Scene.* Cambridge, UK: Cambridge UP, 1997.
Heidegger, Martin. "The Origin of the Work of Art." *Poetry, Language, Thought.* New York: Harper and Row, 1971. Rpt. Mark C. Taylor, ed. *Deconstruction in Context.* Chicago: U of Chicago P, 1986.
Heinze, Andrew. *Adapting to Abundance: Jewish Immigrants, Mass Consumption, and the Search for American Identity.* New York: Columbia UP, 1990.
Hendrick, Burton J. "The Jewish Invasion of America." *McClure's Magazine* 40.5 (March 1913) 125–165.

Higham, John. *Send These to Me: Immigrants in Urban America*. 1985. Revised Edition. Baltimore: The Johns Hopkins UP, 1987.
———. *Strangers in the Land: Patterns of American Nativism, 1860–1925*. New Brunswick, N.J.: Rutgers UP, 1955.
Hoffman, Eva. "The New Nomads," *Letters of Transit: Reflections on Exile, Identity, Language, and Loss*, ed. Andre Aciman. New York: New Press, 1999. 35–63.
Holland, Lawrence. *The Expense of Vision: Essays on the Craft of Henry James*. Princeton, NJ: Princeton UP, 1964.
Hollander, Anne. *Feeding the Eye: Essays*. New York: Ferrar, Straus and Giroux, 1999.
Howard, Alan. "Labor, History, and Sweatshops in the New Global Economy." *No Sweat: Fashion, Free Trade, and the Rights of Garment Workers*. Ed. Andrew Ross. New York: Verso: 1997. 151–172.
Howe, Irving. *World of Our Fathers*. 1976. Abr. ed. New York: Bantam, 1980.
Howells, William Dean. *The Rise of Silas Lapham*. New York: Library of America, 1991.
Hughes, Clair. *Dressed in Fiction*. Oxford: Berg, 2005.
———. *Henry James and the Art of Dress*. Hampshire, UK: Palgrave, 2001.
Hutchinson, John, and Anthony D. Smith, eds. *Ethnicity*. London: Oxford UP, 1996.
Irving, Katrina. *Immigrant Mothers: Narratives of Race and Maternity, 1890–1925*. Urbana: U of Illinois P, 2000.
Jacobson, Matthew Frye. *Whiteness of a Different Color: European Immigration and the Alchemy of Race*. Cambridge, MA: Harvard UP, 1998.
James, Henry. *The Ambassadors*. 1903. New York: Penguin, 1986.
———. *The American Essays of Henry James*. Ed. Leon Edel. Princeton, NJ: Princeton UP, 1989.
———. *The American Scene*. 1907. New York: Penguin, 1994.
———. *Complete Stories, 1564–1874*. New York: The Library of America, 1999.
———. *Complete Stories 1898–1910*. New York: Library of America, 1996.
———. *French Writers and American Women Essays*. Ed. Peter Guitenhuis. Branford, Connecticut: Compass Publishing Company, 1960.
———. *The Golden Bowl*. 1904. Oxford: Oxford UP, 1983.
———. *The Portrait of a Lady*. 1908. Ed. Robert D. Bramberg. 2nd ed. New York: Norton, 1995.
———. *The Princess Casamassima*. 1886. New York: Penguin, 1987.
———. *The Reverberator*. 1888. New York: Grove, n.d.
———. *What Maisie Knew*. 1897. Ed. Adrian Poole. Oxford: Oxford UP, 1998.
———. *The Wings of the Dove*. 1902. New York: Penguin, 1985.
James, William. *Psychology: The Briefer Course*, ed. Gordon Allport. New York: Harper Torchbooks/The Academy Library, 1961.
Jones, Billie J. "The Fabrics of Her Life: Cloth as Symbol in Ozick's *The Shawl*." *Studies in American Jewish Literature* 21 (2002): 39–51.
Kaiser, Susan B. "Identity, Postmodernity, and the Global Apparel Marketplace." *Meanings of Dress*. Ed. Mary Lynn Damhorst, Kimberley A. Miller, Susan O. Michelman. New York: Fiarchild, 1999. 106–114.
Kandiyoti, Dalia. "Comparative Diasporas: The Local and the Global in Abraham Cahan and Alberto Gerchunoff." *Modern Fiction Studies* 44:1 (Spring 1998) 77–122.
Kaplan, Amy. *The Social Construction of American Realism*. Chicago: U of Chicago P, 1988.
Kincaid, Jamaica. *Lucy*. 1990. New York: Plume, 1991.
Konzett, Delia Caparoso. "Administered Identities and Linguistic Assimilation: The Politics of Immigrant English in Anzia Yezierska's *Hungry Hearts*." *American Literature* 69:3 (1997) 595–621.
Kosak, Hadassa. *Cultures of Opposition: Jewish Immigrant Workers, New York City, 1881–1905*. Albany: SUNY, 2000.
Lacan, Jacques. "The Mirror Stage." *Écrits: A Selection*. Trans. Alan Sheridan. New York: W.W. Norton, 1977.
Lauer, Robert and Jeanette Lauer. *Fashion Power: The Meaning of Fashion in American Society*. Englewood Cliffs, New Jersey: Prentice-Hall, 1981.
Laver, James. *Costume and Fashion: A Concise History*. 1982. Revised Edition. New York: Thames and Hudson, 1995.

Lears, J. T. Jackson. *No Place of Grace: Antimodernism and the Transformation of American Culture 1880–1920*. New York: Pantheon, 1981.
Lee, Hermione. *Willa Cather: Double Lives*. New York: Pantheon, 1989.
Levine, Donald N. Introduction. *Georg Simmel: On Individuality and Social Forms, Selected Writings*. Ed. Donald N. Levin. Chicago: U of Chicago P, 1971.
Levitas Henriksen, Louise. *Anzia Yezierska: A Writer's Life*. New Brunswick: Rutgers UP, 1988.
Light, Walter. *Industrializing America: The Nineteenth Century*. Baltimore: Johns Hopkins UP, 1995.
Lowell, Edward J. "Clothes: Historically Considered." *Scribner's Magazine* 14:3 (September 1893) 288–305. *The Making of America*. Cornell University Library. 16 November 2006. <http://cdl.library.cornell.edu/moa. 288>.
Marx, Karl. *Capital: Volume One*. Trans. Ben Fowkes. New York: Vintage, 1977.
McNamara, Kevin R. "The Ames of the Good Society: *Sister Carrie* and Social Engineering," *Criticism* 34 (1992) 217–35.
Michaels, Walter Benn. *The Gold Standard and the Logic of Naturalism*. Berkeley: UCP, 1987.
_____. *Our America: Nativism, Modernism, and Pluralism*. Durham: Duke UP, 1995.
Morris, Linda. "Behind the Veil: Clothing, Race, and Gender in Mark Twain's *Pudd'nhead Wilson*." *Studies in American Fiction* 27.1 (1999): 37–52.
Nackenoff, Carol. *The Fictional Republic: Horatio Alger and American Political Discourse*. New York: Oxford UP, 1994.
Naficy, Hamid. *The Making of Exile Cultures: Iranian Television in Los Angeles*. Minneapolis: U of Minnesota P, 1993.
Nixon, Nicola. "Men and Coats; or The Politics of the Dandiacal Body in Melville's 'Benito Cereno.'" *PMLA*. 114.3 (May 1999) 359–373.
North, Gary. "The Puritan Experiment with Sumptuary Legislation." *Freeman* 24.6 (1974): 341–55.
Núñez de Cabeza de Vaca, Alvar. *Interlinear to Cabeza de Vaca: His Relation of the Journey, Florida to the Pacific, 1528–1536*, trans. Haniel Long. Buffalo, NY: Frontier, 1969.

Excerpted in *Aztlan: An Anthology of Mexican American Literature*. Ed. Luis Valdez and Stan Steiner (New York: Vintage, 1972) 40–1.
Okonkwo, Christopher. "Of Repression, Assertion, and the Speakerly Dress: Anzia Yezierska's *Salome of the Tenements*." *MELUS* 25:1 (Spring 2000) 129–45.
Ozick, Cynthia. *The Shawl*. 1980. New York: Vintage International, 1983.
Patterson, Orlando. *Slavery and Social Death*. Cambridge, MA: Harvard UP, 1982.
Perez-Firmat, Gustavo. *Life on the Hyphen: The Cuban-American Way*. Austin: U of Texas P, 1994.
Peters, John Durham. "Exile, Nomadism, and Diaspora: the Stakes of Mobility in the Western Canon." *Home, Exile, Homeland: Film, Media, and the Politics of Place*. Ed. Hamid Naficy. New York: Routledge, 1999. 17–41.
Posnock, Ross. "Affirming the Alien: The Pragmatist Pluralism of *The American Scene*." *The Cambridge Companion to Henry James*. Ed. Jonathan Freedman. Cambridge, UK: Cambridge UP, 1998. 224–246.
Pressman, Richard S. "Abraham Cahan, Capitalist; David Levinsky, Socialist." *Studies in American Jewish Literature* 12.2 (1993) 2–18.
Reynolds, Guy. *Willa Cather in Context: Progress, Race, Empire*. New York: St. Martin's, 1996.
Roosevelt, Theodore. *The Winning of the West, Volume I*. New York, 1889.
Rosowski, Susan J. *Voyage Perilous: Willa Cather's Romanticism*. Lincoln: U of Nebraska P, 1986.
Rowe, John Carlos. *Henry Adams and Henry James: The Emergence of a Modern Consciousness*. Ithaca: Cornell UP, 1976.
_____. *The Other Henry James*. Durham: Duke UP, 1998.
Sanchez, Rosaura. *Chicano Discourse: A Socio-Historic Perspective*. Houston: Arte Publico, 1994.
Sanders, Ronald. *The Lower East Side Jews: An Immigrant Generation*. New York: Dover, 1999.
Schreier, Barbara. *Becoming American Women: Clothing and the Jewish Immigrant Experience, 1880–1920*. Chicago: Chicago Historical Society, 1994.

Sedgwick, Eve Kosofsky. "Across Gender, Across Sexuality: Willa Cather and Others." *South Atlantic Quarterly* 88:1 (Winter 1989) 53–72.

Seguin, Robert. *Around Quitting Time: Work and Middle-Class Fantasy in American Fiction.* Durham: Duke UP, 2001.

Shields, Carol. *Dressing Up for the Carnival.* New York: Penguin, 2000.

Shumway, David. *Creating American Civilization: A Genealogy of American Literature as an Academic Discipline.* Minneapolis: U of Minnesota P, 1994.

Simmel, Georg. "Fashion." *Georg Simmel: On Individuality and Social Forms, Selected Writings.* Ed. Donald N. Levin. Chicago: U of Chicago P, 1971.

Simon, Rita J., and Susan H. Alexander. *The Ambivalent Welcome: Print Media, Public Opinion and Immigration.* Westport, CT: Praeger, 1993.

Slotkin, Richard. *Gunfighter Nation: The Myth of the Frontier in Twentieth-Century America.* New York: Atheneum, 1992.

Sollors, Werner. *Beyond Ethnicity: Consent and Descent in American Culture.* Oxford: Oxford UP, 1987.

Soper, Kate. "Dress Needs: Reflections on the Clothed Body, Selfhood and Consumption." *Body Dressing.* Ed. Joanne Entwistle and Elizabeth Wilson. Dress, Body, Culture. Series ed. Joanne B. Eicher. Oxford: Berg, 2001. 33–58.

Spivak, Gayatri. *In Other Worlds: Essays in Cultural Politics.* New York: Methuen, 1987.

Spurr, David. *The Rhetoric of Empire: Colonial Discourse in Journalism, Travel Writing, and Imperial Administration.* Durham: Duke UP, 1994.

Stallybrass, Peter. "Marx's Coat." *Border Fetishisms: Material Objects in Unstable Spaces.* Ed. Patricia Syper. New York: Routledge, 1998. 183–207.

———. "Worn Worlds: Clothes, Mourning, and the Life of Things." *The Yale Review* 18:2 (April 1993) 35–75.

Stout, Janis P. *Willa Cather: The Writer and Her World.* Charlottesville: UP of Virginia, 2000.

Stubbs, Katherine. Introduction. Anzia Yezierska. *Arrogant Beggar* (1927). Durham: Duke UP, 1996.

———. "Reading Material: Contextualizing Clothing in the Work of Anzia Yezierksa." *MELUS* 23:2 (Summer 1998) 157–173.

Swift, John N., and Joseph R. Urgo, eds. *Willa Cather and the American Southwest.* Lincoln, U of Nebraska P, 2002.

Takaki, Ronald. *A Different Mirror: A History of Multicultural America.* Boston: Back Bay, 1993.

Thacker, Robert. Introduction. *The Autobiography of S. S. McClure.* Lincoln: Bison Books, 1997.

Thoreau, Henry David. *Walden.* 1842. *The Portable Thoreau.* Ed. Carl Bode. New York: Penguin, 1947.

Trachtenberg, Alan. "Dreaming Indian." *Raritan* 22:1 (2000) 58–81.

———. *The Incorporation of America: Culture and Society in the Gilded Age.* New York: Hill and Wang, 2007.

Tratner, Michael. *Deficits and Desires: Economics and Sexuality in Twentieth Century Literature.* Stanford, CA: Stanford UP, 2001.

Turner, Frederick Jackson. *The Frontier in American History.* New York: Holt, 1921.

Urgo, Joseph R. *Willa Cather and the Myth of American Migration.* Urbana: U of Illinois P, 1995.

Veblen, Thorsten. *The Theory of the Leisure Class.* 1899. New York: Penguin, 1994.

Waldstreicher, David. "Why Thomas Jefferson and African Americans Wore Their Politics on Their Sleeves: Dress and Mobilization Between American Revolutions." Eds. Jeffrey L. Pasley, Andrew W. Robertson, and David Waldstreicher, *Beyond the Founders: New Approaches to the Political History of the Early American Republic.* Chapel Hill: U of North Carolina P, 2004: 79–103.

Warren, Kenneth. *Black and White Strangers: Race and American Literary Realism.* Chicago: U of Chicago P, 1993.

Webb, Wilfred Mark. *The Heritage of Dress: Being Notes on the History and Evolution of Clothes.* New York: McClure, 1908.

Wharton, Edith. *The House of Mirth.* New York: Bantam, 1984.

Wilentz, Gay. Introduction. Anzia Yezierska. *Salome of the Tenements* (1923) Urbana: U of Illinois P, 1995.

Williams, Patricia. "From Folk to Fashion: Dress Adaptations of Norwegian Immigrant Women in the Midwest." *Dress in American Culture*. Ed. Patricia A. Cunningham and Susan Voso Lab (Bowling Green: Bowling Green State U P, 1993) 95–108.

Wilson, Elizabeth. *Adorned in Dreams: Fashion and Modernity*. Berkley: U of California P, 1985.

Yans-McLaughlin, Virginia. "Metaphors of Self in History: Subjectivity, Oral Narrative, and Immigration Studies." *Immigration Reconsidered: History, Sociology, and Politics*. Ed. Virginia Yans-McLaughlin. New York: Oxford UP, 1990. 254–290.

Ybarra-Frausto, Tomas. "Rasquachismo: A Chicano Sensibility." *Chicano Art: Resistance and Affirmation, 1965–1985*. Ed. Richard Griswald del Castillo, Teresa McKenna and Yvonne Yarbro-Bejarano. Los Angeles: Wight Art Gallery, UC P, 1991. 155–62.

Yeazell, Ruth Bernard. "The Conspicuous Wasting of Lily Bart." *ELH* 59 (Fall 1992). 713–734.

———. *Language and Knowledge in the Late Novels of Henry James*. Chicago: U of Chicago P, 1976.

Yezierska, Anzia. *Arrogant Beggar* (1927). Durham: Duke UP, 1996.

———. *Bread Givers, A Novel: A Struggle Between a Father of the Old World and a Daughter of the New* (1925). New York: Persea, 1975.

———. *Hungry Hearts* (1919). New York: Signet, 1996.

———. *Salome of the Tenements* (1923) Urbana: U of Illinois P, 1995.

Zaborowska, Magdalena. "Americanization of a 'Queer Fellow': Performing Jewishness and Sexuality in Abraham Cahan's *The Rise of David Levinsky*." *American Studies in Scandinavia* 29.1 (1997) 18–27.

———. "The Perils of Woman's Americanization: Mary Antin's *The Promised Land*." *How We Found America*, 57.

Zakim, Michael. *Ready-Made Democracy: A History of Men's Dress in the American Republic, 1760–1860*. Chicago: U of Chicago P, 2003.

Index

adamitism 13
Adams, Henry 21, 132, 193
Addams, Jane 6, 41, 46–50, 105, 158, 194, 205
Agnew, Jean-Christophe 62, 67, 69, 71, 73, 196
Alger, Horatio, Jr. 6, 7, 14–19, 25–31, 33–37, 60, 65, 108, 115
The American Scene 62, 72, 73, 78–79, 179
Amerika 122–124, 201
Anderson, Mark 4, 122–123, 124, 192, 201
Antin, Mary 97, 124–126, 132–134, 188–189, 191–192
Antomir, Russia 110, 113, 115, 116, 122, 126, 128, 130
Arrogant Beggar 7, 139, 140, 143, 148, 156, 158–164
assimilation 2, 4, 7, 9, 48–50, 59, 108, 116, 118–122, 124–125, 133, 149, 168, 191, 192, 196, 203, 205
"Autobiography of an American Jew" 7, 131, 133–137
Aztecs 10

Balibar, Etienne 195
Banta, Martha 197
Barrish, Phillip 201
Bennett, James Gordon 36
Berman, Marshall 10
Bloomer, Amelia Jenks 52
Bolles, Albert 25
Boston 39–40, 42, 71, 97, 109, 125
Boston Common 125, 201
Boyarin, Daniel 123–124, 137, 200, 201, 202
Boyarin, Jonathan 123–124, 137, 200, 201, 202
Bread Givers 139, 140–148, 155, 159, 162, 203
Brekke, Linzy 192
Breward, Chris 99, 193, 194
Brooks Brothers 26, 193
Bryn Mawr College 79, 81
Buchanan, James 14
Burk, James 24–25

Burke, Edmund 10
Butler, Judith 171, 206

Cabeza de Vaca, Alvar Nunez 9–10, 19, 177–178, 187
Cahan, Abraham 5, 7, 24, 33, 37, 50, 53, 59–60, 72, 108–110, 112–113, 116–117, 119, 121–124, 128–137, 140, 153, 159, 187, 188, 190, 195, 196, 200, 201, 204
capitalism 18, 24, 85, 95, 105, 107, 144, 199
Caramelo 190
Carlyle, Thomas 10–13, 45, 119, 169, 206
Cather, Willa 5, 7–8, 60, 131, 138, 165, 167–168, 171–186, 187, 188, 190, 206
Cavallaro, Dani 111, 195, 199
Central Park, New York City 78–79
Chesnutt, Charles 50, 55, 57–60
Chicago 6, 82, 86–89, 96, 97, 105, 109, 178, 190
Cinderella 18, 28–30, 65–66
Cisneros, Sandra 187, 189–190
Civil War, American 14, 15, 17, 25, 34, 38, 39, 64
conspicuous consumption 4, 7, 40, 51, 76–78, 87, 89–90, 93, 96, 101–105, 109, 121, 135–137, 166, 188, 203, 207
Corbin, Henry A. 193
Crane, Diana 4, 199
Crane, Stephen 166–167, 172–173
crape 74, 75, 76, 181
"Crapy Cornelia" 73–81, 196
Cunningham, Patricia 14, 191

dandy as social type 63, 118, 120, 121, 137, 153, 167, 168–172
Darwin, Charles 20, 44
Darwin, George H. 44
Davidson, Marianne 207
Dearborn, George Van Ness 194
Dearborn, Mary 203, 205
department stores, history of 97, 99, 199
deterritorialization 111
diaspora 123, 124, 129, 200, 201, 202

Dijkstra, Bram 202
Dreiser, Theodore 5, 6, 7, 18, 24, 31, 60, 63, 82–86, 88, 91, 94, 96–97, 99–107, 108, 123, 134, 140, 198–199
Dubnow, Simon 129
Duster, Troy 195

Edel, Leon 197
Eicher, Joanne B. 193, 195
Emerson, Ralph Waldo 11, 54
Engel, David 200
Ewen, Elizabeth 2, 191, 194, 203

fabric 67, 68, 74–75, 92, 107, 182, 186, 186, 187, 189, 190; as metaphor 3–5, 8, 42, 60, 71, 74–75, 109, 134, 138, 180, 181, 186
fabrication 11, 37, 153, 188; race 55, 58, 181, 186, 195
fashion 1, 7, 15, 23, 37, 60, 62–63, 65, 67, 69, 72, 73–75, 76, 85, 88, 121, 134, 136, 140, 144, 151, 158, 197, 203; assimilation and 49; ethnicity and 108–110; gender and 51–54, 97; historiography and 176, 183, 187, 190; industry 5; psychology of 42–44, 111–112; race and 55–56; social implications of 45–47
Ferraro, Thomas J. 203
fetishism 63, 86, 112–114, 150, 181, 189, 197, 204
Fischer, Gayle Veronica 192
Fisher, Philip 85–86, 88–91, 104, 198, 199
Fitzgerald, F. Scott 149
Fordism 48
Foxlee, Ludmila 49
Frank, Leo 134, 135
Franklin, Benjamin 15–18, 20–21, 24, 30, 36, 191
Freedman, Jonathan 196
Freud, Sigmund 201
frontiersman, clothing of 165, 167, 168, 171, 173–176

Garborg, Hulda 175
garment workers' strike, 1913 7, 133, 202
Gelfant, Blanche H. 192
Gilded Age 2, 18, 40, 51, 109, 137, 139
Girgus, Samuel 202
Glenn, Susan 2, 191, 194, 203
Goethe, Johann Wolfgang von 10
Goldsmith, Meredith 203, 205
Gothic fiction 57, 58, 61–62, 63, 65, 67
The Great Gatsby 149
Greeley, Horace 35–36
Green, David 201
Gubar, Susan 171, 175, 182, 206

Haenni, Sabine 195–196
Hale, Edward Everett 125
Hallab, Mary 65–66
Harris, Susan K. 202
haskalah 129

hats 74, 94, 100, 101, 119, 158, 175, 197
Heinze, Andrew 2, 109, 110–116, 136, 192, 199, 200, 202, 204
Hendrick, Burton J. 132
The Heritage of Dress: Being Notes on the History and Evolution of Clothes 44–46
Higham, John 2, 47, 191, 194
Hoffman, Eva 111–112, 200
Hollander, Anne 1, 4, 29–30, 159, 192, 205
homespun 1, 5, 6, 13–19, 24–25, 37, 53, 64, 78, 131, 166, 192
House of Mirth 51
Howe, Irving 129
Howells, William Dean 39–41, 60, 134, 203
Hughes, Clair 1, 4, 70, 192, 194, 196, 197
Hull House Labor Museum 41, 47, 48, 49, 105
Hungry Hearts 142, 150

immigrants/immigration 1, 2, 5–8, 33, 41, 47–53, 60, 62, 69, 72–73, 78–81, 97, 108–112, 115, 123, 125–128, 133, 137, 140, 142, 147–149, 151, 153, 155, 158–160, 165, 167, 169, 176, 183, 191, 193, 200, 201, 203, 204, 205
incorporation 2, 3, 15, 37, 38, 179, 193, 207
investment, financial 24, 31, 45, 74, 95, 109, 128, 139, 141, 142, 145, 146, 147, 148, 155, 160; as metaphor 15, 27, 38, 88, 95, 109, 116, 118, 130, 137, 139–148, 152–156, 158, 161, 163, 183, 193, 198, 203, 205
invidious comparison 51, 84, 98, 100–102, 130, 135–137, 170
Irving, Katrina 175, 193, 206, 207

Jacobson, Matthew Frye 135, 195, 202
James, Henry 5, 6, 7, 9, 14, 24, 28, 36, 37, 60, 61–81, 82, 108, 181, 192, 196–197
James, William 6, 46–47, 197, 198
Jefferson, Thomas 14, 18
Jewish Daily Forward 109, 133, 200
Jewish Workers' Bund 123, 129, 201
Jews 5, 53, 110, 114, 119, 121, 123, 129, 130–131, 132, 134, 135, 137, 140, 148, 179, 181, 201, 202, 204
Jordan & Marsh's 40

Kafka, Franz 122–123, 124
Kandiyoti, Dalia 201
Kaplan, Amy 2, 85, 87, 104, 192, 193, 198, 199
Kidwell, Claudia 1, 15, 25–26, 191, 193
Kincaid, Jamaica 189
Konzett, Delia Caparoso 203
Kosak, Hadassa 2, 191, 194

Lacan, Jacques 199
Lauer, Jeannette 194
Lauer, Robert 53, 194
Laver, James 53, 194
Lears, J.T. Jackson 3, 196
Lee, Hermione 165, 206

Levitas Henriksen, Louise 205
Lincoln, Abraham 26
Lincoln, Nebraska 183
A Lost Lady 173–174
Lost in Translation 111–112
Lowell, Edward J. 41–43, 47
Lowell, Massachusetts 64

Mann, Horace 193
Marshall Field's 97
The Marrow of Tradition 55, 57–59
Marx, Karl 10, 63, 68, 80–81, 83, 84–85, 117–118, 150, 192, 196, 198, 200, 204
maskilim 129
McClure, S.S. 131, 132, 171
McClure's Magazine 131–132, 133, 134, 136, 153, 202
Mexico, literary depictions 171, 172, 190
Michaels, Walter Benn 2, 85–86, 95, 179, 192, 198, 199, 203, 204, 207
mobile subject 17, 60, 108, 122–123, 130
Montesquieu, Charles-Louis 10, 12
Morris, Linda 56
My Ántonia 167, 169–170, 171, 175, 176, 177, 179, 181–186, 206, 207

Nackenoff, Carol 18, 25, 34
Naficy, Hamid 200
New York City 7, 24, 26, 28, 34, 36, 43, 46, 52, 73, 77, 82, 89, 109, 115, 122, 124, 128, 131, 133, 135, 162, 166, 191
North, Gary 192

O Pioneers! 167–169, 171–172, 176, 177
oilcloth 81, 157, 197
Okonkwo, Christopher 203
Orientalism 52, 114
Ozick, Cynthia 187, 188, 189

Parsons, Frank Alvah 43–44, 47
Patterson, Orlando 195
Perez-Firmat, Gustavo 200
Peters, John Durham 123, 124
Picken, Mary Brooks 54, 60
Pietz, William 197
Poe, Edgar Allan 34
The Portrait of a Lady 47, 70–71
Posnock, Ross 63
post-sumptuary world 16, 17, 22, 42
The Professor's House 167, 170–171, 172, 173, 176–7, 179–182, 184–186, 207
The Promised Land 97, 125, 189, 192, 199, 201
protean subject 17, 19, 22–23
The Psychology of Dress 43
Pudd'nhead Wilson 55–57
Puritans 13–17, 96

race 2, 7, 41, 44–46, 54–59, 129–132, 135, 136, 152, 173, 191, 193, 195, 202
Ragged Dick 27–38
rasquachismo 190

rational dress 53, 194
ready-made 1–6, 14–15, 17–18, 24–38, 41, 48, 62–66, 73, 109, 165, 174, 187
realism, American literary 1–7, 10, 18, 37, 38, 40, 51, 60, 61, 68, 104, 192, 198, 204
The Reverberator 72
Revolutionary War, American 64
Reynolds, Guy 178, 179, 182, 206, 207
Richardson, Ellen 157, 158
The Rise of Silas Lapham 39–41
The Rise of David Levinsky 7, 50, 53, 72, 108, 112–138
"A Romance of Certain Old Clothes" 6, 60, 61, 62, 63–70, 196
Roosevelt, Teddy 7–8, 165–167, 173–174, 176–179, 182, 183–184, 206
"Rosa" 189
Rosowski, Susan 171, 206
Rousseau, Jean Jacques 193
Rowe, John Carlos 193, 196

Salome of the Tenements 149, 151–156, 157, 203, 205
Sanchez, Rosaura 200
sansculottism 13
Sartor Resartus 9, 11, 13, 45, 206
Scandinavians (immigrants) 8, 132, 136, 167, 175, 176, 178, 183
"A Scarf" 188–189
Schreier, Barbara 2, 191, 203
The Secrets of Distinctive Dress 54
Seguin, Robert 3, 103, 104, 192, 193, 194, 198, 199
serge 100, 107, 141, 147, 181
"The Shawl" 189
Shields, Carol 187–189
shirtwaists 37, 49, 100, 133, 161, 162
shtetl 7, 112, 115, 14–42, 147–148, 203
Simkovich, Mary 49
Simmel, Georg 46, 109, 111, 199, 200
simple dress, ideology of 5–6, 11, 13–16, 21, 26, 166, 191; *see also* homespun
Sister Carrie 3, 6, 7, 63, 82, 83, 87–107, 122, 198
Slater, Samuel 15
social Darwinism 41, 45, 50, 125, 194
social mobility 2, 5–6, 14, 16–17, 26, 30, 37, 42, 65, 86, 106, 140, 141, 203
Sollor, Werner 59
Somerset, Charles A. 65
The Song of the Lark 7, 167, 177, 179–181
Soper, Kate 84–85, 102, 107
speculation, financial 139–141, 154, 163, 203, 204
Spivak, Gayatri 197
Stallybrass, Peter 4, 63–66, 70, 74, 77, 83–84, 86, 94, 104, 189, 204
Stewart, A.T. 25, 34, 36
sumptuary laws 13, 14, 17, 46, 112, 191, 196–197
Swift, John N. 207

Takaki, Ronald 194
Talmud 113. 114, 115, 118, 127
Thoreau, Henry David 6, 11, 14, 15, 16, 19–25, 26, 28, 29, 33, 35, 36, 40, 45, 54, 59, 60, 110, 159, 169
Torah 115, 145
Trachtenberg, Alan 3, 15, 179, 192, 193, 206
Tratner, Michael 95, 149, 198, 204
Triangle shirtwaist fire 133
tsedakah 144, 204
The Turn of the Screw 74, 196, 197
Turner, Frederick Jackson 7, 165–168, 170, 173–176, 178, 182–183, 186, 206, 207
Twain, Mark 50, 55, 57, 58, 60
Twenty Years at Hull House 48, 49–50

Valdez, Luis 9–10
Veblen, Thorstein 6, 14, 45, 51, 82, 90, 100, 101, 107–109, 137, 194, 198, 203, 207
"The Velvet Glove" 75, 197
Virgil 183

Wald, Lillian 49, 205
Walden 16–25
Walden Pond 19, 24
Waldstreicher, David 191, 192
Warwick, Alexandra 111
Webb, Wilfred Mark 41, 44–50
Wharton, Edith 50, 51, 60
What Maisie Knew 74, 197
White, Shane 191
Wilentz, Gay 205
Williams, Patricia 175, 176, 191
Wilson, Christopher 193
Wilson, Elizabeth 4, 38, 42, 46, 193, 195
"Wings" 149–151, 155, 159
The Wings of the Dove 82
Winthrop, John 14

Yans-McLaughlin, Virginia 148
Ybarra-Frausto, Tomas 190
Yeazell, Ruth Bernard 51, 196
Yekl 59–60, 195
Yezierska, Anzia (Hattie Mayer) 5, 7, 60, 134, 138, 139–148, 155–159, 162–163, 181, 188, 192, 203
yiddishkeit 123–124, 129–130, 160, 205

Zakim, Michal 13–16, 25, 34–35, 191, 192, 193
Zionism 124, 128–130
Zoot Suit (play/film) 9

www.ingramcontent.com/pod-product-compliance
Lightning Source LLC
Chambersburg PA
CBHW032053300426
44116CB00007B/715